DUDLEY MOORE

DUDLEY MOORE

AN INTIMATE PORTRAIT

Rena Fruchter

EBURY PRESS

First published in Great Britain in 2004
This edition published in 2005

10 9 8 7

Text © Rena Fruchter 2004

First published by
Ebury Press
Random House, 20 Vauxhall Bridge Road, London SW1V 2SA

The Random House Group Limited Reg. No. 954009

www.randomhouse.co.uk

A CIP catalogue record for this book is available from the British Library.

Cover Design by Two Associates
Text design and typesetting by Textype

ISBN 9780091900809
ISBN 0091900808

Penguin Random House is committed to a sustainable future for our business, our readers and our planet. This book is made from Forest Stewardship Council® certified paper.

Printed and bound in Great Britain by Clays Ltd, St Ives plc

In Memory of Dudley

***

For Brian
and for Ruth, Karen, Joel and Elise
my strength and my inspiration

CONTENTS

FOREWORD

Dame Cleo Laine and John Dankworth, CBE

OUR FRIENDSHIP WITH DUDLEY began in a rather unusual but certainly memorable way. He came into our lives by sheer chance before his career even began – although not before his considerable musical talents had begun to make themselves apparent. But the difference between our respective statuses and ages at the time of our meeting made it almost inevitable that in some ways he would come to think of us almost as parents – certainly as family – to whom he could look for guidance from time to time. The fact that he never actually did so was perhaps unfortunate on some occasions. But, of course, parental advice even when given is often not heeded, so as it happened the lack of requests for it meant that we remained good friends to the end.

Dudley's career was – as the ensuing chapters will doubtless show – a quite amazing amalgam of various talents; perhaps their very multiplicity was his problem (whether it was indeed a problem may well be hotly contested by some of his admirers). Or maybe it was not the diversity of his gifts that complicated his life, but the extraordinary extent of some of them. For example, his knack of turning suddenly from laughter to relatively serious musical performance was also the territory of other comic actors such as, say, Harpo Marx. The difference is that while Harpo certainly showed skill and sensitivity in managing a difficult instrument, Dudley's piano interpolations showed only a tiny fraction of yet another gift, that of musical composition. His work in this creative capacity indicated not only an originality of concept which was quite refreshing, but a latent greatness clamouring for more time to develop and mature.

Do we have regrets about our failure to find more time to spend with our friend over the years? Of course we do, since things that we would like to have told him about our admiration for his work remained unsaid. And – who knows? – we might have succeeded in helping him through a few sticky patches of which we had previous experience ourselves, had our relationship been a little closer – geographically and otherwise.

But basically we rejoice in our good fortune to have known a remarkable – and remarkably kind – man who had the rare disadvantage of possessing enough talent to last for several lifetimes – and having only a single one (and a cruelly curtailed one at that) in which to explore and enjoy them all.

Dudley Moore's good fortune, however, was to have been aided in the latter (and most difficult) part of his life by two true friends – themselves musically gifted – to succour and comfort him through the last tormenting stages of his affliction. One of them has become an author to record the compelling story of Dudley's bitter but heroic struggle against the forces of nature – a tale which will move us and no doubt sadden us, but will at the same time perpetuate the memory of a remarkable and lovable man.

FOREWORD

Eric Idle

'People who indulge in comedy tend to be more and more isolated as the years go by.' Dudley Moore

I SAW HIM FOR the first time on the London stage in *Beyond the Fringe* in 1962. A show which totally changed my life. It made me want to become a comedian. I never realised before that you could laugh at everything that oppressed you. Dudley in many ways was the Ringo of this extraordinary comedy group, his pantomiming and clowning being slightly at odds with the imperious Cook, the flamboyant Miller and the neurotic Bennett. He was the only musician in the group, effortlessly mocking Mozart operas and Benjamin Britten arias, but what impressed me was that he was equally at home in the jazz clubs of London, where he confidently led the Dudley Moore trio. I would go and listen to him play at Ronnie Scott's and at the Marquee on Oxford Street, where for many years my only claim to fame was that I had taken a piss next to Dudley Moore's bass player. (See *Famous People I have pissed next to . . .* Oxford Unscientific Books.)

When it hit the BBC in 1967 I became a huge fan of *Not Only . . . But Also*, which saw the full flowering of the Cook–Moore partnership. This led to such delights as the Pete and Dud monologues and the sheer joy of 'The Leaping Nuns of Norwich'. *Monty Python* has always been fortunate that the parsimonious BBC wiped most of the tapes of this show so no one can see just how influential they were, or how much we owed to them. Alas for them they were still in black and white, so that we burst on to a multi-coloured TV landscape without having to pay the debt of gratitude we owed them both. Dudley was the one in the funny cap trying desperately not to giggle as Peter mercilessly attempted to crack him up every week in their wonderfully bizarre dialogues. This partnership came to perfection in their movie *Bedazzled* (which Peter wanted to call *Raquel Welch*, so that they could bill it as Peter Cook and Dudley Moore *in* Raquel Welch) and would lead later to the classic filthy records of Derek and Clive, quoted interminably by every travelling British rock group (*What's the worst job you've ever had?*)

I met Dudley on only three occasions. Once in LA in the nineties when Mick Jagger and I took him out to dinner. We had heard from Marcia Strassman that he was glum and decided that precisely what he needed to cheer him up was dinner with us. So we called him up out of the blue and invited him. Dudley was puzzled. Polite. Bemused. He suggested his restaurant (72 Market Street) and dined with us. I expect he was waiting for us to make a pitch. That's what happens in Hollywood when people you don't know invite you to a meal. But we had no pitch. We were just fans. He was polite but diffident and I'm pretty sure he picked up the tab though I don't know whether that cheered him up or not.

The second time I saw him was at a memorial evening for Peter

Cook held at the Improv. Dudley was downright weird. Everyone thought he might be stoned but in fact it was the beginning of his sickness. The final time was in New York in 2001 when Rena organised a splendid evening for him at Carnegie Hall. It was a genuine glittering occasion, with Dames and fancy film stars all singing and performing for him. My part in the evening was to play Peter Cook opposite Jimmy Fallon's Dudley as we committed the lèse-majesté of performing the 'One-Legged Tarzan' sketch in front of him. He was a wasting figure in a wheelchair and afterwards I shook his hand and mumbled something. How can you say, 'Thanks, Dud, for making it all possible, for all the laughs – for just being you?' He was right. Comedy is isolating. His disease was the most isolating of all. Or maybe that's comedy . . .

PRELUDE

IT WAS A RECURRENT dream that began about six months after Dudley's death. In it, I am trying to find his new phone number. He has moved to a new place and nobody knows the number. It isn't just 'unlisted', it is completely unavailable. In the dream, I start to panic. I need to speak to him. Where is he? How is he? Who is helping him? Does he have a piano? Why doesn't anybody have his new phone number? Then, every time at the same point in the dream, I wake up and remember that Dudley is dead.

Dudley was always very good at interpreting dreams. When I didn't get the meaning of my dream, he would say, 'Well, that one is so *obvious*,' and launch into a lengthy explanation, always using the longest words he could muster and the deepest psychological analyses, even towards the end of his life, when the words were increasingly difficult for him to form.

What would he think of this one? I ask myself, curious, and

slightly amused. He would probably laugh his inimitable laugh and say, 'Oh, that one is so *obvious*. I *have* moved to a new place, and there are no phones here. You don't have to be a genius to figure this one out.'

In truth, Dudley would be very frustrated without a telephone. It was his lifeline. The phone would be significant in this dream because we talked endless hours by phone – during the early years of our friendship we spoke on the phone nearly every day. Later, when we were piano partners and when Dudley was living as part of my family, we continued to speak many times a day by phone.

My first mobile phone was a birthday present from Dudley in 1996. When I expressed delight, he said pragmatically, 'It was impossible to get in touch with you.'

'How long do I keep it?'

'For life,' he said.

'Whose life?'

'Whoever goes first,' he said, laughing.

Just when I thought the recurrent phone dream would never end, there was one more, stranger than the rest. In it, I'm sitting at the piano playing one of Dudley's 'Songs Without Words', and the phone rings. It is Dudley. 'What are you doing?' he asks, a question he often asked me by phone.

'Practising your "Songs Without Words",' I reply. 'I've had no luck getting your new number. What is it?'

'I don't have a number. There are no phones here.'

'Then how did you call me?'

'I didn't. This is your dream. And I'm just here to remind you.'

'Remind me what?'

'I taught you to interpret your dreams, didn't I?' Strange as dreams tend to be, I can also see him on the other end of the phone.

He is looking at his watch, and I'm sure this is another clue, as he spent a lot of time looking at his watch, especially when he was feeling impatient.

I wake up, startled, and annoyed to wake from the dream without the answer. It feels like a riddle that I will have trouble solving. I really do have to interpret the dream by myself, but I can use the skills I learned from Dudley. 'Remind me what?' The words stick in my brain. It is days later before I begin to wonder if it is as simple as my own subconscious insisting it must be time to tell the story we agreed I would write one day – the story of the last years of Dudley's life.

'You know me better than anyone ever has,' Dudley had said more than once during the last decade of his life.

Still, I had resisted writing, although I knew he had in effect assigned me the task, and not given me much choice about it. But writing Dudley's story seemed so difficult, and I was filled with self-doubts, the same kinds of doubt that had filled Dudley all his life. I had written about many subjects, but none as close to me as Dudley and our friendship, or Dudley and his struggles. It couldn't be a biography, or a factual historical account. Dudley's story is one of a struggle to overcome obstacles, to come to terms with the changing direction of his own life, and to change enough to really, fully, accept himself. It's about laughter and music and relationships. Could I find the emotional strength it would take to relive the past decade and a half while writing about his life and our time together? Yet I had made a promise to Dudley and to myself, and I had to keep it.

For more than five years, and for very good reasons, most of the details of Dudley Moore's life were kept private. From time to time, the press would try to learn what was going on in his life and with his health, but with only a few notable exceptions, the details were sketchy and the information was inadequate or inaccurate. Dudley wanted the truth of his struggle to be known, but he also valued his privacy at a time he needed it, and in a way he had never needed it before. The two were conflicting emotions – his need for everyone to know his struggle, because of who he was, and the need to have a private life that, for the first time in his adulthood, could really be private.

Dudley was a part of my family, and my entire family sheltered and protected him, helping him to lead a life as close to normal as was possible for someone who was a brilliant artist and a celebrity, and at the same time struggling with a debilitating disease. It was a difficult and powerful journey for all of us, and we all learned from each other what is truly important.

PART I

PART 1

1

THE END

THIS IS A STORY about courage in the face of adversity. It's the story of a man loved by the world, a man who rose to the top of the world and then struggled to maintain his life as a devastating condition took from him everything that had given him his identity – everything that made him Dudley Moore.

The tragedy is that Dudley Moore had so much left to do, to give, when his life was taken from him at the age of sixty-six. But this is not just a sad story. Dudley left a legacy of brilliance in music, comedy and film, and his life touched many people. This is a story about music and laughter, courage and triumph, friendship and love – and what it took for Dudley to rise above his struggle. It wasn't easy for Dudley to understand and appreciate his own strengths and gifts the way others understood and appreciated them, but his remarkable journey took him to that point.

This is the story of the last years of Dudley's life, and what those years meant in the context of his extraordinary earlier years. It's a story he wanted the world to know. During his last years, Dudley was constantly in transition. He knew something was physically wrong, but it would take him years to find out what, as he grappled with difficulties in his personal life, difficulties in his career, difficulties with his finances. But in the midst of the journey he also found peace. He learned to accept himself and to accept a rare and devastating medical condition from which nobody has ever recovered. As fighting his condition became more difficult, he gained strength and awareness he hadn't found before.

During his last decade, Dudley changed. He stepped down off the podium and into real life. His life was difficult and turbulent, but Dudley also blossomed – he searched for, and found, contentment. He finally learned to identify what was important to him. He learned how to say no. He learned how to look inside himself and to see what was good. He stopped letting people hurt him and take advantage of him. Sometimes he wanted to die, but he fought to stay alive, knowing his condition would only get worse. It was a time of revelation for Dudley. He looked at the world through music and humour and it was music and humour that helped him to keep going as his illness progressed.

At the end of his life, Dudley could barely speak, but he could still communicate and listen to music, and he could still laugh. He became weaker physically, but stronger in spirit, closing his all too short chapter proud of what he had given to the world and finally knowing how to trust and how to be close.

This is my story too. It is about Dudley's relationship with me, and with my family. We worked and lived closely together for years; our lives were intertwined and we changed each other's lives.

Dudley and I were the closest of friends, as well as partners and colleagues. He lived in New Jersey as a part of my family for the last five years of his life, with my husband Brian Dallow and me, in a small community that included our adult children and small grandchildren, and close friends and colleagues. We were together for some of his triumphs and we were holding his hands as he died on 27 March 2002, while listening to his own music playing softly in the background.

It was a terrible Wednesday morning at the end of March. Dudley had pneumonia, the death knell for anyone with Progressive Supranuclear Palsy, a degenerative neurological condition that had sapped Dudley's strength over the course of five years. Dudley had been spared the death he had feared most, from choking – one of the dangers with the condition – and he had fought death back, surprising everyone with his will to live despite the quality of his life towards the end.

Normally, when a friend or a family member dies, there's time to absorb the loss, to sit quietly with one's grief. Not so on 27 March 2002. Nothing could have prepared my family for the eye of the tornado, for the moment when Dudley became a screen on the television, a still photo with the caption: 'Dudley Moore, actor and musician, dead at the age of 66.'

His body was carried from the house by an undertaker who knew that this job had to be done before the press learned of Dudley's death. Dudley's sons had to be notified, and his sister in England, his closest friends, and his agent, his attorneys and his press representative. We stood, frozen in place. Brian, me, our daughters, Dudley's doctor, the hospice nurse. The moment had been so long in coming, no surprise and barely a shock. But we were stunned, motionless, holding each other. The tears flowed. Dudley dead? It was incomprehensible.

Then the phone began to ring. The Associated Press, Reuters, *People* magazine, the *Daily Mail* – everyone who knew how to reach us, and the calls were simultaneous. On mobile phones and the house phone. 'Can we have a statement? What was the cause of death? Was it expected?' The television in Dudley's living room was on, and his picture was flashed on the screen, with his dates underneath: 1935–2002. So final, and the obituaries were already prepared.

Tiny Dvorah, my nearly four-year-old granddaughter, had sung for him the night before. 'Twinkle, Twinkle, Little Star', her favourite comforting song, just to make him feel better. Nobody had thought to shelter her from the onslaught. She stood in front of the television, a tiny person in the midst of chaos, looking at Dudley's picture. 'What happened to Uncle Dudley?' She began to cry. Uncle Dudley was her best grown-up friend. Her mother scooped her up in her arms and together they sobbed.

The house was filled with people, but the silence without Dudley was deafening. Later that day, when Brian and I returned from making arrangements at the funeral home, the street was lined with video cameras, reporters with large lenses, asking how we felt, what we thought, when the funeral would take place.

The day we had dreaded had finally arrived. And yet Dudley was finally at peace. How could anyone reconcile the two?

In accordance with his wishes, he was to be buried at the beautiful Hillside Cemetery less than half a mile from where he had spent his last few years. The funeral was to be a solemn and dignified event, but also a celebration of his life by people who loved him. Not thousands of people, but under a hundred. It was not going to be a media circus, and was by invitation only to those who had been a meaningful part of his life during the last years.

There would be music, Bach and Dudley's (his two favourite composers), and stories about Dudley, serious moments and moments of high comedy. And everyone would go from the funeral to lunch at a country club near the cemetery.

Because a number of people were travelling long distances to attend the funeral, the date was set for Tuesday, nearly a week after his death. Dudley had four ex-wives — Suzy Kendall, in London; Tuesday Weld, in New York; Brogan Lane, and Nicole Rothschild, both living in Los Angeles. Dudley and Suzy had maintained a close friendship that lasted until the day he died. She was devastated by his death, and decided not to attend the funeral but to help plan a memorial service a few months later in England. Tuesday and Brogan both planned to come to New Jersey for the funeral. We hoped that Dudley's son Patrick, then aged twenty-six, would come too. Their relationship had been distant in recent years, although they continued to care about each other. And Dudley rarely saw his six-year-old son Nicholas. He had learned the hard way that seeing him meant tangling with Nicole.

By two days after Dudley's death, all we had left to do was to figure out the order of the programme and how the security could be handled graciously. We had been dodging the persistent tabloid press for those two days, hoping we would be able to keep them from knowing the exact location of the funeral.

Whenever we drove away from home, a photographer and reporters from one of the American tabloids would set up a relay team in a couple of old cars. We were followed everywhere, including a trip to one of Dudley's favourite restaurants for Dvorah's fourth birthday. Typical of Dudley, who always kept track of birthdays, he had selected a gift and a card for her weeks earlier, just before his condition had taken a rapid downturn. Dvorah understood what it all meant. 'I miss Uncle Dudley,' she said quietly.

In the months before his death, Dudley had only briefly discussed his funeral arrangements, but had asked that only one person not attend – his fourth ex-wife, Nicole. It had taken Dudley several years, and in-patient therapy, to break his addiction to Nicole. He provided financially for her, but after 1999 he had wanted nothing further to do with her. He had escaped from the situation, he said, and he didn't want her to see him in a casket.

Tuesday Weld, Dudley's second ex-wife, had gone to Los Angeles to find her son Patrick and bring him back to New Jersey for the funeral. Dudley had spoken to Patrick a few months earlier by phone, and a meeting that was going to be arranged between the two had not taken place. Dudley had intended to set a date, but did not feel a sense of urgency, and Patrick had a tendency to disappear for weeks or months at a time.

Now, Tuesday was concerned about Patrick's emotional and physical well-being. She knew where he was living in Los Angeles, but when she got there she was told he had left. Nobody knew what Patrick's condition would be. Patrick had hoped to reconnect with Dudley, and that hope was gone. He was at a difficult point, struggling to find a path in his own life. Tuesday checked into a hotel and did the only thing she could think of doing. She began driving the streets looking for her son. It was Saturday and there were three days left until the funeral.

Tuesday Weld wanted to attend the funeral, and she wanted to help Patrick begin the long healing process. She remained upset that Dudley had not tried harder to reach out to Patrick, but she had also expressed her sadness about his degenerative condition and his death.

In addition to the swirling of emotions surrounding Dudley's death, the complex arrangements, the search for Patrick and pursuit by the press, there was one other incident. Nicole, angry that Dudley had wanted to exclude her, hired an attorney on behalf of her six-year-old son in an attempt to stop the burial and bring Dudley's body back to Los Angeles.

After a tense couple of days, late on Saturday night the phone rang. It was Patrick. 'I'm sorry about your dad,' I said. 'And that you didn't get to see him. I hope you know that he loved you very much.' Patrick was quiet. It was easy to hear that he was hurt, in shock and angry. But he had stopped running, and asked his mother to help him get back to New Jersey for the funeral.

When it came to the test, Patrick, having full rights as the eldest son, took a strong stand and saved the day. With twelve simple words of support and his signature, sent by fax to a small army of attorneys in New York, New Jersey and California, Patrick allowed his father to rest in peace in the place he had chosen. Dudley's final power struggle with Nicole was over.

So much had been left unsaid between Dudley and Patrick. In earlier years, they had shared many happy times, but Patrick's relationship with his father had not been good since his difficult teens; both had wanted it to be different, yet they didn't know how to change it. Patrick had never really been able to help his father, but in this one strong action, he carried out his father's last wish.

2

LUNCH AT THE RITZ
(THE BEGINNING)

I FIRST MET DUDLEY over the phone in 1987 when I was writing a weekly music column for the *New York Times*. He was performing the piano solo in Beethoven's 'Triple' Concerto for violin, cello, piano and orchestra. Dudley was part of an esteemed trio that included Itzhak Perlman and Yo-Yo Ma with the New Jersey Symphony Orchestra, and I volunteered to interview him for a *Times* article that was to appear on the Sunday before the event. We spoke by phone for forty-five minutes, all about Beethoven, piano technique and performing with orchestra.

He asked if I wanted to attend a rehearsal, 'although I'm not sure how good it will be,' and we met briefly at a press conference set up afterwards by the concert promoters. He said he had enjoyed our conversation, and asked if we could discuss music one more time. I agreed. He phoned the following week at a time we had chosen and we spoke about Debussy.

'I don't suppose this *has* to end today, does it?' he said. 'I know you are busy and probably thinking to yourself, Why should I talk about music with some actor from Hollywood?, but would you mind *terribly* (he became extremely British for a moment) if we did this just once more, if you aren't too busy,' he added. He was phoning from his Los Angeles home. 'Everybody here is so busy getting tanned and blonde. They don't seem to have the time to discuss Chopin *at all*.'

His request was so simple, and so touching. There seemed an implication on his part that I might object to his being an actor, that it would detract from our conversations or that I had better things to do with my time.

'I don't mind the Hollywood part. I'm a pianist and a writer,' I said. 'But people find that difficult to accept – I should be one or the other. It's too confusing. Who am I? I'm a pianist first, and I make a more steady living as a writer, but I'm a writer second, in my heart.'

'That's exactly the same with me,' he said. 'I'm a musician in the depths of my heart and soul, but I have to confess, I do make more money as an actor. Well, a few million more. What a mystery . . . So we have that in common,' he added.

After that, we began speaking regularly on the phone, usually about piano music. I had been surprised and impressed by the depth of his musical knowledge, by his intellect and by the quality of his performance with the orchestra a couple of weeks earlier. Brian and I had attended the concert. Having grown up in England, Brian was more familiar than I with Dudley's career and his musicianship. I was surprised, but as a music critic, I wrote an objective and favourable review. I told Dudley I would send him a copy. A week later, he phoned and said, 'I was afraid to open the envelope. I generally dislike critics, and reviews. Thank you for this nice review.'

We continued to speak often on the phone. Sometimes Dudley would call very briefly from a set where he was filming. At other times we would have long conversations about music, or about articles I was writing for the *Times* or other publications. Dudley loved to discuss grammatical minutiae, and would debate points of punctuation. Sometimes it seemed as though he would read more for grammatical perfection than for content. He loved the intricacies of language, the meanings of words, and intentionally using a large vocabulary that included words most people would have to look up in the dictionary. When I mentioned I was visiting relatives in another city, he mused, 'Now would that be relatives, or relations? I'm always wondering about that one. Or is it an American/British distinction, and would it be relations in England and relatives in America, or vice versa?'

We would always make a serious effort to resolve such important issues, but would end up laughing. And if at all possible, Dudley would have to find a sexual connotation. 'But I suppose if you were in England, and having relations with your relatives, or vice versa – oh, how would that go – it wouldn't work if it were relatives with your relations – it would have to be relations with your relations. Well, I'm sure you see my point. And who cares, anybody besides us?'

'Possibly the relations having the relations would care,' I suggested.

This could always go on for minutes, a huge pair of parentheses encircling the distraction from the main topic of conversation. It could be trivial points, but underlying the humour was his fascination with language. It wasn't hard to understand why. Dudley had a remarkable brain – a quick wit and a conversational ability that extended to a wide range of subjects, largely excluding politics, which he thought boring. He was well educated and well read, absorbing and retaining information that he could recall at will if the topic was of interest to him. Dudley's public might have assumed that his intellect had taken a back seat to his musical and comedic achievements, and his Hollywood stardom, but in reality his intellect was very much intact and craving engagement.

The library in his home was massive, although even at this point in his life he was too distracted to read much. He would begin reading many books but would rarely finish them.

Dudley would usually end the parenthesis: 'Now, where were we? Oh, I remember, discussing my cadenza for the Mozart Concerto. You were saying it has a moment of Bach in it. But do you really think that's a problem? The cadenza is intended as a personal statement by the performer – me – to encompass my musical tastes, and I think it needs a *touch* of Bach.'

I hadn't objected to it. I thought his Mozart cadenzas were superb. A short and virtuosic solo section generally played near the end of a concerto movement without the orchestra, the cadenza was traditionally improvised by the soloist. It was extraordinary that Dudley was among the minority of pianists still in a position to write and perform their own cadenzas. Most pianists went to the store to purchase cadenzas. Dudley always wrote his own and they were very good.

We had these discussions once or twice a week after the Beethoven concert in New Jersey. A few months later, Dudley was filming in New York and suggested that we meet. Lunch at the Ritz, he said. On the way I phoned to ask if he wanted to go somewhere out of the city instead.

'Where?' he asked.

'A museum – the Cloisters?' I replied.

'I would *love* to,' he said. 'Yes. Get me out of here. I've been cooped up here, doing interviews. Being a celebrity. But . . .' He stopped talking. I waited for the silence to end. 'I just remembered. I'm starving. No, no Cloisters. We must have lunch. You are probably starving too, after driving all that distance.'

'It's nineteen miles,' I said. 'Yes, lunch would be good. That was the plan. We can do the Cloisters another time.'

I made my way through the Lincoln Tunnel, into Manhattan, over to the end of Central Park, a little nervous because the traffic was heavy and I knew I would be late. I found the first available parking spot on the street, right across from the hotel. When I arrived, Dudley was already seated in the restaurant, looking at his watch – even though I was only about ten minutes late. He had watched me park, cross the street and enter the restaurant. He waved at me from a corner table, and I felt self-conscious as everyone watched me cross the room to his table.

Dudley was wearing jeans and a casual shirt, contrasting with every other male in the restaurant, all of whom were dressed in suits and ties, looking formal. A jacket hung on the back of his chair. He seemed out of place in the Ritz. He was aware that people in the room were looking at him; he half smiled but pretended not to notice, resting his arm on the table but jumping up quickly when I approached.

'It's nice to see you,' I said, arriving after what felt like much longer than the ten seconds it had probably taken me to walk from the door to his table.

'Really?' he replied, sounding surprised, and sitting down again after I was in my chair.

'Especially after all these phone conversations.'

'It's nice to see you too. I've been waiting to see you. Why haven't we had lunch until now?' he asked, looking quickly around the room to take stock of the watchers, who were no longer paying attention.

'You live in LA and I live here.'

'Oh. That's right. I forgot.' He was quiet for a minute, studying the menu. 'I don't know what you like to eat. Do you like fish?'

'Depends on the kind.'

'Chicken?'

'Not fried,' I said.

'Beef?'

'Occasionally.'

'Good. Do you know about my trout habits?'

'Not really. We've only talked music. Not fish. So I don't know all that much about your eating . . . or fishing habits. What do you mean by trout habits, anyway?'

'I cook trout . . . every morning, for breakfast. With steamed vegetables – Brussels sprouts and mangetout.' I had no idea what mangetout were then, but I didn't want to interrupt. 'Most people ruin Brussels sprouts by overcooking them to a mushy pulp,' he continued. 'Yuck. They must be steamed for exactly six minutes, then they are *perfect*. This is the most difficult thing to train somebody to do, by the way. So now you know everything *important* about me and my trout habits. And while we're on the subject of trout, I should tell you that I love Schubert's "Trout" Quintet. Do you think there's some connection here?'

'There must be. I'm glad we've had our first trout conversation,' I said.

'Of many, I'm sure,' he said, mock pompously. And he was right.

The waiter was hovering, afraid to interrupt, being very aware that it was Dudley Moore. But this was the Ritz, so the waiter was also pretending not to be too impressed.

'I thought *everyone* knew about my trout and steamed vegetables.' I didn't yet know that Dudley could sometimes discuss a subject to death. Equally, he could dismiss an entire subject in three words. It depended on the subject, and how closely connected it was to him or his life.

I didn't yet know how complex Dudley was, or how many facets there were to his personality. He often encompassed opposite emotions or thoughts simultaneously. He could be despairing and hopeful at the same time. Sometimes he had no clue how to weed out his extraneous feelings and get to the core of how he felt about something, and he could quickly go from one extreme to another. Several people could know him well and yet know completely different sides of Dudley. We had talked on the phone for months, and I was only beginning to get the smallest clue as to who he was.

'I haven't really read all that much about you, yet.'

'*Good*. Then you're not really a fan.'

'I admire your work. I like your playing. I like talking to you. Does that make me a fan?'

'God no, thank goodness. I get so fucking tired of people thinking they know everything about me. What I do. Who I screw. What I eat. What I like. Usually they are wrong.'

'Well, I think we're starting on the ground floor here. What I know about you is pretty much what you've told me. Oh, and I have seen *Arthur*, like every educated person.' Something about that made him laugh.

'So what would you like for lunch?'

That was how my first lunch with Dudley began. I had apparently passed the non-fan lunch test and was able to proceed. It was one of thousands of lunches we would share over the next decade and a half. Lunch was one of Dudley's favourite experiences in life, second only to music and probably coming slightly above, or maybe equal to, sex.

We looked at the menu again and decided on fish. He had trout. I had salmon. Later I was to learn that Dudley rarely ordered trout in a restaurant, because nobody else could cook it to his satisfaction.

The rest of the time we talked music. Debussy. Mozart. Beethoven. Childhood piano teachers and piano technique. The size of my hands. The size of his hands. Our hands were just about the same size, which seemed to amuse Dudley, except that his were more muscular.

'I can stretch a ninth. What about you?' he asked, demonstrating on the edge of the table. 'C to D.'

'Same for me, although it would probably be A to B.' It was such a dumb joke I suddenly wished I could take it back. A ninth is a ninth. Stupidly I had demonstrated on my plate and had mashed potatoes on my little finger. He stared for a moment, then let out an amazing guffaw.

'That's good,' he said. 'I'll have to remember that one. A Victor Borge-ism. Oh, his name doesn't take an "ism" very well, does it? But "asm" would be even worse,' he added, whispering, 'especially in a place like the Ritz.' He looked around the room again at the suits and ties. 'So, do you practise . . . scales?' he asked softly, raising his water glass, with a pained expression on his face – and a feigned slightly intoxicated voice, as though he were asking a risqué, and very personal, question.

He didn't wait for me to answer, only for the laugh he expected. He answered his own question. 'I don't. I did, but not now. But I play Bach every morning. I come downstairs and it's the first thing I do every morning, for about an hour.'

Dudley seemed very interested in the fact that I had started my piano career as a child prodigy, dressed as little Mozart and playing my first public performance at the age of four. Philadelphia Orchestra at the age of six. Boston Pops with Arthur Fiedler at the age of eleven. To me, being a child prodigy was something I had to overcome in order to become an adult musician. Child prodigies get special attention for their ability to play works usually reserved for adult musicians. There's an advantage – an edge – but as an adult musician the circumstances are different. Many prodigies quit rather than struggling to function without the advantage of precociousness.

Dudley admitted that my prodigy career was a source of slight jealousy. 'If I'd had that start, my technique would be better now. You were fortunate. You shouldn't think of it as a handicap to be overcome. My club foot – that was a handicap to overcome. I still struggle with it sometimes, although twenty years of therapy helped a bit,' he said. It amused him that he was such a slow learner when it came to his own psychological issues. He was very sharp about everybody else's issues.

His jaw dropped when I told him that Brian and I had produced triplets (then aged 15) and a 17-year-old daughter as well. He *never* stopped being amazed, either. It was usually the second thing he told people about me, after my name. 'This is my friend, Rena Fruchter. She gave birth to triplets.' Later, when we were a piano duo, this information would be included in his on-stage introduction of me.

Nobody in the audience ever believed the bit about triplets. But they laughed at the way he said it.

Halfway through our fish, I glanced out of the window and noticed a tow truck across the street – in fact, just behind my car, and a policeman writing a ticket and talking to the tow-truck driver. 'Excuse me,' I said, too surprised to speak and just pointing across the street. 'I'll be back. Wait for me.'

I dashed out, annoyed at having to interrupt my first lunch with Dudley. I moved the car and returned to lunch after a fifteen-minute intermission. Dudley was waiting, extremely amused by what he had witnessed; he had been patient and was not looking at his watch, but he was eating all the bread that was on the table, with butter, dipping it into large amounts of salt, which he adored, from the hill he customarily piled on the edge of his plate. Out of breath, annoyed, I sat down with the ticket in my hand. 'Give me that,' Dudley said, grabbing the ticket out of my hand.

'What for?' I asked.

'Don't you remember? I invited you for lunch . . . and a ticket!' He tucked it in his pocket and insisted on paying for it.

We went on to an extravagant dessert and coffee, continuing to talk about our respective childhood music teachers. By the time lunch was over, we felt like old friends. We agreed to talk again soon, hugged quickly and said goodbye.

3

STREISAND AND DUTOIT
(THE BEGINNING OF THE END)

IT WAS NOVEMBER 1995 and Dudley's film career had been floundering for five years. He was doing a lot of musical performances as soloist with orchestras, but his last films had been *Blame it on the Bellboy* and *Parallel Lives*, both released in 1992. In 1995, he was personally in turmoil, and in the middle of his fourth and most difficult marriage.

Dudley was in New York rehearsing for the Barbra Streisand film *The Mirror Has Two Faces*, the last film he was ever offered. Dudley had experienced highs and lows in his film career, and his major hits *Arthur* and *10* had propelled him into a stardom he could never have anticipated. Acting had always come very easily to him, and he memorised lines instantly.

With *The Mirror Has Two Faces*, it was a different story. He was having trouble remembering his lines, even after studying them twice as long as he would normally have needed to. He couldn't understand what was going wrong. Anybody with a good crystal ball would have known that Dudley was showing the early signs of Progressive Supranuclear Palsy, a degenerative neurological disease with wideranging symptoms affecting many areas of the body. He was also affected by the stresses of his personal life. He was on a physical and emotional roller-coaster heading towards disaster. But all he knew that day in New York was that he couldn't remember his lines, and couldn't understand why.

Streisand eventually arranged to have his lines held up on big cue cards, an action that Dudley found demoralising. He was doing his best, but nothing was going the way he expected it to. He couldn't muster the energy he needed for the small part in the film.

In the middle of filming, he was scheduled to go for a short trip to Montreal to perform as soloist with the Montreal Symphony, led by the renowned conductor Charles Dutoit. At that point in our friendship, Dudley and I were talking almost every day. But while in New York, Dudley was evasive. He tried to confine himself to his hotel room, but eventually responded to my urging him to talk. By the time he agreed to let me in for a visit, he had almost completely withdrawn. He was obviously deeply depressed and wasn't taking most of his phone calls – very unusual for Dudley, who was always ready to grab the phone at the first ring, and usually willing to talk for a long time. Even Dudley had been able to laugh at himself and appreciate the humour of a nine-minute message he had once left on my answering machine. The humour of it was the fact that it seemed perfectly normal to him.

When asked how he was, Dudley was nearly always an emphatic *fine*. This time, in New York, after talking about nothing much for an hour over lunch, we went back up to his suite. As soon as the door was closed, he blurted out that he was in a black depression because nothing in his life was going right. He wanted to die. He didn't see the point of living any longer, or of talking about it, as there was nothing that could fix his problems, he explained. This, too, was a significant departure for Dudley, who was usually ready to talk for hours about himself and his problems, even knowing they couldn't be solved. I knew that, despite his dark words, he wasn't suicidal, so had no real concerns about leaving him alone.

The next afternoon, I flew from Newark to Montreal, arriving a few hours before Dudley, and in time to join a representative from the orchestra and meet Dudley at the airport. A wise decision, as Dudley's arrival through customs that evening was the only time I ever saw him drunk – the only time in our entire friendship. It was obvious that something had happened, but we couldn't talk about it at that moment. Often Dudley would discuss personal things or problems in front of whoever was around, but this time he was deliberately holding back. On the way to the car, Dudley managed a superficial conversation with the orchestra representative, who seemed unaware of any problem. There were a few good distractions as people stopped him for his autograph or to have their photo taken with him. As always, he was cordial, though this time a little disorientated.

'I wouldn't ordinarily ask you for something like this,' he whispered at the car's open door. He wasn't good at shortcuts designed to get to the point quickly. How was he going to squeeze in his request in the few seconds before we got into the limo, I wondered.

'Could you pretend you are really talkative? I don't think I can keep up this act for more than a few minutes.'

'I can try,' I whispered back, and spent the whole trip in frivolous conversation with the young man, who pretended to be mildly interested but would rather have been talking to Dudley, nearly asleep on the back seat.

When we were finally alone in his hotel suite, Dudley let out a huge sigh. He was deflating before my eyes. He collapsed into a large soft armchair, unbuttoned his shirt, took off his shoes. 'I feel ill,' he said. He had had three Bloody Marys on the plane – unheard of for Dudley. One Bloody Mary on every plane trip, no matter what time of day, was a ritual for him, but never more than one. And when not on a plane, he maintained that he did not like hard liquor of any sort, and would select a glass of wine with a meal. One of Dudley's many idiosyncrasies.

'My life is falling apart,' he said. 'Everything is going wrong. Barbra Streisand called me in and asked what was the matter with me. It was horrible. She was condescending and treated me like a child. I just couldn't remember the lines, that's all. I promised to do better when I get back to New York.'

He was talking very fast and seemed both angry and frightened. Defensive and upset, and truly puzzled by what was happening to him.

'She wasn't very nice about it – I can understand that, from her perspective, but it wasn't for lack of trying. I can't concentrate on anything.'

It was all just pouring out. He had never sounded so desperate in all the time I had known him.

'Nicki is moving everything to Colorado. I'm not sure how this concert will go. I haven't been able to practise in days. What do you think I should do?'

'What do you want to do?' In the past I had always tried to offer solutions if he asked, but this time it was all much worse. I didn't know where to begin, how to help. He was right. His life *was* falling apart.

'I don't know. I just want things to be better, but it's all a miserable murky morass.' He chuckled at the alliteration. 'A moment of comic relief,' he said. It was a good sign. 'Shakespeare was famous for it. The buffoon in the tragedy. Oh fuck, look at me – I'll do anything to distract myself.'

'What about the film? What can you do to save it?'

'Nothing. I don't give a flying fuck about that. Something is happening to me, and I don't know what.'

This was all completely out of character for Dudley. He had approached most of his films with the kind of enthusiasm that made him an inspiration to others in the cast. On the set, he had a reputation for being funny, lively, unconventional and easy to work with. He had a positive attitude and inspired others. And if he wasn't thrilled with the way a film was going, he was not a complainer. He made the best of it. He made suggestions to improve things. He ad-libbed lines if it was appropriate. He was completely comfortable on the set of a film. Dudley got along with most people, and it was extremely unusual for him to clash with his colleagues.

Dudley originally hadn't wanted to do the film, *The Mirror Has Two Faces*, but had agreed 'because everybody thought it was such a good idea. Lou (Dudley's Los Angeles agent Lou Pitt, at the time with ICM Artists) really wanted me to do it, and I couldn't argue with his logic. I couldn't turn Lou down. He's been trying so hard to find a film for me.

'But I have to get out of the marriage. I can't live like this any more. This marriage is killing me. I just want to play the piano and have everybody leave me alone.'

He had said it all, and I was powerless to help. He was distraught, devastated by the turn of events, unable to understand how life had gone from so good to so difficult in such a short time.

He was finished, out of words, the way it often went with Dudley. There was silence for the first time in half an hour. He looked around the room, as though waiting for somebody who wasn't there to speak, and wondering why there was silence.

'Well, goodnight. I shall see you in the morning. Breakfast at eight?' He walked me to the door, although it was only ten feet away, and opened it. 'Be careful,' he said.

'Of what?'

'Goblins. Thieves. Streisand. Fairy-tale characters. People who speak French. Mozart themes that invade your brain when you are asleep, then transform themselves into dissonant Schoenbergian tone rows, hard as it might be to do that, and eat away at your sanity. That's probably what happened to me. God, three Bloody Marys. What on earth was I thinking?'

I laughed. That was what he intended.

It was hard to know which way it would all go. For the first time ever, I felt, Dudley was being blocked at every turn. I didn't see the sparkle I had always seen. His eyes were sad, almost fearful, and he was struggling to find humour to deflect, something he had always done so easily in the past.

This film had seemed like the perfect way to rejuvenate his film career. And the Montreal concert should have provided a respite from the problems in New York. As it turned out he was at a low point and trying to deal with two tough taskmasters – Streisand and Dutoit – known for being equally demanding perfectionists.

Nothing improved much the next day. His rehearsal with the orchestra was filled with problems. Dudley sounded unprepared, although he was playing a repertoire he knew inside out. He played wrong notes, seemed unable to focus and looked like he didn't care. Charles Dutoit was quietly fuming. He had hired Dudley to bring in the audience, knowing that his fame as an actor would fill the hall, and assuming that his performance would be good and solid, if not virtuosic.

By the end of the rehearsal, however, he felt it had been a mistake to engage Dudley. Dutoit took him aside and told him, point blank, to go back to the hotel and practise. Dutoit looked me in the eye, took my hand gently and said, 'Make him practise.'

Dudley bristled at Dutoit's condescension. In the space of two days he had been reprimanded by Barbra Streisand and Charles Dutoit, highly respected masters of his film and musical worlds. He didn't really give a damn about the film – only what it represented in terms of an attempt to rescue his acting career, and out of his genuine concern for Lou. But with Dutoit, it was a different story. This was the world he now wanted, more than anything. At the piano, he felt most alive, in touch with his emotions. He desperately wanted his concerts to go well.

After the rehearsal, a small group of reporters from the top Montreal newspapers assembled for the brief obligatory pre-concert press conference with Dudley in the green room. Dudley was both flippant and witty, but the undercurrent of depression was clear, if unspoken, to everyone present. He focused on ageing, and told the rather sedate group assembled that he had recently turned sixty, despised the ageing process, and that 'this reminds me of a joke I've heard. The problem with ageing is that everything that should be soft gets hard, and everything that should be hard gets soft.' There was subdued laughter from the group.

The concert was much better than the rehearsal, and whatever was lacking in the more formal part of the programme Dudley redeemed with his riotous encore parodies at the end of the evening. The audience, as always, was with him, cheering him on, loving him. Dudley came through the experience commenting that it had been a 'very close call'. Dutoit patted him lightly on the shoulder and we knew that he would never be invited back to play in Montreal.

Lou Pitt came to Montreal at the last minute for the concert. It was only the second time I had met Lou, and we were drawn together by our mutual concerns about Dudley. Lou hoped the Streisand situation would be resolved, but before Dudley had a chance to make good his promise to do better in the next session, she fired him. Selected to replace Dudley in his role in *The Mirror Has Two Faces* was George Segal, whom Dudley had replaced sixteen years earlier in *10*. With *10*, Dudley had been thrust into Hollywood superstardom. It was hard to miss the symbolic beginning and end to Dudley's film career. He had been holding the imaginary Hollywood baton for sixteen years. Having returned it, he was never offered another role in a film.

Dudley felt that, in some bizarre way, he was the victim of the Fates, who had been kind to him in lifting him out of a working-class family background in Dagenham and sending him to success beyond his wildest dreams, but who could just as easily cast him down again. He wondered if he had reached his peak, 'if everything that goes up really does come down – I'm the goddamn victim of gravity', or 'if I've done *something* to offend the gods'. He began to obsess on this theory, not knowing it would be his reality. Not knowing that a mysterious condition had already taken hold in his body and that there would be no climb back up to that peak, which had become so familiar – and so comfortable – to him.

Despite Dudley's fame and success, however, he never lost sight of his roots, never forgot the journey that had brought him to such an enviable spot. At his core Dudley remained the kid from Dagenham, still struggling to overcome his club foot and his difficult childhood. It was no secret that John (Jock) Moore was quiet and distant as a father and Ada Moore was inconsistent – sheltering Dudley, loving him, at the same time telling him his club foot was a terrible handicap. He shared the hereditary club foot with his maternal grandmother, Bammy, who was very fond of Dudley and extremely protective of him. She died when Dudley was very young. Dudley was attached to his elder sister, Barbara, but as adults theirs had become a distant, though caring, relationship.

Dudley's natural talent, easy humour and musical genius, both as composer and performer, 'some hard work, and a lot of luck', in his words, had catapulted him to the top of the world. He was one of only a handful of celebrities who were international household names. Dudley's films ranged from superior to mediocre, but he retained his position as the darling of the public.

Until now, he thought. A month before his marriage to Nicole, a year and a half earlier, he had been arrested in a domestic dispute, falsely accused of abusing her. Everyone who knew Dudley was 100 per cent certain that he could not have been violent, but his reputation was tarnished. A lucrative television advertisement he was scheduled to film was cancelled because of his now questionable reputation.

All of his professional activities had previously been a breeze. He had composed music, always on tight deadlines, with lightning speed. He had performed jazz and classical piano music with ease. He had learned his lines effortlessly for every film and television project. He had always kept up the brilliant wit and quick repartee. *Until now*.

His life was changing, and he had many theories as to why, but there was no real explanation.

PART II

PART II

4

OUT OF THE CLASSICAL CLOSET

DUDLEY CALLED ME ON the day my mother died, in 1989, before I had called to let him know. 'Just checking up on you,' he said. 'I had the strange feeling that something was wrong.' My mother had died two hours earlier, at the age of eighty-four.

'I'm so sorry,' he said. 'I'm sorry I never got to meet her too.' We had had many 'mother conversations' over the years – all the good and bad things our mothers had done to us, but shining brightly in the 'good mother' section was providing a piano and lessons early in both our lives.

We still hadn't even begun to make her funeral arrangements, and probably nobody else would have felt safe at that moment broaching the subject of a concerto performance I had coming up exactly ten days later. I was going to play Beethoven's Third Piano Concerto with an orchestra in New Jersey. Dudley went directly to the heart of the subject. 'You're not going to cancel the concert, are you?'

'I thought I should. How can I play it ten days after her death?'

'You know the piece, don't you?'

'Of course. It's ready to play.'

'What would your mother have wanted you to do?' he asked.

I was sitting in my mess of a study on the first floor of my house, with the door closed, the box of tissues that I had been carrying around for two hours placed directly in front of me, my eyes red from crying. Brian was downstairs, calling people who needed to be notified. I had intended to do the same, and had come upstairs to pick up my address book. Friends and family were on their way to the house. I knew the last thing I should be thinking about was the concert. It didn't seem right.

'When it was planned last year, I thought she would be able to come,' I said, the tears starting all over again. 'It was her favourite concerto. She took me to hear it for the first time in Philadelphia – I was twelve.'

'So she would ask you to cancel your performance because of her death? Correct me if I'm wrong. You had your problems, she could be difficult, but she gave you music, told you that you had the talent. Where's the logic in your thinking? Call me tomorrow,' he said. 'Call me today if you need anything.'

'Tomorrow is your birthday,' I said.

'Then call me tomorrow and wish me a happy birthday. Today is too early.'

He was sharp, quick, right to the point. Everyone else was so focused on her death, not daring to talk about anything else except the sadness of it. Dudley always had difficulty expressing the more expected and conventional sentiments at such times, but he had let me know he cared, and he had reminded me what her life had meant, how she and I were connected. I would have got to it eventually, but probably not on the first day.

The following day, I called Dudley in Los Angeles. 'Happy birthday,' I said. He had turned fifty-four. 'Are you OK?'

'I'm *fine*. My body fell apart when I turned fifty, so it's more of the same. How are you? What did you decide?'

'I'm sad, and I'm going to play the concerto and dedicate it to her memory. You were right. Thanks for helping me.'

'I only asked the right questions. You had the answers all along,' Dudley said. 'Yuck. I sound like a cliché. But that's what twenty years of therapy did for me. I'm good at this. It cost me a fortune, so it ought to be useful for something or other once in a while. Other people's lives, if not my own.' He went on: 'What about the California tour?'

I was scheduled to play a few recitals in California about three weeks later. I hadn't thought of it as a tour. I had never been to California, and I also planned to visit several friends and relatives – or was it relations – living in Los Angeles and San Francisco. I would have cancelled it all had it not been for Dudley's words the previous day.

'I'm going to play that too,' I said. 'It's your fault, but thanks.'

'Good. I shall clear my schedule for the next month. Will you come to my house and play the programme for me?'

I liked the way he put it, and laughed out loud. I knew he would not change anything on his schedule, but that we would hope to find a couple of hours for my visit.

'I'll call when I get to LA, but if I do play for you, I want your honest opinion. No flowery praise unless it's incredibly well deserved!'

When I arrived in Los Angeles, I phoned Dudley from my hotel to say hello. 'This place is different,' I said. 'I've never seen palm trees that look like huge pineapples.'

'You've probably never seen as many fake tits as you'll see here either. Or skateboards. Be careful you don't get knocked over by one or the other,' he said. He immediately gave me directions to his Marina del Rey house. However, our schedules did not coincide at all, and in my three days there, the only time we could find to meet was on the day I was leaving for San Francisco.

I arrived at his house early afternoon and joined him in a strong coffee he had made, followed by a quick tour of the house, a brief introduction to Brogan Lane, his wife at the time, and their two dogs, Chelsea and Minka. Dudley and Brogan never mentioned that the process of their divorce was already under way.

I was playing a programme of Beethoven, Chopin, Debussy and Berg, and Dudley was most interested to know all about the Berg Sonata, a twentieth-century work he hadn't yet heard. After nearly two hours at the piano, and discussion of every work I played, interrupted by Dudley's talk of his miserable efforts to lose weight in a place where you had to 'be thin or die', I needed to leave for the airport.

Dudley gave me directions to Los Angeles Airport, but they were so dreadful I missed my flight and had to catch a later one. I had no idea that he was infamous for completely lacking a sense of direction. He would get lost everywhere, except in New York City, where he was fully in command of how to get around.

At that time, Dudley was beginning to play a lot of classical concerts. It was as though his classical musicianship, which had lain dormant for years, was now springing back to life. Dudley had sung in his church choir and studied piano and violin as a child. 'I began life as a *choir boy*,' he would tell his audiences. 'I know some of you will find that hard to believe.'

Dudley was firmly rooted in the classical repertory while an organ scholar at Magdalen College, Oxford. At first, it was not easy for him to transcend his working-class Dagenham background, where he had lived in council housing and struggled to rise above the constraints his background might have placed on his talent, but his intelligence and skills as an actor helped him to adapt as needed. He changed his accent and mannerisms. He was a serious composer and performer there, a scholar; while simultaneously developing his comedic and acting skills, and his jazz playing. When he graduated from Oxford in 1958, he was offered, and turned down, an extended organ scholarship and residency, and was instead swept along by life onstage as a jazz pianist and as part of the brilliant comic quartet that created *Beyond the Fringe*.

After Oxford, Dudley toured United States army bases with the Vic Lewis Band and played in New York jazz clubs for a few months, then returned to England, where he was invited to join John Dankworth's band, continuing to play jazz clubs after hours – 'so I could meet women,' he always explained. In 1960, Dudley asked Dankworth for three weeks off to perform in *Beyond the Fringe* at the Edinburgh Festival. 'I knew he wouldn't be back,' Dankworth said.

Dudley teamed up with Peter Cook, Alan Bennett and Jonathan Miller for a partnership that would occupy his life for the next four years. It was John Bassett, Dudley's friend from Oxford and fellow jazz band student, who thought of putting together a comedy revue of Oxford and Cambridge performers. Nobody could have imagined at the time that the iconoclastic ensemble would alter British comedy and forever change the lives of its unsuspecting young members – four different personalities who combined onstage to brilliant effect.

'We had no idea what hit us,' Dudley said of the early and instant success of *Beyond the Fringe*. 'It was pure blind luck. Oh, of course, we were amazingly talented, brilliant and all that – it goes without saying. But each of us in a different way. It just happened – lightning struck, and we had no idea it could possibly take off that way. It could just have easily gone the other way.'

It was in 1959 that Bassett had approached Jonathan Miller, a highly articulate Cambridge graduate and Footlights star, who by this time was in medical school. He reluctantly agreed to the idea of a comedy revue, and he recommended quick-witted fellow Cambridge comedian Peter Cook, already acting in professional theatre. Bassett then approached Dudley, whom he had known at Oxford, and Dudley introduced Bassett to Alan Bennett, a shy and scholarly young man from Yorkshire, whose comedy had impressed him. Bennett was as reluctant as Miller.

Dudley recalled their first meeting, watching the other three hesitant and competitive, with Peter completely stealing the show. They were all six foot two inches – a foot taller than Dudley, and he consoled himself with the fact that he was there to provide music more than comedy.

Dudley felt immediately more comfortable with Peter than the others, although their origins – Dudley's working-class background and Peter's upper-class background – could not have set them farther apart. Later, when they became partners, their differences and the contrasts between their personalities set them up perfectly as a comic duo, their characters drawn from life, satirical eye always clearly focused.

Beyond the Fringe opened at the Lyceum Theatre in Edinburgh in

August 1960, to good reviews and a small but enthusiastic audience. After its Edinburgh run, the show had an unsuccessful Brighton try-out before going on to a very successful West End run, where it changed the face of satirical revue. Peter Cook did about two-thirds of the script-writing, the others sharing the remaining third.

Dudley seemed forever surprised at the way *Beyond the Fringe* altered his own life – and Cook's, Miller's and Bennett's, each in a different way. For Dudley and Peter this was the foundation of a legendary partnership that continued long after the quartet disbanded, and was to include *Not Only . . . But Also* and *Behind the Fridge* as well as several films, among them *The Wrong Box* and *Bedazzled*. After their deaths, much of the material they produced together has taken on new life.

In 1964 producer Joseph McGrath asked Dudley to star in a one-hour-long television show, and Dudley wanted Peter Cook as his partner. On the first programme in 1965, Peter was one of several guests, among them also John Lennon. At first planned as *The Dudley Moore Show*, the title was changed to *Not Only . . . But Also* (*Not Only Dudley Moore But Also* John Lennon, Peter Cook and others). Their 'Pete and Dud' characters developed from here, with loosely structured sketches that had an improvisatory feel. Pete and Dud became cult figures, discussing their fantasies about sex and women (such as being pursued by Brigitte Bardot), their philosophies of life and their bizarre views of the world. They pushed the BBC's censors to their limit, Dudley said. Dudley always played to the audience, taking it as far as he could; Peter was more aloof. The contrast was part of their success. Every show closed with their comic 'signature' song, 'Goodbyee', ending with Dudley soaring into a falsetto range.

Peter and Dudley's partnership began to fall apart while they were performing their show *Behind the Fridge*, which had gone to Australia and to America under the title *Good Evening*. With Peter's drinking and Dudley's desire to strike out on his own, the partnership was by now in trouble. It was in the late 1970s that Dudley, now living in America and touring with Peter Cook, decided to take a chance on a new career on his own, and went on to major stardom in Hollywood.

In the early 1980s, when he looked back on his achievements over the previous twenty years, Dudley knew that music, his first love, had somehow taken a back seat to everything else in his life. He wanted this to change. But it was more by chance than intention that it began to happen.

His friend Robert Mann, first violinist of the Juilliard String Quartet, helped Dudley to turn the corner from jazz into the classical world. They played sonatas together, and Mann was so impressed with Dudley's musicianship and ability to sight-read works which others would have to practise for hours that in 1982 he persuaded Dudley to give a formal recital with him at the prestigious small recital hall in the Metropolitan Museum of Art, New York City. Dudley was hesitant, but agreed, performing a programme of Bach, Delius, Ravel and Bartók with Robert and friends, including cellist Joel Krosnick. The success of this first programme gave him the courage to believe he could take the next step 'out of the classical closet', as he put it.

Dudley had known Mann for many years. The first time they met was in 1960, the same year *Beyond the Fringe* opened at the Edinburgh Festival. Robert Mann clearly remembers the occasion. Violinist Isaac Stern was in Edinburgh, and tipped Mann off about a 'new hot thing going on. *Beyond the Fringe*. So we went, and went backstage — we talked about music, and about each other's work.'

The Juilliard String Quartet was playing the Bartók Quartets at the festival. 'Dudley told me he loved Bartók,' Mann said, and attended the quartet's concert the next night. Their friendship developed quickly. Whether they met in New York, London or later in California, Dudley and Robert would always play sonatas together, covering many works in the violin and piano literature. 'That was the core of our relationship,' Mann explained.

In 1992 the Martell liquor company set up six programmes — the Martell Cordon Bleu Concert Series — intended to bring classical music to a large and new public audience. Who better than Dudley to be the star of these programmes? The series was wonderfully successful and led to his management, ICM Artists, adding another dimension to their work with Dudley, booking him in classical concerts all around the United States.

Then in his mid-fifties, Dudley was thrilled with this development, although completely outspoken about the fact that he was entering the serious orchestral concert stage through the back door. He worked diligently to improve his piano technique and his musical presentation. But he was having a hard time, and we spent a lot of time on the phone talking about some of his technical problems.

While his jazz technique and improvisation were sparkling and on top form, he found playing classical concertos a challenge of a different sort. He learned the music very quickly, memorising easily, but he wasn't satisfied with the results. The allegro passages were not quite as smooth as he wanted them to be. He was having trouble sustaining a melodic line the way he thought it should sound, and his arms felt stiff.

He could hear it all clearly in his head, but was very critical of his own playing, and not happy with the tapes of his playing he listened to after the concerts.

Dudley cautiously asked me to listen to a rehearsal of Mozart's Piano Concerto No. 21 and Gershwin's *Rhapsody in Blue*. 'If you really wouldn't mind, and if you can spare the time.' He was usually not very good at asking for help, but it was clear that he was eager for it this time. His classical engagements had increased again, and he was feeling overwhelmed. I had offered to attend a rehearsal and take notes.

Two weeks before the Minneapolis concert, he phoned and said, 'I practised the Mozart, but it is still *eluding* me. I'm not sure what to do to make it better. I tried what you said, practising it really slowly, and the tricky parts from the end, adding four notes at a time, but it's still sounding . . . bumpy.'

I knew exactly what he meant, as well as what to do about it. 'Do you want some help, in person?'

'YES, *please*. Would you really do this? You have to let me pay you.'

'No. We've been friends for ages. I won't do this if you pay me. That's my only condition.'

'Then will you allow me to pay your airfare and hotel? That's *my* condition.'

'That's fair,' I said.

Strictly business, he had mumbled, a throwaway line. He later told me that as I was 'moderately respectable', he had wanted to be certain his intentions were not misunderstood. 'And, you may know by now that I have a bit of a . . . reputation,' he said in one of the various British accents he used for seasoning, 'but tell Brian not to worry – not on this trip, anyway. I've got to improve my technique – um, I mean my piano technique, of course.'

I had to laugh. The master of *double entendre*, Dudley in this instance really wanted to sound honourable, but not to risk his reputation (of which he was proud) by sounding *too* honourable.

This was to be the first of many such trips. I arrived at Dudley's hotel suite to discover that he had been at the piano six hours a day for the past week. He looked tired and worried. 'I've never practised this much in my life,' he said. 'This stuff is not easy!'

He was nervous about playing Mozart's Piano Concerto No. 21 and Gershwin's *Rhapsody in Blue*, and, surprisingly, admitted that he was anxious about getting help. He had been working on his own for a long time and was not used to anyone else making suggestions.

'What if you spend all this time and I don't improve?'

'Then we will both know you're a hopeless case,' I said, and so we began.

He knew he could trust me to keep the arrangement confidential, and it remained so until he wanted people to know that I was travelling with him to help, to be another pair of ears at rehearsals and concerts. When that day arrived, he was very outspoken about my role. He would defer to my judgement on questions of balance or tempo. At rehearsals he would look out into the hall during the breaks to make sure I had a chance to say whatever needed to be said.

After a couple of these trips, he sent me his 'before' and 'after' concert tapes, with a scribbled note taped to the 'after' tape, simply saying: 'Thanks. I think I've improved. Let me know what you think. I shall sit by the phone, awaiting your imminent, or perhaps I should say eminent, reply. Love, Dudley.'

Dudley's technique had improved substantially, and his ability to put across his interpretation of a classical work to a large audience was increasing all the time. I thought the improvement was due a little to my help and a lot to his absolute brilliance as a musician, and to the fact that once he caught on to something that worked, he could apply it to many different situations. He insisted it was 'my brilliance, a little – your help, a lot'. We agreed to toss a coin for the true answer.

Over breakfast one morning somewhere in the Midwest, after an excellent programme the previous evening, Dudley was in one of his more communicative moods, pouring out his thoughts on every subject, in no particular order.

He was curious about the progress of Music For All Seasons, a fairly new organisation Brian and I had created to provide live musical programmes for people in all types of residential institutions. It had been my inspiration a year or so earlier, while trying out a piano programme at hospitals and nursing homes. Close to the start Dudley had offered to head the Advisory Board, became President (a title he cherished) and was taking an active role in the organisation. I had assumed it would be enough for Dudley to lend his name to the fledgling charity and was surprised that he wanted to be a working president, to participate in all decisions and hear regular progress reports.

This was a breakfast filled with progress reports of one sort and another. 'While we're on the subject of progress,' Dudley said, 'you should know that the divorce is moving forward quite well.' I barely knew Brogan, but she had seemed very warm and caring.

'Why are you getting a divorce?'

'I don't know exactly. I have to. I married her because she was so beautiful. But she tries to interfere in my business. She's also very jealous. She doesn't trust me — with good reason, I'm sure — but she could at least try. I know we'll continue to be friends. I just have to do this. I have to divorce anyone I marry, in fact. As soon as it's on paper,' he said, picking up his serviette to demonstrate, 'the marriage is over,' he explained, crumpling it up and tossing it aside.

'What about marriage counselling?'

'Oh, I hardly think *that* would work. I had twenty years of therapy — *twenty years*, and I'm much better. I mean, it made a small dent,' he said, laughing. 'But it would take another twenty years to fix my problems with marriage, and I'm sure I haven't the time.'

'So . . . you won't marry again, knowing what you know?'

'I wouldn't go as far as to say that. But I think the whole idea of being faithful in a marriage is totally overrated. And absurd. And impossible for a man. And this seems to irritate women no end. God knows why this should be so . . . important to women.'

Dudley had met Brogan Lane, an aspiring model and actress, during the time she was working as a waitress and doing parts as an extra in occasional films. A brunette, her good looks and extremely outgoing personality appealed to him. She was friendly but unsophisticated and not accustomed to formal social situations. She was constantly encouraging him to expand his horizons, to engage in recreational activities, such as whitewater rafting, that he had never considered before. Brogan was devoted to him, pushing him to go out more, socialise more. She also loved entertaining at home. Brogan, a talented photographer, make-up artist and interior designer, was hoping to establish a film career, and her attempt to star opposite Dudley in the film *Sketchlife* in the late 1980s — a film that was never made – became a source of friction in their marriage.

While Dudley's marriage to Brogan was dissolving, Nicole was already waiting in the wings. If it hadn't been Nicole, it would have been someone else. Dudley had no idea how to be alone. And he didn't ever have to be alone, as he had discovered in his early twenties when he began playing jazz piano in London clubs. He had quickly learned that, despite what he considered his physical flaws – being short and having a club foot – women found him irresistible. He had a magnetic, boyish charm, and women wanted to mother him, to make him happy. Women adored his vulnerability, his talent and his wit. He was outgoing, but at the same time projected a sadness that challenged women to come to his aid, to bolster his ego. He knew exactly how to draw women towards him.

Dudley was on his second espresso and covering a toasted muffin with apricot jam. He had already finished his Eggs Benedict.

'I think the concert went really well last night,' I said.

'I love this,' he exclaimed. 'I know I wouldn't have these concert dates if it weren't for the films. They can fill the hall with my name, and then they are surprised I can really play the piano. I always love *that* part, when they are surprised, even *shocked* that I can play. But I was a musician first. That's who I am, and I wouldn't really care if there were no more films. I would just be at the piano all the time.'

He had been playing the same programme – Mozart and Gershwin – over and over, and knew it well. 'Is there a concerto you've always wanted to play but never had the chance to do?' I asked.

'Absolutely – the Grieg Piano Concerto.'

'That would probably be a good fit for you.' Dudley loved big romantic works like the Grieg where he could pour out his emotions. 'But it's harder than the Mozart and the Gershwin.'

'I know. That's why I've never tried it. But I will some day. In some big splashy programme . . . in . . . Oh, God – are you thinking what I'm thinking?'

'Not Carnegie Hall?' I said.

'Precisely! Another espresso please,' he said to a waiter who was twelve feet away. 'We need to be more awake for this conversation,' he said, turning back to me.

'This could be amazing, but not easy,' I said.

Dudley was energised by the challenge, and wanted to double the effect of the programme by donating the proceeds to Music For All Seasons – 'the least I can do as *President*,' he said, smiling.

The idea of doing this concert was totally insane, but hard to resist.

5

ORIGINS AND CHAOS

DUDLEY LIKED ALL THE obvious advantages of being a celebrity, but he never forgot his modest beginnings. He was born in Dagenham on 19 April 1935 – a small baby with a club foot. His parents, Ada and John (Jock) Moore, also had an older daughter, Barbara, who Dudley always believed was the favoured child because she had no physical deformities.

Dudley remembered having a distant relationship with his father, and a mixed relationship with his mother, who was extremely proud of his musical, academic and theatrical achievements, yet ashamed of his deformity.

'It's only a smaller leg,' his friends would tell him as a young adult. But it was much more than that to Dudley. Dudley felt that much damage had been done to him early in life. Ada had told him that at his birth she wished he had died. This confession, he later understood, was made in the light of how much her feelings towards him had *improved* – how she loved him as he grew, but not at his birth. It was a hard concept for a child to comprehend. She tried to love him the way mothers are supposed to love their children, but she was filled with conflicting emotions. Dudley felt he had inherited his ambivalence from his mother, as well as his nervousness and inability to clarify his own feelings, and he had learned detachment as a father from his own father.

There was little doubt that Dudley's club foot – and his mother's reaction to it – had a major impact on his life. Dudley's left leg was smaller and thinner than his right leg, and his left foot was shorter and noticeably smaller than the right one. *Talipes equinovarus*, or club foot, is a congenital deformity in which the bones in the front part of the foot are misaligned, with the front half of the foot turning in and down. In order to walk with ease, he had a special insert made for his left shoe. Until his sixties, when he began to feel the effects of Progressive Supranuclear Palsy, he was able to walk and run well.

'My mother said I should not let anyone see my left leg. She thought it was horrible, disgusting.' As a child, he had believed her, absorbed her feelings about it, kept it a secret. As an adult, he knew otherwise rationally, but could not reverse the damage her words had caused. Dudley was sensitive, vulnerable and easily hurt. He obsessed over little things. Often he wouldn't show his real feelings and would carry small resentments for years without saying anything.

Dudley was serious as a small boy, but said that he discovered at the age of eleven or twelve that he could gain attention in school for being funny. He learned more and more to depend on that, to deflect attention away from what he considered his flaws by making people laugh. As an adult he continued to use humour, sizing up his 'audience', whether one person or a group, and trying to get a reaction.

Over the years, Dudley's feeling of deformity and his conviction that he had been neglected had taken a major toll on his self-esteem. The image of deformity was always in his mind, in the physical portrait of himself he carried inside his head. Despite the acclaim and attention he received, he struggled with negative feelings throughout his life. The fact that beautiful women wanted to be with him was a boost to his ego but did not erase the damage that had been done. Dudley recognised that he was talented, brilliant and attractive, and had a substantial intellect. But he continued to battle feelings of inferiority.

Dudley struggled with fears of abandonment. He said that there had been many operations on his club foot, and that he was left in hospital for weeks at a time, with few and infrequent visits from his family. Dudley's sister, Barbara Stevens, said that had not been the case, that his hospital stays were short and that the family did visit. It seems likely that the truth lay somewhere between the two – that Dudley's childhood mind exaggerated the time and the neglect, until it felt intolerable to him. It is also likely that his family did their best to make the journey to visit him, but that in the 1930s and 1940s hospital conditions for children, and family visiting hours, were not what they are today. Dudley recalled lying in a ward side by side with soldiers who had been wounded in battle. Listening to their suffering was sad and frightening for him.

Long stretches of time passed for the young boy lying in a hospital bed, with little company and without the music that he loved. But the whole story will never be known. The most significant part of Dudley's childhood is how it made him *feel*, and how much of it stayed within him throughout his life.

As an adult, he spent much time in therapy dealing with his feelings, trying to understand those of depression and inadequacy, and why he had trouble forming lasting relationships. He embraced therapy enthusiastically. At first the idea of talking in a group about his emotions was foreign to him, but he quickly got into the American spirit of sharing feelings openly, and he found it comforting. Dropping the secrecy about his club foot was a major breakthrough.

Still, he remained best able to express his feelings through music, and by the early 1990s he had finally made a commitment to himself to pursue as many musical opportunities as he could.

A few months before the Carnegie Hall concert, scheduled for September 1994, I had arranged to spend a few days in Los Angeles functioning as 'the orchestra' – playing the orchestral part of the concerto, transcribed for piano. Dudley had three nine-foot concert grand pianos in his Marina del Rey home – a Steinway and a Yamaha piano in his large living room, which looked out onto the beach, and a magnificent Bösendorfer – his favourite – in the recording studio on the second floor. In addition, he had a small Steinway grand in the bedroom, and his childhood upright piano – located after many years by Brogan Lane and presented to Dudley as a surprise – had a special place on the ground floor of the house.

It was mid-March. Dudley had been divorced from Brogan for two years, and was in the midst of his newly renewed relationship with Nicole, which had been on and off for years, between and during several other relationships. Years earlier, Dudley had been driving his Bentley in Los Angeles when Nicole, an infatuated fan, had spotted him and shouted out of her window, asking for an autograph. They had pulled their cars over and exchanged phone numbers. She was eighteen at the time. Later she had married and divorced Charles Cleveland; they had two children. Dudley's relationship with her had always been a secret. Now, finally, that was about to change.

The Marina del Rey beach house was purchased in the late 1970s, while Dudley was married to Tuesday Weld. At the beginning of his relationship with Brogan a decade later, the house underwent a major renovation that took a year; Dudley recalled the work on it costing $5 million. The newly remodelled house was filled with touches provided by Brogan, a talented interior decorator with a fine eye for style. Set on the beach, the large pink house was in Mexican adobe style, with polished pine floors and large furniture made from stripped pine logs. Dudley's professionally equipped recording studio comprised most of the top floor of the three-storey building.

Considered modest by Hollywood standards, the open-plan main floor of the three-bedroom house contained a huge living room overlooking the beach, and a dining room dominated by a large country-style pine table with enormous chairs and benches. The two grand pianos were covered with pictures, glass animals and various awards, including the two Golden Globes Dudley had won for *Arthur* and *Micki & Maude*. The bookshelves were filled with collected works of famous authors, and the shelves of the entertainment unit with tapes, CDs and LP recordings, as well as a substantial collection of sheet music.

Brogan's influence was still visible in the house. It was strange to think that she was out and somebody else was in, although Nicole, during her marriage to Dudley, kept the house Dudley had purchased for her a few blocks away and never became a full-time resident in his home.

It was also odd to think that Dudley felt compelled to move from one relationship to another, especially since he could only give what sounded like flimsy reasons. All of Dudley's friends and colleagues had liked Brogan. She was warm, outgoing and uninhibited. Everybody liked her efforts to get Dudley out, to introduce him to new adventures, to things he would never have thought of doing. But her positive, outgoing era was over, to be replaced by a turbulent time.

Performing a virtuoso showpiece like the Grieg A minor Concerto was a big stretch for Dudley, but he wanted his playing to grow, to develop. And presenting a concert in Carnegie Hall was also a stretch for a new organisation like Music For All Seasons; however, the small board of trustees voted to move forward despite the financial risks.

'Use my name. That's why they called me Dudley Moore, instead of, oh, I don't know, what else *could* they have called me?'

Dudley mentioned that somebody else in London was named Dudley Moore and kept receiving his fan mail. He didn't mind sharing his large volume of fan mail, but was not happy about sharing his name. It seemed 'strange' to him, he said. Dudley often used the word 'strange' in situations where somebody might have used a stronger term, such as 'really horrible'.

I had objected to the fact that at least three others I knew of (none of them related) had the same name as mine. We consoled ourselves with the knowledge that it was better than John Smith, or some other name millions might share.

'Or Fiona,' he added.

'What's wrong with Fiona?' I asked.

'Nothing much, except that every British journalist is called Fiona.'

'I doubt that.'

'Three Fionas called me just last week, always first name only,' Dudley said. 'They all sounded alike – fifty-five, brown hair, deep voice. I had to say, "Are you Fiona MacPherson or Fiona MacSomebodyelse?" Well, I thought it was funny. They didn't, apparently . . . End parenthesis.'

But we had completely lost the original topic. 'Where were we?' I asked.

'I've *no idea*,' he replied. 'Sex? Food? Literature?'

I told him it must have been the Grieg, which was dominating all his waking hours – Grieg and his relationship troubles, hardly related topics.

Dudley's involvement with Music For All Seasons made it possible to get backing for the concert and a level of visibility that would normally have taken several years longer to achieve. Dudley was determined to make it a success, and willing to talk to anyone to make it happen. In press interviews, he would say, 'I'm President. I've *no idea* what that means, but I *love* this title. I feel so . . . presidential.' Usually he would go on to speak eloquently about the purpose of the organisation and the emotional power of music, particularly for those confined in institutions of whatever kind.

With the help of Norman Dee, an EMI executive and an old college friend of Brian's and mine, we obtained high level support from

EMI, as well as a recording contract for the Grieg Concerto that assigned a small percentage of the proceeds to Music For All Seasons.

Dudley had been working hard, and had already memorised the first movement and part of the second movement of the concerto. But this was twice as challenging for him as the Mozart concerto or *Rhapsody in Blue*. Some of the passagework would just dissolve halfway through. Rather than get upset, Dudley would laugh. He wasn't yet on deadline, the pressure wasn't on — yet. The next time he tried the same passage, it was likely to go more smoothly.

His spirits were good and his energy high, but in moments away from the piano, over lunch or driving to and from my hotel in his Lexus, there was a new level of agitation I hadn't seen in him before. On the third day of my visit, he came at about 11 a.m. to pick me up for our rehearsal session.

He had come to my room to find me. We were walking towards the front door of the hotel when he turned abruptly and said, 'Let's have lunch first,' leading the way into the hotel's dining room. Often he liked to face out into the room, to be seen. This time he chose a seat facing the wall.

He began, out of the blue. 'I told Else what's going on in my life, and she said I need to get *out* of the relationship.'

'I think I've missed a chapter,' I said. 'How did that happen? We've been talking every day, twice a day. I didn't know there were problems.'

'I thought you might worry. I didn't want to say anything.'

Else Blangsted was among his few very close friends. I had not yet met her, but I knew that she was in her seventies and that she and Dudley had been friends since working together on the film *Six*

Weeks, for which she was music editor. She had a deep affection for Dudley, and liked telling him she was like a mother to him. He liked her straightforward, down-to-earth approach to life, and the fact that she could tell dirtier jokes than he could, and would sprinkle foul language liberally to make a strong point. Dudley trusted her and valued her opinion.

'This relationship is not going well. It's crazier than the others. Nicole wants me to marry her, but I don't think I should. We've been arguing over that. She's irrational, erratic. She has phobias. There are drugs. I've tried them – just the tiniest taste of powder on the tip of my finger,' he said, demonstrating with a few grains of sugar, 'but it affects me badly. I don't like it. That's why Else says I need to get out.'

It was clear that he was in trouble. I was wondering why he needed the relationship if he was so unhappy with the situation. I felt concerned for him. As he went on, I began to understand that he was trapped, but felt obliged to take care of Nicole.

'She's like a child. She depends on me. She's never worked a day in her life. She doesn't know how to take care of herself, or her children. She needs my help.' He stopped, and stared at the table for a minute. 'But at the same time, I don't like how this is affecting me. I thought I would feel good with her, but I feel worse. Like a noose around my neck. That sounds horrible when I hear myself say it.'

'Sounds like you've got a decision to make.'

'I shall have to get out. But I seem . . . strangely unable to do it.'

'What if you were to look at it from the outside, as though it were somebody else's life?'

He looked around the room, satisfied that he had been spotted and a few people were whispering, although it wasn't such a big deal in Los Angeles, where people were used to seeing celebrities regularly. They would notice, whisper, then go on with whatever they were doing.

He had thought about it long enough. 'Oh my God. It's a disaster. I should tell Else she is wise beyond her years.' He chuckled. 'Else made me promise not to die before her. I told her it's not likely, if she's really planning to turn *seventy-four* next month.'

The next morning, I left Los Angeles and returned to New Jersey, an all-day trip going east. The Academy Awards were on television that evening. The following morning I was awakened by a phone call from a family member giving me the news that Dudley had been arrested in a domestic dispute with Nicole.

I picked up the phone and got Dudley's voicemail. A few hours later he phoned me back.

'What happened?' I asked. 'Are you OK? The news reports say you attacked her. Is that true?'

'I'm *fine*,' he replied. 'Although I did NOT like being taken off in a police car. And, no, I did not attack her. I yelled at her to leave my house. She lunged at me, and I grabbed her. But I didn't hit her. I'd had enough. I wanted to break it off, to get her out of my house, out of my life. We both called the police. It got blown out of proportion. Don't worry. I'll call you this evening. I've got dozens of calls to return. People keep calling me about this, as though it were some *big important thing*! It was nothing. We had an argument. They have some rule that says they need to arrest somebody, so I was the one.'

I got off the phone and told Brian what was going on. 'Well, maybe now he can get away from her,' Brian said. I told Brian I thought he would probably marry her. I felt his need to placate Nicole would be stronger than his need to protect himself.

A month later, he did. In the intervening weeks, I had spoken to Dudley every day. But I learned of the wedding on a late-night television news programme.

It didn't feel right. I was disturbed. The pieces of this puzzle did not fit together. The following morning I phoned Dudley. He answered the phone on the first ring, his habit.

'Congratulations,' I said. 'But you might have mentioned you had a wedding coming up when I spoke to you – the night before your wedding.'

'I tell you the important stuff,' he replied.

'How are things?' I asked when I arrived in Oklahoma, where Dudley was trying out the Grieg two weeks before Carnegie Hall. We had barely discussed his marriage of a few months ago.

'How are things? *Fine*,' he said.

'What kind of fine? Is that an English "fine"? An American "fine"?' We had discussed these *fine* distinctions at length in the past. An American 'fine' was closer to the surface, easier to crack. 'One's real condition will ooze through the cracks much faster,' Dudley had said. An English 'fine', at least from his generation, was ironclad. 'Takes a sledgehammer to crack.'

'So, what type is this?'

'American: eggshell.'

'Oh,' I said, mulling it over. But we would not get to the bottom of it in Oklahoma. We were here to work. He wanted to be distracted, to immerse himself in the music and forget the turmoil – to play the piano uninterrupted for hours on end.

'She wants to have a baby,' he said, the strain of this pressure apparent in his eyes.

'And you?'

'I had a baby. I mean . . . my second wife, Tuesday Weld, had the baby.' Dudley's wives all had numbers. By now everybody knew their order, but even in concerts, when talking about his wives, he would count them on his fingers. 'My – one, two, three – third wife, Brogan Lane.' It was always good for a laugh.

'And I'm sure I messed up Patrick. I don't know how to be a good father. My father didn't know how to be a good father. Patrick won't know how to be a good father. This goes down from generation to generation, along with the fine china, if there is any.'

'It doesn't *have* to be,' I said. I felt sad for Patrick; equally sad that Dudley would probably agree to father another child. But I knew that people could break the pattern he was describing. He cared deeply about Patrick, and maybe their relationship would never be ideal, but I thought he could make it better.

'You are so intelligent,' I added. 'You see things other people don't see.'

'Intelligence has little to do with emotional baggage. Like a huge boulder on top of my head. That's why I'm not taller.'

'But you love Patrick, don't you? Wouldn't that help you to change?'

'I do. I love him. He's my son and I want the best for him. I've tried but I can't sustain it.' He meant it. This was just too much for him.

'Some people can change. Not me. I'm just the way I am, the way I've always been. Not a good father. I don't think this would be fair to another child. But she's insisting. We'll see what happens,' he said, abruptly ending the subject. We did not discuss it again until he brought it up a few weeks later.

Dudley was, as usual, and not by request, in a lavish suite, upgraded by the hotel from the suite that was in his concert contract. No matter how many times he was placed in the presidential suite of one hotel or another, he always found it comical. On one particular occasion, he found himself getting lost in a suite that seemed designed not for one president, but for a presidential entourage. And there we were, just the two of us, and a piano, except that he couldn't remember where they had put the piano. We wandered from room to room until we found it. Then we began work. In one presidential suite he claimed it took him fifteen minutes to find the bedroom. 'An extraordinary confession for me, I can assure you.'

After a couple of hours of working on Grieg's fiendishly difficult finale, we needed a rest and a lunch break. Opening doors until we discovered a dining room, we sat down, Dudley very relieved that he had found a spot where lunch, his favourite meal, could be delivered. The table was twelve feet long and had ten chairs. We sat at either end, and Dudley said, 'This should be the board room. We should start a company.'

'What sort of company?' I asked.

'I don't know,' he replied. 'A production company?'

'To produce what?'

Dudley looked very serious for a moment. He picked up a pen from the table and stared at it. 'Videos,' he said firmly. 'We should produce videos, and CDs. And documentaries.'

'Documentaries?' I asked, surprised. 'On what?'

'Bach, my music, circumcision.'

'Circumcision?'

'It would be interesting. We could interview people. Show pictures.

Discuss the pros and cons. I would do the interviews.'

He was completely serious.

'This has always been a great fascination, as . . . well, you know, I'm not.'

'Well, no, I didn't know,' I said. I wasn't sure I really needed to know, but this confession seemed important to him.

'We could have board meetings, just the two of us . . .'

Dudley usually despised 'meetings'; he would do anything to avoid a block of time that came under the heading of a 'meeting'. We could call it a 'discussion' or a 'conversation relating to a specific and important topic', but 'meeting' conjured up something horribly boring in his mind – unhappy people in suits and ties discussing things they didn't much care about, just in order to make money.

Dudley wanted to be sure the company ground rules were clear. He was adamant that he would not wear a suit.

'Dressing gowns, in fact, would be most appropriate.' Dudley usually remained in a dressing gown until he was forced to get dressed, so he was right about it being appropriate for him.

'And today,' he said, pretending to be an executive speaking to his staff, 'we'll work on the script for our documentary, *Dicks of the World.*'

'What will we call this company?'

'It will have to be Fruchter-Moore Productions,' he said.

'I think it should be Moore-Fruchter Productions.'

'No, I insist – Fruchter-Moore has a better ring. It flows better. We can call it F&M for short – sounds like S&M.' He was serious. 'We'll need a logo, stationery, envelopes, and a BOARD ROOM,' he added.

And so, with little fanfare and a lot of enthusiasm, our production company was born. I thought it had to be one of the more memorable corporate launchings. Dudley thought that's the way all corporations were begun. Dudley and I became, respectively, President and CEO, with the understanding that he would never have to attend a meeting wearing a suit. It was a corporation he called 'a company with a twist', and we agreed we would donate to charity the proceeds of our various projects.

This was no ordinary company. We had 'board meetings' – just the two of us – in every city where we performed. We would sit at a table, create a detailed and comprehensive agenda, covering all the company's planned projects. And we would vote, keenly and often. We would engage in spirited debate over everything that was on our list, until every item had been checked off. I was appointed to take notes.

Dudley always wore a dressing gown, a point of honour with him. Usually he wore the robe that came with his hotel suite. If we were discussing what he considered a particularly important subject, he would change into a silk robe from his suitcase. In all the years of running the company, he only twice attended a meeting wearing both a suit and a tie, once for a meeting in an upscale restaurant with a top Disney executive.

It was his choice – 'Once in a while I should look like an "executive", and don't forget, I am a double-president – you may call me President President. I don't suppose a dressing gown would be appropriate for a lunch meeting in a restaurant,' he said. He didn't wait for my reply.

The company didn't produce much for a while, but the first real project was to be a competition for young writers, open to young short-story writers, under the age of twenty, from all over the United States. Dudley set the winning story, by teenager J. Erin

Sweeney, to music and it was premiered in Carnegie Hall in 1996. Later there were other projects, including the CD *Live From an Aircraft Hangar*. Whatever projects were in the works, Dudley took his role as president of the company very seriously, and was involved in the smallest details of the process.

'This is such fun,' Dudley said once. 'I always thought being an executive would have to be terribly boring.'

Finally it was almost time for the big Carnegie Hall event. Brian and I, and a devoted band of volunteers committed to putting together the first big fundraiser for Music For All Seasons, were totally unprepared for the onslaught from the press, and the complex web of organisational details.

Dudley had insisted on adding Beethoven's Triple Concerto to the programme. It was a work he had previously performed twice – many years earlier in Carnegie Hall and a few years earlier in New Jersey. He asked Steven Isserlis, the renowned British cellist who had participated with him in the five-part 1993 television series *Concerto!*, to join him. Joshua Bell, a member of the MFAS Advisory Board and a close friend of Steven's, completed the trio.

The brilliant soprano Roberta Peters, also an Advisory Board member, was to open the programme, with the Orchestra of St Luke's, led by the Israeli conductor Yoav Talmi. The conductor and all the soloists would donate their performances, but paying for the orchestra, paying the Carnegie Hall charges and publicising the event still made it an expensive project.

While all the artistic elements of this grand production were coming together beautifully, it seemed that the tickets were not sell-ing themselves, even with the star-studded cast. A week out, we were in danger of losing money. The high-priced concert-and-dinner tickets were selling well, but seats in the house were selling slowly. Nobody had warned us that September was the worst month to book a non-subscription concert in Carnegie Hall.

Brian and I peeked into the concert hall. 'Look at it,' Brian said. 'It's incredible.' Most of the hall was filled. The two tiers with box seats were packed, much of the balcony, and with the exception of the last few rows downstairs, most of the seats were taken. It was hard to believe. We had made it, and by the end of the concert MFAS would show a small profit. The event would also put the organisation on the map, and allow MFAS to begin expanding into other states. But for now there was a concert to put on.

Dudley was standing in the wings as the lights went down. Brian slipped into one of the first-tier box seats, and I stayed behind, as Dudley had asked me to turn pages for him in Beethoven's Triple Concerto. First the overture, then Roberta Peters, then the concerto.

Dudley wasn't the slightest bit nervous, but stood backstage, joking with Steven and Josh. A few minutes later, they were on. Dudley got a thunderous ovation simply walking onstage. He pulled together all the energy he usually had for a concert, and it was going beautifully. In the last movement of the Beethoven, however, there was one passage that had never gone smoothly in any rehearsal. Steven and Josh had ribbed him about it, knowing that they could cover for him in that one spot. I was sure that Dudley, who was a perfectionist, would be worried. The first two movements were over, and he was now moments away from the dreaded passage. I turned the page for him and the moment was beginning. Josh and

Steven both gave Dudley a look of support. Dudley began, and was holding his breath. He was halfway through, and now into the trickiest moment, a finger-twisting array of rapid sixteenth notes in a pattern that Dudley said Beethoven must have written purely to test Dudley's skills at this very moment. But he was still going. Somehow, he met the challenge, passed the test and the passage was over. He turned his head slightly towards me and winked – the only time I ever saw him wink. He sat up straighter. Josh and Steven glanced over. A tiny but monumental triumph.

But there were more challenges to come in the second half of the programme. The Grieg. Either the Beethoven or the Grieg would have been enough for most pianists. Had Dudley known the prestigious group of artists, musicians and executives from several recording companies who were in the audience because they had heard the phenomenal news that he was about to tackle the Grieg concerto, he might indeed have been a little nervous. This took guts, and many of those people did not believe he could get through the concerto. Not Dudley Moore, the actor.

His performance of the work was neither a musical triumph nor a disaster. His musicianship came through, but he struggled to put across the effortless technical performance that he wanted. The tempo was slower than it should have been. But for Dudley, who a year earlier had only dreamt that one day he might play the Grieg in Carnegie Hall, it was an important personal triumph. He had stretched to do it, and he was glad that he had.

The New York Times review praised all his efforts, and his warm-heartedness in putting on the concert for a charitable cause, calling him 'kind and generous', as well as 'uncommonly brave . . . he got most of the notes out . . . and negotiated some bravura octave runs with surprising success, but he muddied phrases, perhaps mercifully, with excessive pedaling' and gave him glowing praise for the collection of parody encore pieces that followed, adding: 'This was Mr. Moore in his element, and wondrous to behold.' The evening was so enjoyable that nobody really noticed the concert had been three hours long.

Nevertheless, it had taken its toll on us. 'Never again,' we swore once the concert was over. And we stuck to that pledge – until a few months later, when Brian and I reserved the hall for another MFAS event in April 1996.

The next morning, the EMI representatives announced to Dudley that the performance of the concerto was not good enough to release as a CD without additional work, and arranged with Dudley to meet him in their Los Angeles studio a few days later to re-record much of the piano part, and re-insert it back into the orchestral backdrop.

Dudley took the news well, and thought of it as a chance to improve his performance. He continued to practise every spot that had not gone perfectly. EMI allocated a full five days for the project, figuring they would be finished in a day or two.

It wasn't to be that easy. Fitting his part into the orchestra part from the concert, using headphones, was challenging, and Dudley began having more and more problems trying to recreate his performance in a studio setting, feeling under fire and under more pressure than he had onstage. He was uneasy, impatient, distracted by the process. After five full days, the work was done to everyone's satisfaction and some months later the work was released. But Dudley had concerns about the process, and when he heard the finished product he felt that it had been the wrong decision to piece it together bit by bit.

Each morning that week, we drove from Marina del Rey to the recording studio, onto the freeway for twenty minutes and off at a downtown exit. The first day, I experienced Dudley's legendary sense of direction. He knew exactly where we were going in downtown Los Angeles, but upon taking the freeway exit, he wasn't sure which direction to take.

First north for two blocks. 'No, this doesn't feel right.'

Then south for two blocks. 'No, this doesn't feel right either.'

Then north for the same two blocks. And south again. We repeated this exercise six times, each time bringing the busy downtown Los Angeles traffic to a screeching halt while he turned the car round. The last two times I just shut my eyes and hoped we would live.

Finally I said, 'What about asking somebody?'

'Well, I've been there before. I should know the way. But I suppose I *should* really ask.' He pulled the car phone out of its cradle and began to dial.

'Not 911?' I said. He was already through the 9 and heading for the 1. He stopped. 'Oh, I see your point. Point *well taken.*'

Fortunately a petrol station was just coming into view. But I could see his hesitation.

'I don't mind getting out and asking,' I said cheerfully.

'Oh, thank you. Thank you,' he replied. 'I suppose you do know why Mozart wandered the desert for forty years.'

'I thought it was Moses,' I said. 'Because he didn't want to ask directions?'

'Right. Mozart would have wandered Vienna, but only for thirty-five years. He wouldn't have asked for directions either.'

On one morning of the five-day re-recording marathon, Dudley said, 'Would you mind if we make a five-minute stop along the way?'

'Fine with me,' I said. 'Where are we going?'

'To a doctor. I've got to produce a sperm sample. Nicki is ovulating right this minute, so she'll go to the doctor later this morning.'

'Is this what you want to do? I thought you had concerns.'

'It's not what I want. This is what she wants. It will link her permanently to me, after we are eventually divorced.'

'Then why are you going along with it?'

'I can't stand the nagging any more. She wants a baby? Let her have a baby.'

A few years later, during the divorce, Dudley questioned whether he was really the father, despite the process of insemination. Dudley said that he was no longer intimate with Nicole, and that her ex-husband Charles was living with them at the time and was HIV positive. Dudley did have a paternity test that showed 99 per cent probability, virtually conclusive evidence, that he was the father of Nicholas.

We stopped in front of a building that housed the doctor's office. 'Would you like to come inside?' he asked.

'Thanks, but I think I'll wait in the car.'

About ten minutes later, he emerged from the building.

'Everything go OK?' I asked.

'No problem at all,' he replied. 'Now off to the studio.'

The following summer Nicholas was born. In order to avoid more chaos in his own home, Dudley agreed to Nicole's suggestion that they rent a large house in Corona del Mar, high up and overlooking the ocean, for $6,000 a month, he said. The house was large enough to accommodate Dudley, Nicole, Nicholas, Charles,

Nicole's two older children from her marriage to Charles, and other family members who would visit, and stay. They continued to maintain their two Marina del Rey houses.

The process of working through the Grieg concerto on two pianos made it clear that we were a good musical team and enjoyed playing as a piano duo. It didn't take long for Dudley to suggest the idea of exploring the two-piano and four-hand (one piano) repertoire over the next few months. Initially, we had no concerts planned as a piano duo, but after reading through *Carnival of the Animals* by Saint-Saëns, Dudley thought that – despite our earlier protestations of 'Never again!' – we should play the work in Carnegie Hall.

With a 1996 Carnegie Hall date in place, Jeff Berger, an agent then working with Dudley at ICM in New York, suggested using Dudley's already-scheduled dates with the National Symphony in Washington, DC to give our duo a pre-Carnegie Hall début three months in advance.

Arriving in Corona del Mar for a working visit, I walked through the front door and Dudley handed me the baby, saying he needed to wash the bottles. Nicholas was screaming. He didn't know where Nicole was. 'Probably shopping for more baby clothes that we don't need.' Charles was wandering around the house in a dressing gown. He was out on bail and had a court hearing later that day, to which everyone in the house was cordially invited over the intercom, as though it were the day's entertainment. After an hour, Nicole came back, arms laden with bags of baby clothes.

'These are so cute,' she said, pulling out more clothes than five babies could possibly use. Dudley was quiet. I was still holding the baby.

The house was in a gorgeous spot, and while staying in the attached guesthouse I found a route to the beach, a deserted spot that looked out onto massive and impressive rocks some feet from shore.

'Do you know what's down there, on the path beyond the house?' I asked Dudley. It was early in the morning and no one else was awake yet.

'No idea. What?'

He had been living in the house for months but had never set foot on the beach. I led the way and we walked onto the beach, across the rocks and to a large flat rock where we finally sat down.

'Look out there. This is such a beautiful place. If you came out here once a day, for ten minutes, it could restore you. Give you the strength to continue with—'

'With the path I've chosen? You don't have to say it.' It had been less than a year and a half since that lunch in Los Angeles when Dudley had said he needed to get out of the relationship. Less than a year and a half since his arrest. He was looking worn and tired. His eyes lacked their traditional sparkle. He had lost weight. He had very little work. And he was trying so hard to make sense of it all.

We sat on the same rock, not moving, for half an hour, not speaking, just listening to the waves hitting the rocks. Dudley put his head in his hands. 'What have I done? What have I done to myself, to my life?' There were tears in his eyes. He took my hand to help me off the rocks, but stopped. We were in a precarious spot, trying to maintain our balance on slippery rocks – a bit like Dudley's life, I thought. 'You won't ever . . . just give up on me, will you?' he asked. 'Decide I'm a hopeless case? Because I don't know what I would do then.'

'Never,' I said.

I felt that Dudley was trapped in a situation he had not anticipated, and responsible for more people than he could count; yet he
seemed alone, isolated, lost.

We climbed across the rocks and back up to the house. Everyone
else was awake, and several people were arriving at the front door:
Charles's mother, and a couple of people somehow related to her. I
never caught the connection and didn't ask. She was visiting from
Las Vegas, where she lived rent-free in a townhouse Dudley had
purchased for her at Nicole's request. That morning, the television
was on full blast in the living room, but nobody was watching it.
Dudley bristled, turned it off and walked out into the garden. 'How
many times do I have to tell them the same thing?' he said.

We drove back to his Marina del Rey house for some peace and
quiet, took our places at the two pianos and began work on the
Carnival of the Animals, which we were scheduled to play several times
in the coming concert season.

6

TELLURIDE-UPON-MARS

TELLURIDE, COLORADO WAS FILLED with skiers, as it normally was in December. Before I flew there for the first time, Dudley kept calling to warn me about the last few minutes of the flight and the scary landing of the small jet. I could tell from the way he described it that he had been nervous, and he wanted to be sure to warn me enough times so that I was well prepared.

'An extra couple of feet, one is convinced, and the little plane would hit the mountain.' He wasn't *trying* to frighten me, but the words just popped out of his mouth. 'Don't worry about it,' he said, not very convincingly. Dudley had a way of sounding very protective when he cared; very detached when he didn't. In this instance he was overly reassuring, and his own fear was completely transparent. 'Those pilots seem fairly good. You have to just believe they haven't been drinking. If I were ever to become religious, it would have to be while flying into Telluride Airport.'

'You aren't helping,' I said. I had a fatalistic attitude about the trips. Every time I'd landed in the past, I had said to Dudley, 'That's one more flight that didn't crash. Let me see now, the total is . . .'

'Stop it,' he finally said. 'I need you at the other piano. This stuff would sound dreadful with only half the music. No more talk of crashing, or you'll jinx the flight.' That was the last time I said it. But I did offer what I thought was a rational explanation of why I was safe.

'My plane can't crash until I clean up my study,' I said, genuinely believing it. I was sure that my life was protected by some divine force that would not inflict upon my heirs the job of cleaning out my study, which always looked as though a train had driven through the middle of it. One time it looked worse than usual. It took me a while to figure out that a squirrel had climbed in through a slightly open window and moved things around.

Dudley had agreed to play a 1995 New Year's Eve concert at the little Telluride theatre that doubled as a movie theatre – the only place in the tiny, snowy town with anything going on to draw an audience. He had agreed at the beginning of December, and added me to the programme later while I was in Telluride to rehearse for the concerts we had coming up in Washington, DC in January and Carnegie Hall in April. Dudley's Telluride concert was to benefit a local cause. He insisted on covering expenses for both my trips to Telluride, although no fees were paid to either of us for the concert.

The first night of my four-day stay, I attended a movie there with Dudley. More accustomed to the comparative luxury of the Hollywood cinemas, he found the Telluride theatre amusing, and said it reminded him of his childhood. The seats were uncomfortable and the movie was shown on an old projector. There was time out to change the reels, and sometimes it didn't go smoothly. About fifteen people attended on an average night, and the crowd let their feelings be known when the pause between reels seemed long enough to try their collective patience.

'Give the guy a chance,' Dudley shouted, when the complaining from the tiny group became loud. 'It's not his fault he's got poor equipment,' he added, hoping somebody would get the *double entendre* and he would get a few comedy points. A couple of the locals recognised Dudley's voice and he got the intended reaction. The impatient audience listened to his advice and calmed down, but after a few quiet moments began heckling the projector operator again, who took it as a matter of course.

When Dudley first met Nicole, a pretty, five-foot five-inch brunette, he had been struck by her extrovert personality and quick smile. When relaxed, she had a good sense of fun. She also had a hot temper, and the stresses of life made her look for ways to escape. She did not like being in the spotlight, and was not comfortable being in the public eye, a requirement as part of Dudley's celebrity lifestyle. She was devoted to her mother and sisters, and her ex-husband Charles, and preferred staying at home with family and friends rather than attending Dudley's concerts or other professional obligations. He kept her a secret from his friends for a long time.

It was now just a few weeks since the disturbing day in November when Nicole had insisted on moving the entire household, sisters and all, from Los Angeles to Telluride, while Dudley was trying to film with Barbra Streisand in New York. Nobody quite understood why this move took place – it was another of Nicole's many 'escapes', Dudley said. It was only a few months earlier that they had moved from Marina del Rey to rent the house in Corona del Mar. The bigger mystery was why Dudley had agreed to go to Colorado, when he did nothing but complain about the move to anyone who would listen, saying, 'Telluride . . . Colorado,' as though he were saying 'Mars'.

A great place for skiers, but Dudley didn't like any winter sports.

For Dudley, enduring the weather and life that he disliked in Colorado seemed easier than worrying about the careless use and frequent damage to his possessions in the Marina house – at least, until he really found out what living in Colorado meant to his lifestyle.

'I've told them we would add Carnival to my programme,' he informed me, shouting through the bathroom door of my hotel room. 'I assume that's OK with you.'

I opened the door and came out. 'What did you say? I heard that you assume I'm OK with something about Carnival, but I'm not sure what exactly.'

'Oh, I just said we should play some or all of Carnival on New Year's Eve.'

'Here? In Telluride? That's in about two weeks! You think I'm coming back to this airport in the snow in two weeks?'

He was quiet. He acted like he hadn't thought to ask me first, but I believed it was a calculated move on his part, intended to appear innocent. He had already given them my name for the programme.

'We need to rehearse for Washington. We have work to do,' he said, sounding a little hurt. 'I thought you would like to do this.'

'I would,' I replied. 'You know I love doing this, but I'm usually home on New Year's Eve. I'm not sure how Brian will feel about this, and I would normally at least discuss something like this with him first.'

'Do you want me to ask him?' Dudley said. I smiled. The idea was sweet. I knew I had little choice. He was right that we needed to rehearse, and this would give us a good chance to try *Carnival of the Animals* in front of an audience for the first time, even if it was a slightly different arrangement of the work.

'It's *fine*,' I said, looking him in the eye. He caught the irony. 'I'm fine', closely seconded by 'It's fine', were Dudley's most overused, and least truthful, expressions. It wasn't easy for Dudley to say what bothered him. It was a lot easier to dismiss everything and just say it was 'fine', even if resentments were building up. In this instance, he knew I was teasing him. It really *was* fine.

Dudley liked the challenge of attempting a two-piano version of *Carnival*, even though it meant learning two different versions of the work – one containing the orchestral part built in to the two pianos (a lot of extra notes), and the other, for the performance with orchestra – a slightly easier version. Because each movement was preceded by a brief and witty Ogden Nash poem, *Carnival of the Animals* was a good work for Dudley – one that effectively combined his musical and theatrical skills.

For Dudley, who was already irritated by life in Telluride and had little other work on the horizon, this was an important project; he wanted to work and to accomplish something.

We needed two pianos. We had planned to rehearse at his Telluride home, where Dudley had one piano and for a week would rent another. Nicole, however, had other ideas. She wanted him out of the house. She didn't want to listen to hours of rehearsal every day, especially classical music, which she disliked. So Dudley was told to move his own piano out of the house and into the theatre, which he did, without a word of protest.

The manager of the theatre was intrigued by the request and immediately agreed. There weren't many productions taking place at that time, and the crew simply moved both pianos, Dudley's and the theatre's, to the side of the stage whenever the stage was required for a show. The arrangement proved a good one; Dudley was relieved to be out of the noisy household, away from the baby and Nicole's two older children.

Because of the chaos in the Telluride house, I was staying in the hotel adjacent to the theatre. Dudley was glad to have a place to go. He had taken up the habit of driving around the area when things at home were difficult – a very bad habit for him. He wasn't the best driver under any circumstances, and with his lack of experience at driving on ice and snow, he had more than one close call. After driving with him a few times in the snow, I firmly believed that the same divine force that kept my study a mess in order to preserve my life was moonlighting in Dudley's Lexus.

Sound finances and a clean legal record were extremely important to Dudley, and he was disturbed about the word he had received from his business manager that there were legal troubles surrounding the move to Telluride. On the first visit to Telluride, Nicole had found a house she wanted to rent, and they had signed a contract on it. When Dudley was in New York filming, Nicole moved the household. Most of his possessions stayed behind in the Marina house; Nicole largely moved her own. However, she could not get everything into the Telluride house they had selected.

So she simply selected another house on the same street, in the process violating the existing contract. The owners of the first house had many thousands of dollars at stake and were not about to let the money go without a fight. They were threatening to sue, and ultimately they did. This action cost Dudley thousands to settle, and added fuel to his growing anger towards Nicole.

Telluride was not the haven Nicole expected it to be. 'What did she expect? She brought herself along,' Dudley said wryly. There were drugs and chaos in the house, he said. Dudley said he had used Ecstasy and speed a few times with Nicole, but he wasn't happy about it, and he said he was worried about the effect drugs had on Nicole's personality. Nicholas was five months old at the time, but Dudley found himself unable to bond with the baby the way he had hoped. Before Nicholas's birth, he had been optimistic, thinking of it as a second chance at fatherhood – an opportunity to put right some of the mistakes he had made with Patrick. But he had even more quickly fallen into the same patterns. He cared, and wanted the best for his sons, but was still detached as a father. This was proof, he said, that he could not escape from the patterns of detachment passed along by his own father.

Dudley had no friends in Telluride, and after growing a beard was generally able to walk around town without being recognised. This was not the Dudley Moore anyone knew. Wearing a big, thick, beige ski jacket down to his knees, and sporting a beard that, unlike his dyed-brown hair, was sprinkled with grey, he blended into the local scenery like many of the other cold, slightly ageing men. He began wearing the same clothes for two or three days at a time, a departure from his normal habit. He was feeling too morose to care.

This was out of character for Dudley, who normally loved getting attention wherever he went. He would go out of his way to speak to people, give autographs and do wacky things just to be noticed. In Telluride, he said he was in 'some cold kind of hell. Whoever said hell was hot?' He didn't know who he was any more, or what was becoming of the life he had known. He was sinking into a place that was lower than he had ever been before.

Dudley's favourite thing about living in Los Angeles – and one of the reasons he said he had left England – was the consistently beautiful weather. Being away from his familiar California surroundings on the beach, isolated in the snow of Colorado, pushed him over the edge into a deep depression. He was beginning to be aware of his financial problems too. For years, he had left his finances in the hands of his business manager and rarely asked for details. Nicole chose the moment Dudley was just realising he had financial troubles to decide she would open a store to sell upscale children's clothing and furniture. Dudley thought it was 'a ludicrous idea'. This was a ski resort, and tourism was the means by which the town survived. Anyone with half a brain for business, Dudley said, could see that a shop selling high-priced children's items was 'the last thing on earth that Telluride needs'.

He told her so, but she was insistent. 'I'll sell *cute* things. We'll make money. I need something to do here.'

Dudley had thought of telling her she might try taking care of the children, or cooking occasionally, or picking up the clothes that were strewn all over the floor, but he bit his tongue. He never knew what would set off a streak of violence – yelling, throwing things – and it scared him. Especially stuck in the middle of nowhere in the snow. He was more inclined to pacify her with whatever she wanted.

'She keeps moving from one place to another,' I said to him. 'And she has no command of finances. How will she run a store?'

'I've *no idea*,' he added, the emphasis extended over the last two words. 'But she says she wants to do it and needs $60,000 to start. What choice do I have? She wants me to "lend" her the money — I'm sure I'll be throwing it away.'

Dudley couldn't lend her the money because he didn't have easy access to it. He was already borrowing to pay for the expenses of living in Colorado, and he didn't have enough work. Hugh Robertson, his business manager, refused to let Dudley put $60,000 into a store. Nicole was furious with Robertson and begged Dudley to help her. She came up with a list of people Dudley should ask for the money, including his agent Lou Pitt and many of Dudley's other friends, whom she had never met. Dudley was proud of the fact that he had never asked anyone for money in his entire life. He was always the one to offer, to lend, to give. But with Nicole at first begging him, then insisting, he felt he had to obey her. As humiliating as it was for him, he dutifully went down her list, asking all of his friends and some people who were only casual acquaintances. In turn, every single one said no. And it was reported as a nasty piece of Hollywood gossip that sent Dudley deeper into his depression.

Finally, he borrowed the money from the bank. Nicole ordered thousands of dollars' worth of furniture, but she never opened the store. Dudley was at first furious, then swallowed the loss as just another bad turn in his failing marriage.

One afternoon we were taking a rehearsal break at the theatre.

'Do you suppose 911 is still 911 in Colorado?' he asked me.

'I'm pretty sure 911 is the number for emergencies everywhere in the country,' I said. 'Why?'

'Oh, I was just *wondering*, in case it comes up.' He was quiet for a minute, removing a piece of lint from his cardigan. 'In case I'm lying in a pool of blood, for example, or if I should do anything out of character.'

'Such as?'

'You know, things people do when they go berserk.'

We were sitting in the front row, drinking coffee.

'Did I play too many wrong notes?' I said.

'Not *you*,' he said.

I didn't really like what was going through his head, but I thought it was probably good for him to talk about it. 'Well, Dudley, don't you think if you were the one who went berserk, somebody *else* would have to dial 911?'

'Oh, I suppose you're right. I hadn't quite thought this through.'

'What are you thinking, anyway? Are you really having violent thoughts?'

'Fantasies, not actual thoughts. Half-dreams. I'm asleep and she starts hitting me and I grab the nearest thing I can find. A large heavy lamp. And everyone is watching as I hit her with it. In this dream/fantasy, I'm finally able to say, "Fuck you, I've had enough of this. Enough of you." But I can never say it in real life. What's wrong with me?'

Just saying it was a relief. His hands were shaking and mine were freezing cold. He was having trouble breathing. There were tears in my eyes and I was powerless to do anything except listen. I hoped that, for the moment, it was enough. I knew that he could never carry out the fantasy. I put my arm through his and we stood up together, climbed the few steps back up to the stage and went to our pianos.

'"Stars and Stripes Forever"?' he asked.

'Sure, why not? It fits the moment.'

He laughed. We had found a two-piano version of 'Stars and Stripes Forever' and planned to play it some day with strobe lighting. It wasn't until Australia that we did actually do it — a moment of high comedy that the audiences loved. The piece itself was enough of a contrast to erase the heavy topic we had just discussed. It was the most difficult moment of the four days we had in Telluride, and he seemed better, lighter, afterwards.

With Dudley hating life in Colorado and Nicole finding that life contained the same chaos as in California, only colder, the Colorado household began falling apart. In Los Angeles, they maintained separate houses. His was neat and well-run, with a housekeeper and a maid. Household chores went like clockwork in his Marina del Rey residence. Nicole's house was disorganised and, Dudley said, 'there's shit all over the place. I have to step over piles of trash to get to the bed.' He disliked having Nicole and her children in his home, and tried to set it up so that he would spend days at his house and nights at hers. He had treasured the solace of his own home.

Living together in Colorado was stressful for him. Nicole would regularly send Dudley to the store with a shopping list. Since he knew that was the only way he could get the items he liked, he agreed. He was also glad to get out of the house by himself. One afternoon, at the end of a long rehearsal in the theatre, Dudley and I went to the supermarket and wandered up and down every aisle while he selected fish, berries, cereal and San Pellegrino, his favourite sparkling water, the most expensive one in the store. I teased him about it, calling it his 'celebrity water', which normally would have made him laugh, but this time he said it was the only thing that reminded him of what his life was like in LA.

While we were in the cereal aisle, an announcement came over the loudspeaker. 'If Dudley Moore is in the store, could he please come to the courtesy desk.' I gasped. Dudley stopped dead in his tracks. I could sense every muscle in his body tighten. The one thing he loved about shopping in his grey beard and bulky coat was his anonymity, being able to read the cereal boxes without being asked for an autograph.

We went to the desk, as people who had been unaware of his presence began to stare and whisper. 'Your wife wants you to pick up a box of Pampers for the baby,' the young attendant said with a smile. 'Nice to meet you, sir. I had no idea you were living here. Wait 'til I tell my mom!'

That box of Pampers was the final item, which he dutifully picked off the shelf and loaded into the cart. We went through the queue and loaded the bags into the car. People who had passed him in the aisles before the announcement suddenly knew who he was, and stared in the checkout queue.

'I'm sorry that happened,' I said when we were in the car.

'It's OK,' he replied, his hands tightening on the steering wheel. 'That's just the way she is. She has no clue what's appropriate and what's not.' It seemed a strange comment coming from Dudley, who loved to shock people when he could, and never seemed to measure appropriateness by anybody else's gauge of normality. But he wanted to be the one to decide. Despite his apparent addiction to Nicole, he didn't want her telling him what to do. He needed to feel as though he was in control, in charge – and she had trampled all over that feeling. He hesitated a moment before turning the key in the ignition. 'Guess I have to go home,' he said, starting the car.

It had been light when we started the shopping expedition, but it was pitch-black outside, and freezing cold, when we got back into the car. It had been driven from Los Angeles to Telluride by Nicole and her sisters, and it was one of the few possessions Dudley had in Telluride that gave him any pleasure. The Lexus had never been used in a cold climate before but it did have heated seats. 'Finally, I'm able to use this remarkable feature! My arse is burning. How's yours?' he said, as we drove down the road. He dropped me off at the hotel and took my hand. 'Wish me luck,' he said. 'I never know what I'll find when I go home. See you in the morning. Would you like a wake-up call?' Dudley didn't sleep well and was usually up early, functioning at his best in the morning. He wanted to be sure I wouldn't sleep past 8 a.m.

'Sure, a wake-up call sounds good. But not before eight!'

By Los Angeles standards, the Telluride performance was a low-key event. The audience packed into the theatre responded kindly, treating Dudley more as an old familiar friend than either a celebrity or a great performer, and there was a favourable review in the local paper.

'I started life as a choir boy . . .' he began, as he liked to do, opening the programme with stories of his childhood, and playing his very first composition, created at the age of eleven. 'It's called "Anxiety", a precursor of things to come, I suppose.' The audience laughed, but his short composition was a serious one, filled with dramatic tension. Still, he continued to be amused by the fact that he had been so serious as a young boy.

Dudley hadn't really planned what he was going to say onstage. He rambled on about his childhood and his music; it was clear that he was ad-libbing the whole thing. But the audience liked it; people felt he was speaking directly to them, and he was honest, direct and spontaneously witty. He was completely at home onstage, and comfortable with the audience.

I waited for my cue, a very long introduction that included information about Music For All Seasons and the fact that I had given birth to triplets. Later, in our concerts together, he expanded on that theme, turning to the audience and saying, 'Ooh, that must have *hurt*.' He would set it up so that by the time I did make my grand entrance from the wings, the audience was laughing, and so was I. It was impossible to have any stage-nerves with Dudley.

After the concert there was a festive New Year's Eve reception. Dudley stayed until he had received hundreds of compliments on the programme. Although it was a smaller event than most of his concerts, it had gone a long way towards restoring him to being Dudley Moore. Without work and an audience, he was being suffocated. A good response from an audience was like oxygen for Dudley. He had told his friends that, because of the altitude, the air in Telluride was thin and oxygen was in short supply. He was doubly deprived. The little New Year's Eve programme had saved his life, for the time being.

On 1 January, Dudley drove me back to the airport for my flight home. As we started the last mile to the airport, going uphill, the car seemed slightly unsteady. The road had been ploughed but it was snowing lightly. I felt a little nervous, and checked to make sure our seatbelts were properly fastened. We were talking about the New

Year's Eve programme and the next rehearsal we would have for the concerts in Washington, DC.

'I hate this,' he said. 'I hate this place. I hate the weather. Do you have to leave?'

'I'll see you in a couple of weeks. I'll call you when I get home.'

The snow was coming down more heavily, and Dudley turned the windscreen wipers onto a higher setting.

'We should have checked if the flights are going,' I said.

'They nearly always go, unless it's a blizzard,' he said. 'Otherwise the planes would be backed up here for weeks. Half of California would have to just live here. There wouldn't be enough hotels.'

Suddenly, the car swerved a few feet to the right and we were in a snow bank. Had it been on the opposite side of the road, we would have gone over a cliff, but I tried not to think about that, and Dudley seemed not to notice. His Lexus was firmly wedged into about three feet of snow. I couldn't open my door at all. Dudley lifted his car phone and made a call to the local garage; we settled in to wait for help. When the truck arrived, we both got out — I had to climb over Dudley's seat — and the truck driver took us to the airport and then drove Dudley back home. It took several hours to remove the Lexus from the snow bank the following day.

At the airport, Dudley and I hugged goodbye, and I joined the dozens of skiers waiting to leave Telluride. The large body of travellers had so much luggage and equipment that the airport attendants reported they could not get it all on the small plane, and nobody knew when the luggage would be able to travel. It was days before my suitcase made it back to New Jersey.

A couple of weeks later, Dudley flew back to Los Angeles and asked me to meet him there to rehearse. 'I've shaved my beard,' he said. This was an important announcement. I knew he had climbed out of the depression pit and was looking forward to Washington, DC.

7

TRIUMPH IN WASHINGTON, DC

DUDLEY HAD BEEN LIVING in California for nearly twenty years, and the Telluride episode was the only time since establishing his Hollywood film career that he had attempted to live anywhere else. He first went to see ICM agent Lou Pitt in 1976 when he was living in Los Angeles with his second wife, Tuesday Weld, and performing *Good Evening* with Peter Cook. Lou Pitt was familiar with Dudley's career in Britain and recalled seeing *Beyond the Fringe* in New York while still in his teens.

At that moment, Dudley was ready to leave behind both Peter and his British career, and to start anew in the United States. Tuesday Weld's agent, Sue Mengers, introduced Dudley to Lou, but their first meeting in Lou's office was awkward. 'We sat across the table from each other, and it felt too formal,' Lou recalled. They ended the meeting quickly, and instinctively knew that rescheduling it for another day, when they could have dinner, would be more productive. During the second meeting, things fell into place and they began building a relationship —both professional and personal — that lasted until Dudley's death twenty-six years later.

In approaching Lou Pitt, Dudley was very clear about his purpose. 'He wanted to do films, and felt he could succeed as a film actor,' Lou said. Although still in the middle of touring with Peter, Dudley made it very clear to Lou that he felt locked into a world that no longer suited his needs and he didn't want to work with Peter any more. 'He had deep feelings about that,' Lou recalled. 'He was trying to break through for himself, and to separate from Peter as much as he possibly could.'

But Peter and Dudley had been a team for years, and 'it was inevitable that they would work together again'. Although the duo split in 1979, there were periodic reunions for another decade and a half. It was commonly believed in the entertainment world that Peter never forgave Dudley for abandoning him for the temptations of Hollywood. Peter was left behind, and was openly critical of Dudley's Hollywood success, making negative or sarcastic comments about Dudley's American career to members of the press.

Dudley and Peter were cult figures in Britain, and Dudley's reputation had followed him to the United States, but not in the same way. 'He was a star in his world, but his celebrity was not transatlantic,' Lou said. 'Dudley knew he had accomplished a great deal, but I never got the feeling he thought he *had* to be a star. He just wanted the opportunity.'

Lou Pitt had confidence in Dudley's abilities from the start. Dudley was already forty when he began his career in Hollywood, although he had made several films in Britain, most notably *The Wrong Box*, in 1966, *Bedazzled*, in 1967 and *30 is a Dangerous Age, Cynthia*, in 1968.

'He was starting from scratch in Hollywood, a totally different world,' Lou said. But he was viewed as 'good, fresh, charming and outrageous', and Lou knew that Dudley would do whatever it took to create a new career in America. 'He understood the risks involved.'

Lou was always aware of Dudley's personal issues – problems with his relationships and a tendency towards depression, and feelings of low self-esteem that continued despite his success. Dudley shared his problems openly with Lou. But Dudley was also 'a very private person, while needing to be sociable in spite of all the angst,' Lou added.

The first Hollywood break came for Dudley in *Foul Play*, in 1978, at the urging of actor and comedian Chevy Chase. Chevy wanted Dudley for the role of a sex-starved orchestra conductor in *Foul Play*, but Dudley turned down the role twice before it was altered to suit him better. Chevy believed Dudley had actually turned down the part because of his club foot, although Dudley never said so. The original script had semi-nudity, and at that point he wasn't ready for people to know about his club foot. He had a small part – just three scenes – but with the film he launched his American career.

Chevy Chase had been head writer for *Saturday Night Live* when he met Peter and Dudley. 'They came as a team,' Chase recalled, 'but Peter was drunk during the week.' When Chevy had the opportunity to do *Foul Play*, his first film, he thought immediately of Dudley, as they had really hit it off during *Saturday Night Live*. 'We made each other laugh.' The two had in common 'music (jazz piano), painful childhoods, and comedy covering up deformity, in a metaphysical and other sense. I was covering up low self-esteem with comedy,' Chase said.

The timing of Dudley's move from Los Angeles to Telluride somehow coincided with the end of his film career, although he did not know it then. When we next met in Los Angeles, Telluride felt like a distant memory. But it was only a couple of weeks earlier that we had been stuck in the snow on the way to the airport. Dudley didn't say anything right away, but he appeared stronger, a little more able to deal with things, more hopeful about his career. The little concert date in Telluride had been a turning point. Dudley had remembered the importance of an audience – of his relationship with an audience. When he made the decision that we would rehearse in Los Angeles, it was a decision to be back on home turf, to return to being Dudley Moore, although his Telluride era wasn't quite over.

I came through the gate at Los Angeles Airport, and Dudley was standing there with his driver. He was in a good mood. There was no sign of the Telluride depression, and he was waiting to get back to the two pianos in his Marina del Rey home – the nine-foot Steinway and Yamaha concert grands that took up only about a quarter of the space in his living room. He didn't want to waste a minute, although he acknowledged that I might well be tired from the flight, and we stopped at 72 Market Street for a leisurely lunch that had a slightly impatient edge to it.

Dudley had a habit of looking at his watch frequently, something he only stopped doing while at the piano. He believed his incessant time-checking was inherited from his father, a railway electrician. Dudley had a tendency to blame all of his quirks on heredity.

'Should we skip dessert and rehearse?' I asked, after he seemed to be checking the time every two minutes. He wasn't yet at the *final* level of staring at his watch. 'Level 4' I called it. Sometimes I referred to it as 'Code Red'. Eventually he would stare at his watch without blinking, and then you knew it was time to stop whatever was causing the problem. Dudley never minded talking about his unusual and quirky habits. He loved discussing the smallest details of his personality, where the habits originated, how they affected other people, why they couldn't possibly be changed.

'Skip dessert? No, no. Of course not!' he said, as though the idea were totally ludicrous. 'That would be nuts.'

Dudley loved sweets. Skipping dessert was out of the question, and would also have meant skipping his espresso. Both were essential components of any good meal.

Dudley liked his espresso with sugar and artificial sweetener, and it didn't matter what else was going on, this was not an option – it was a requirement. Backstage before a concert he never hesitated to ask an attendant for coffee the way he liked it: espresso if possible, but regular coffee would do, 'as long as it has four sugars and one Equal'. The Equal was his attempt at dieting.

Dudley was one of the principal owners of 72 Market Street, a trendy and popular restaurant in Venice, California, a ten-minute drive from his home. He ate lunch there nearly every day, sometimes alone, but it was a place he was always proud to show his friends. In better times, he used to turn up and play the piano that was in the dining room there.

After ordering dessert and coffee, Dudley turned to me and said in a whisper, 'I don't like the espresso here very much. I've had better in many other places. They don't get it quite right.'

'How long have you felt that way? Is somebody new in the coffee bar?'

'Since the beginning. It's always been . . . oh, *je ne sais quoi* . . .

mediocre. Not *superbe*,' he said with a French accent. He was still whispering, as the coffee bar was only a few feet away.

'But, Dudley,' I whispered, 'you *own* this place. Surely you have some say in what kind of coffee is served here.'

'I wouldn't want to hurt his feelings. This is his *job*. I'm sure he would be upset if I said something.'

He added extra sugar to his espresso when it arrived. Just the additional spoonfuls (on top of the original four) would have been shocking to most people.

'That's better. Now I can't really taste the coffee,' he said.

We never put into words the importance of the Washington, DC concerts that were coming up at the end of January. But there was a clear understanding on Dudley's part that these programmes had to go well – that he had to turn things around. Over the past year, Dudley's solo orchestral dates had become increasingly problematic and his management had felt that the change in his programme to include Saint-Saëns' *Carnival of the Animals* would improve the situation. With the Telluride programme, Dudley had confirmed that he was comfortable with the combination of music and comedy in this work, and he was already confident in our partnership onstage.

We both knew that adding the orchestra to our two-piano partnership could only strengthen the combination. Although we had been playing informally together for a long time, our début with the National Symphony was a critical date for Dudley, and one that his management hoped would go a long way towards eliminating the problems of the past few months.

This was our last rehearsal before meeting in Washington, and Dudley was determined that we eliminate all the rough spots in the work. There were fourteen short movements in *Carnival*, varying in degrees of difficulty. Many of them were humorous, not only because of the Nash poems, but because of the humour inherent in the music.

But one of the pieces, the famed 'Le Cygne' ('The Swan') for solo cello and the two pianos, touched Dudley so deeply that he was on the verge of tears every one of the hundreds of times we played it, and more than once he brushed away a few tears while turning towards the orchestra so the audience wouldn't notice.

We struggled with 'Hemiones', a musical representation of 'Wild Asses', and both felt very proud when we got it up to the frightening tempo at which it should be played.

Towards the end of a rehearsal session that lasted for several days, with time out to eat, sleep and go to the movies, Dudley pronounced the work: 'Ready to go. We sound damn fucking terrific. Do you agree?'

'Damn fuckingly,' I said.

'Cursing doesn't suit you,' he said. 'Once more, from the top, for damn fucking good luck.'

'I'm exhausted. That's six hours so far today.'

'I thought we agreed to practise six hours and twenty-three minutes today. From the top . . . please. In the words of Ogden Nash: "Camille Saint-Saëns was wracked with pains when people addressed him as *Saint Sains*."' And he signalled across the long expanse of two pianos for the start of the opening phrase.

When Dudley arrived at the Watergate Hotel in Washington, DC, he looked badly shaken. Pale, strange, as though he was trying not to let me know that something was wrong. I persuaded him to join me

in the hotel restaurant, and we sat across from each other and each
ordered a glass of Chardonnay, always Dudley's first choice on th
wine list.

I knew that he had gone back to Telluride after our LA rehearsal
– to pick up his concert clothes, which he had left behind – but w
had not spoken in any detail about what was going on there.

During dinner, he was quiet, trying to be witty but forcing it. 'I neve
really liked Michael Tilson-Thomas very much. He was so . . . stiff . .
and not much of a sense of humour,' he said out of the blue. Tilson
Thomas had nothing whatsoever to do with the Washington concerts.

'But he had one good joke . . . and I shall tell it to you right now
Dudley was trying very hard. 'A Chinese man walked into a bank i
New York and wanted to exchange yen for dollars. The clerk gav
him eighty dollars. "What's this?" the Chinese man said.' Dudley
was speaking in a very bad mock Chinese accent. '"Last week I gav
you the same yen and you gave me a hundred dollars. Why is that?"

'"Fluctuations," the bank teller said.

'"Well, fluck you Americans too," the Chinese man said.'

I laughed. It was the best he could do at the moment. The
Dudley was quiet for a few minutes, waiting for me to say some
thing. I asked him what had happened.

'I had an accident,' he said.

'What kind of accident?'

'I was following a tow truck,' he said. 'It was snowing heavily. I
couldn't see a thing.' I was thinking of our trip to the airport in th
snow. I knew that Dudley and driving in the snow was a deadly
combination. 'All of a sudden, I couldn't see his lights. All I could
see was snow. I was rolling down an embankment. I thought it wa
all over. Then I thought I was dead.'

'Oh my God.' It was about all I could think of to say. 'Are you hurt?'

'No, I'm *fine*,' he said. 'My two little fingers got very cold, frozen, in fact.' He held them up. 'I wasn't really dressed for winter.'

'You were living in Colorado.'

'But I'm used to LA. I never really believed I was *living* in Colorado. Who could believe that?'

I imagined he had rolled the car 10 or 15 feet into a ditch. I remembered our accident a few weeks earlier in Telluride and wondered for a moment if the pattern of accidents meant that something else was going on, other than Dudley's always questionable driving and his inability to drive in snow or ice. But it wasn't the right time to pursue the thought. Dudley needed to talk about his accident.

'What happened when you went into the ditch?'

'It wasn't . . . well, it wasn't exactly a ditch . . .' He was hesitant. I knew he didn't really want to tell me. But, at the same time, he *had* to say it. He needed to hear somebody gasp, because he hadn't yet uttered the words to anyone. 'I rolled a hundred and fifty feet.'

I tried not to, but I gasped. I felt thankful that he was OK, or seemed to be OK. But I was worried about what it all meant.

'It was all in slow motion. The car rolled over but I wasn't aware of it until the end.' I wanted to tell him I couldn't listen to any more of this story, but I was also drawn in by his words, and the images flashing across my mind of his guardian angel saving his life. Dudley wanted to tell his story, and he needed sympathy. But he didn't want me to overreact either. There was a perfect balance that had to be struck. I was making an effort, and he knew it. There were some people Dudley liked to shock, for the effect or the sympathy; I wasn't one of them. I knew my role was to cushion his experience, to let him talk. Dudley wanted me to share his sense of awe and amazement at the forces of nature that had dealt him such a blow and yet spared him from death.

'Then . . . there I was at the bottom of the embankment. I was shivering, and scared. I thought I would die down there.'

Somehow, Dudley had managed to extricate himself from the car. He had no idea how, but he half remembered climbing out of the window of his now-totalled Lexus, a car he had always loved.

I was thinking that Dudley would always be safe, that nothing really terrible could happen to him, but that he was tempting fate by driving in the snow.

Luckily, Dudley's Lexus and the tow truck had been the only two vehicles on the road. The tow truck had met Dudley at the airport in Telluride by prior arrangement. Dudley was flying back from LA after an absence of two weeks and was concerned that the Colorado winter would have drained his car's battery and he would need help to get it started. He was following the truck on the road home, and the truck driver noticed that the lights behind him had disappeared. He turned round and retraced his route, and managed to find the spot where Dudley's car had gone off the road.

'I was at the bottom, and I began trying to climb up the hill,' Dudley said. 'But I kept slipping back. I had no gloves, and I was digging my hands into the snow and trying to climb up. It wasn't working. I knew it was the end. My life was going to end at the bottom of a fucking ravine. An icy hell. I tried and tried and kept slipping back.'

I wondered if he recognised the symbolism of his words a few weeks earlier. But, in the telling of it, he wasn't scared. He seemed strong, although the scene kept replaying itself in his mind over the next few days, when he was awake, and when he was asleep.

It had felt to him like hours before he was rescued, but in reality less than half an hour had passed when the truck driver shone a flashlight down the hill and saw the car. Then he saw Dudley, and quickly climbed down to help him.

And that was the shape he was in when he arrived to rehearse the next day for one of his most important orchestral dates, with the National Symphony in Washington, DC.

Typical of Dudley's ability to bounce back, when we started to rehearse on the two pianos in his hotel suite, everything went incredibly well. He was glad to be back in action, relieved to focus on the music again. He said he felt 'fine'. His two frozen fingers were operating well, and he was quick to capture every humorous nuance of the Ogden Nash verses for *Carnival of the Animals*.

The first rehearsal with the National Symphony went surprisingly well too. I was nervous. While we had been playing as a duo for what felt like years, this was our first big orchestral date, and a lot was riding on its success.

On the night of the performance, we stepped onstage to thunderous applause and everything clicked into place. Dudley was on top form – funny, witty, and with flawless comic timing.

'Candy is dandy but liquor is quicker' was the first Ogden Nash phrase he uttered before we began playing *Carnival*. He shared the audience's knowing laugh that it was a subtle reference to *Arthur*.

Looking directly across the piano and into my eyes, he blurted out his favourite Nash quote, as though totally unrehearsed, 'Women would rather be right than reasonable.' He believed it. And I feigned annoyance. There was a noticeably male laugh from the audience after that quote.

Then we launched into the music, and it felt as though Dudley's accident had been erased from his memory.

The audience loved the performance and the conductor and orchestra were with us every step of the way. We had tremendous support from a large entourage of friends and from my family, Brian and our children and some of their friends, who turned out in full force to see our début with the National Symphony.

Dudley played Gershwin's *Rhapsody in Blue* in the second half of the programme, and this was a format that was soon to be scheduled repeatedly with other orchestras.

At the end of the performance, he seemed pleased, content, relieved. We returned to the hotel, tired. Before going back to my room, I gave him a hug and some of the flowers. He looked me in the eye and said, 'It was wonderful.' It was rare praise from Dudley. He had really enjoyed the performance. He wanted this to continue.

In the review a couple of days later, the *Washington Post* critic described us as 'a formidable duo', reinforcing in print what we were beginning to believe ourselves.

With the success of the pair of Washington concerts, there were now eleven orchestral dates for the two of us between the end of January and the 26 April Carnegie Hall date. All our concerns about being ready to play the work in a high-profile Carnegie Hall concert vanished.

Sometime during the course of the next couple of months, Dudley and Nicole moved the household from Telluride back to Los Angeles. His totalled Lexus went to an icy grave in Telluride and

Dudley ordered a new one, leasing a Lexus in the interim. Nicole, the children, her sisters and her ex-husband Charles were all back in LA now, and Dudley resumed the task of trying to keep them in separate houses. Dudley had taken responsibility for all of them, including Charles, claiming he helped in the house and provided companionship for Nicole when Dudley was busy or out of town. Some of Dudley's friends had suggested that Charles, who had a criminal record, had put Nicole up to marrying Dudley so they could all be supported Hollywood-style. It seemed like a believable theory, especially when Charles moved into Nicole's Hurricane Street house.

In March, just a few weeks before the Carnegie Hall date, we had a seven-concert tour to Cerritos and Palm Springs, two small affluent Southern California communities within a two-hour drive from Los Angeles. Dudley told me that life was becoming stormy and chaotic again, and that he was looking forward to the tour. But he wasn't counting on the shattering incident that would occur when the Palm Springs portion of the tour began.

When I came through the gate at Los Angeles Airport, Dudley looked triumphant. He usually took a chauffeur-driven limo to the airport when travelling or picking up friends, but this time Dudley stood alone with a luggage cart. I didn't have to ask even one question about this surprising turn of events.

'I drove here, and I parked the car,' he said, almost too proud to say the words one at a time.

'That's great,' I said as effusively as I could. 'I can hardly believe it. Is this the first time?'

'Well, I suppose it is! I'm an LAX virgin.'

I didn't ask why he needed to do this. He was elated and we simply enjoyed the moment.

'Thanks. This is really nice,' I said. He took my carry-on bag, which was attached to wheels, as usual. We stopped at baggage claim. I collected the other bags while Dudley signed a few autographs. Together we wheeled the bags, with difficulty, across the street and near the parking lot. He stopped dead in his tracks.

'What is it?'

'I have absolutely no idea where I put my car.' He was staring at two buildings, several storeys each. He was silent, looking troubled. Finally he laughed out loud. 'What an idiot. People write these things down, don't they? That's how you know where you've put your car,' he said, realising he had done everything right except the most important thing.

'Most people do this . . . once,' I said, reassuringly.

'Now what?' he asked. 'What do people do after they've done this idiotic thing that they only do once?'

'I think they start on the ground floor and walk a lot.'

'Well . . . all right then. Are you wearing the right shoes for this?' he asked, looking at my feet. It only took forty-five minutes to find the car, and Dudley thought that wasn't bad at all.

8

DUCK IN THE SWAN
(ERUPTION IN PALM SPRINGS)

'CELEBRITY,' SAID CHEVY CHASE, 'is awful, and isolating. It's so odd to be famous, and it's frightening.' Dudley might well have uttered the same words. He loved and hated his own celebrity, and it made him feel guilty for what he had.

When Dudley was first living in Los Angeles in the late 1970s, he had enrolled in a group therapy programme dealing with psychological and emotional issues. Director Blake Edwards recalled being in the same group as Dudley for about two years. It was a group that got to know each other very well, and Dudley was not only outspoken about his own problems, but observant about other people's difficulties as well. Led by a psychotherapist, the members helped each other. Dudley was finally beginning to address some of his emotional issues in an atmosphere where he felt comfortable.

Blake was set to direct 10, which he had written and was co-producing with Tony Adams, and was disturbed to learn that

George Segal had pulled out at the last minute in a dispute over his wife, whom he wanted the producers to hire as editor for the film. 'He became insistent, and everybody said no.'

Blake immediately thought of Dudley as a replacement. 'In my mind, I had a camera focusing in on Dudley as the group went on. He came into focus time and time again. It was like my muse said, "There he is right in front of you. Everybody is calling him Cuddly Dudley, for heaven's sake."

'I said, "Excuse me," and grabbed Dudley right in the middle of some kind of seduction of one of the female patients. We were out in the hall. "Do you want to do a movie?" "Sure," he replied, "what movie?"'

Dudley, only half listening, told Blake he was in the middle of another project. '"Oh fuck that, Dudley," I said to him. "I'm not going to audition you. There's a leading part. You're a schmuck if you don't take it." So Dudley agreed.'

Persuading Blake's wife, Julie Andrews, was not so easy. 'She told me, "Dudley? I'm a giant. I'm just too tall for him."

'We're losing her, I thought, and if I'm right about Dudley, I can't afford to lose her. She was wrong – right because that was how she felt, but *wrong*! I told her it was too much emphasis on height. I asked her what if it was André Previn. She loved him, loved his work.'

That was a persuasive argument, since Dudley's role in *10* was that of a successful songwriter.

'I thought I was too hefty,' Julie explained. But Blake was relentless; he also gave Sinatra as an example – 'someone hugely charismatic, and not tall,' Julie added. 'That's exactly what Dudley was – hugely charismatic, and it was easy to work with him.' They had met only once before – backstage at a performance of *Beyond the Fringe* in London.

Julie finally responded to Blake's arguments and realised that Dudley's height in the role was unimportant. Nevertheless, Blake said, they did agree to try 5-inch platform boots, which were 'so silly, they were hysterical' – and quickly abandoned.

'Working with him in the film,' Julie said, 'our friendship and closeness came about. I was tremendously struck by his courage, knowing the kind of childhood he had – his struggle, his foot. He was such a dear man, a lovely guy. On the set – eternally funny, and played the piano every chance he had.'

Bo Derek recalled first meeting Dudley before they were officially supposed to meet on the set of *10*. She was not enthusiastic that he had been chosen for the role – until she began working with him 'and fell completely under his spell,' she said. In a meeting almost comical enough to be a scene in a film, they ran into each other in a local LA supermarket – Dudley having just stepped off a plane and looking tired, and Bo, as she described it, feeling 'absurdly bloated'. Their 'official' meeting in Blake Edwards's office a few days later went much better.

'My part in *10* was as a weird fantasy creature. I was shy in general, shy with Dudley. And he was shy around me.' Bo was only twenty at the time, and Dudley was very protective of her. The black market tapes of *Derek and Clive* had just found their way to California, and the crew of *10* would play them as they travelled in cars and vans. When Bo was there, however, Dudley insisted that the tapes were turned off, she said.

Bo and Dudley developed a warm friendship, and Bo saw him several times in the last couple of years of his life. 'There was a comfort level, attraction, familiarity, and I always felt like crawling into his arms,' she said. For both, *10* was a 'life-changing experience. I don't think we ever thought our careers would take off the way they did.'

Producer Tony Adams worked with Blake and Dudley on two films: *10* and *Micki & Maude*. Adams, still in his twenties at the time, recalled Dudley as 'incredibly polite and respectful, which given my youth and inexperience at the time was exceedingly generous. Through the course of the film we formed a very strong bond. I wouldn't say friendship – it was hard to be friends with Dudley. Like most comics, he deftly deflected his personal feelings with humour.' Dudley always spoke highly of Tony Adams, although their contact was infrequent. Tony said. 'I don't think Dudley respected or trusted anyone immediately. Respect had to be earned, and trust, if it was granted, had to be hard won.'

The next time Blake, Tony and Dudley worked together was five years later, on the film *Micki & Maude*, a comedy in which Dudley ends up married to two women, played by Amy Irving and Ann Reinking, both of whom are pregnant and due at the same time. Although Julie Andrews wasn't in the film, she visited the set, completing the reunion of good friends. Both Tony and Blake observed that, although Dudley's career had taken off during the intervening years, he hadn't changed a bit.

For Ann Reinking, working with Dudley was 'one of the best times – the whole process of filming with Dudley was a delight. The cast couldn't wait to get to work. If Dudley made you his friend, if he *believed* in you, he was always there for you.'

Later, Dudley was encouraging to Reinking when she was given a chance to do a serious play. 'Being a dancer, there was a certain prejudice,' she said. 'He told me, "Don't listen to the prejudices. Just do it." He really understood.' On one occasion, he was watching her in a dance class. 'He said to me, "You *know* you're good, and you *don't* know you're good – just like me."'

Dudley objected to being pigeonholed, typecast, and he encouraged those whom he admired to stretch themselves to reach their full potential. Many of his fellow actors spoke about Dudley encouraging their efforts, drawing them out, listening to them. Reinking remembered him as a strong influence on those working with him.

Dudley was an inveterate letter writer, corresponding regularly not only with his close friends, but also with fans. If someone wrote to him on a subject of interest, he would write back and continue the correspondence – long, detailed, personal letters. His most striking opinions about his work sometimes showed up in his letters.

Corresponding with Hugh Macdonald, a producer from New Zealand, he wrote about *Micki & Maude* and other films. '*Micki & Maude* I hope you will enjoy, since I think it is the best thing I have done since *Arthur*.'

It was a great disappointment to Dudley that '*Six Weeks* was pretty butchered by everyone . . . some people cannot take the feeling that I am putting out.' He loved the music he had written for the film. 'It is a very tender, poetic, joyful story, despite having at its center enormous sadness . . . but that's life, isn't it!?' And he would always feel regret that it had not been better appreciated. He knew he had composed a wonderful score for the film, and the fact that it hadn't been more generally acclaimed did not change his own appreciation of the music.

In March 1996, having completed a successful run of concerts in Cerritos, we arrived at a resort in Palm Springs on a hot, sunny day. Dudley was feeling pressured by the demands placed on him by Nicole, who had said she might join him for the three remaining days of the tour. Dudley had some radio ads to record in his spare time on the trip, and he had promised to write a chapter for Lin Cook in England. She was assembling and editing a book of memorial tributes to her late husband, Peter Cook. Dudley had promised for weeks that he would write something, and the fact that his was the only tribute that Lin still needed – and he was having trouble focusing on the task – was another pressure he didn't appreciate.

'I don't want to write this, but I told her I would do it.'

'Why don't you want to?' I asked. I could probably have answered the question myself.

'I had a lot of problems with Peter. I think it will colour what I have to say. I still resent some of the things he said about me when we were no longer working together.'

Dudley had made some comments in interviews since Peter's death that had been neither tactful nor politically correct. He had said that he wasn't really upset, didn't miss Peter and that Peter's death hadn't affected him much. And this in highly public forums – newspaper interviews, television interviews, at a time when the press was eager to hear kind and sad words from Dudley on the subject of Peter's untimely death at the age of fifty-seven. Those close to Dudley were sure that he wasn't in touch with his emotions on the subject. His reaction seemed so callous, so out of character. I had said it seemed hard to believe he wouldn't feel anything.

'That's not what I said, is it? I told you I didn't feel what everybody else thinks I should feel. That doesn't mean I don't feel anything. I feel angry that he was jealous of my success in Hollywood. I feel angry that sometimes he was drunk onstage when we performed together. I feel angry that he wasted his talent, and that he felt superior enough to ridicule me. And of course I'm upset that he's dead. But what am I supposed to say when everybody asks me about this? That I'm mostly angry? That we weren't close in the end? What?' I knew that after Peter's death, Dudley had called Peter's answering machine several times to hear his voice.

Comedian Eric Idle has often spoken about the influence *Beyond the Fringe*, as well as Pete and Dud, had on the Monty Python group. And he credits them with making him want to become a comedian. He watched Peter and Dudley's careers, and relationship, closely. 'Peter seemed never to quite forgive Dudley for becoming a successful movie star. But then Peter needn't have been so drunk at the London premiere of *Behind the Fridge* that you were grateful for Dudley's sobriety and professionalism. Indeed, a year later when I saw the same show in Los Angeles – now called *Good Evening* – Dudley had become the funny one and Peter the other one. A strange transformation, like seeing the doll suddenly controlling the ventriloquist.'

Journalist Barbra Paskin, who at that time was completing her biography of Dudley, had argued persuasively with Dudley about all the good reasons to write his tribute for Lin Cook's book, and he had finally acquiesced. Barbra offered to interview Dudley and write the tribute chapter for him. She had already written about us in her own book, but had not yet heard us play a concert together. Dudley suggested that she meet us in Palm Springs on the second day of our stay there, attend the concert and spend the next morning discussing Peter Cook with him. Dudley agreed to handle his tribute that way. He could well have written the tribute to Peter Cook himself, but he hadn't done it in the several months since first being asked. This was an easy out for him; in the end he was glad Barbra had offered.

The first of the three Palm Springs concerts went well. Having played the programme several times with the same orchestra and conductor, we were comfortable and well prepared, and an easy rapport had developed with the ensemble onstage. Dudley was relieved that Nicole wasn't there and we returned to the hotel after the concert, planning to meet the next morning.

Late that night, however, Nicole arrived, with all three children, her ex-husband Charles, one of her sisters and a stray dog that they had picked up along the way. The next morning, Dudley was clearly under some strain. His eyes were troubled; his face had a pained expression. He said he hadn't slept much and wasn't feeling well. The children were noisy, and there were trays of food everywhere from several orders of room service. Clothes were all over the chairs and the floor, as though the suitcases had been upended. Not exactly how he had hoped to rest before a performance.

Dudley and I settled in to practise in the living room of his suite, the one spot still more or less untouched by the invasion. Barbra arrived a short while later, while we were practising The Swan, and settled herself on the couch, the lone audience member in the suite. Dudley was playing a piano whose sustaining pedal needed some repair and squeaked exactly like a loud duck – not the sound needed for the most melodic and serious piece of the set. After the first couple of squeaks the contrast between the sweet melodic line and the raucous duck was so out of character that we both began to laugh so hard we could barely play. It didn't matter how many times we went over the piece – we couldn't stop laughing. I had to leave the room once to catch my breath and stop the pain in my ribs. I was certain that the evening's performance would be interrupted by our laughter just thinking of the rehearsal piano.

The suite was huge, with several large rooms that might have accommodated eight or ten people, and Dudley had told Barbra that if she needed to stay that evening after the concert, there was plenty of space in the living room, which had several massive couches and a separate bathroom. She had just put down her things in the room when we all heard a commotion in one of the other rooms. Nicole opened the door and stormed into the living room, followed by her older son and her sister.

'What the hell is she doing here?' Nicole said, looking at Barbra. 'You didn't tell me she was coming. I know you are having an affair with her, or you would have told me about this. You didn't think I was coming here, did you?'

'I certainly did tell you she was coming. I told you last night and this morning,' Dudley said.

'After I was already here!'

'Nicole, I am here because we are *working*,' Barbra said. 'I thought you knew that. You certainly have nothing to worry about. I'm not having an affair with your husband. I never have.' Barbra was telling the truth. They had been friends for years, and Barbra had interviewed Dudley many times, for publications, for television and for the biography. Their friendship was platonic, though close after more than a year of working with Dudley on her book. Once, Dudley had become so irritated with Nicole's jealousies that he had told her he couldn't remember if he had slept with Barbra or not, as there had been so many women. To him, it had been a joke. To Nicole, it was serious, particularly since by that point in his life, his womanising was legendary. At this moment, it looked like Nicole' memory of Dudley's flippant comment about Barbra months earlier only served to fuel the fire.

'I want her out of here. Just get her out of here or I'll tell the papers about your hookers. How would you like that?'

'Fine with me. Tell them everything. Tell them whatever the hell you want. Barbra is here to work. We have an interview to do.'

'I don't care why she's here. I want her to leave,' Nicole said. 'She has no business being here.'

'Neither have you,' Dudley said. 'You never understand what it means when I have to work.'

'I'm your wife. I have every right to be here.' She was starting to yell, and Dudley went into the bedroom and slammed the door. Nicole followed him into the room. Dudley then left the room, and Nicole began throwing things.

'Don't you run away from me,' she screamed. 'Where are my cig arettes, you fucking little midget.'

'Don't you dare say that,' I yelled at her. 'You need to leave. Dudley is here to perform. He has a concert in a couple of hours.'

I felt angry, devastated for Dudley that his wife could insult and belittle him. I remembered him saying that once, while cutting the ribbon for a dedication ceremony, he overheard someone comment ing on his height, saying he looked like a midget. Dudley had felt deeply wounded and never forgot the incident. Now, I couldn't imagine how he would cope with this comment from Nicole.

Nicole was livid. She was in the hallway, and her sister was now with her. Nicole picked up a huge vase and was getting ready to throw it at Dudley when her sister grabbed it and restrained her.

Barbra was frightened and moved to the door.

'Yeah, you get the hell out of here, you bitch,' Nicole shouted.

'I'm leaving,' Barbra said. 'I'm not here to cause a problem. I'm going.'

Dudley was standing, frozen in place by his anger, coupled with his fear of confrontation. It was hard to tell which was going to be the winning emotion.

I turned to leave. 'Are you going to be all right? Do you want me to get help?' I asked.

Nicole answered, 'You fucking get the hell out of here, and we'll all be fine.'

Dudley looked for a moment as though he was about to leave, hesitated, and said, 'Come by in an hour. I'll get dressed for the concert now.' I left feeling disorientated, in shock and disbelief, and certain that however I felt, Dudley must have felt much worse.

An hour later I was calmer, but worried about what was to come. Dudley, Barbra and I went to the concert hall. Dudley and I went backstage to our dressing rooms and Barbra took her seat in the hall. Nicole didn't come to Palm Springs to attend the concert. Although she had requested twelve tickets, which were being held at the box office, she stayed behind with her entourage and ordered more room service.

We were scheduled to be onstage at 8 p.m. I was wearing a long formal black skirt and a black top with red sequins that I had picked up as a joke while visiting my daughter Ruth in Las Vegas. Normally I dressed more conservatively, but I thought the bright colour might be a good idea that evening. I sat down in his dressing room.

'That's enough to keep the audience awake,' Dudley said, blinking twice as the light in his dressing room bounced off some of the sequins.

'I've been to Vegas to see Ruth. I must have caught something there.'

'Good,' he said. 'You should be flashy once in a while.'

'I'm sure it's temporary. So . . . are you OK?'

'I'm *fine*. Oh, fucking hell. I'm not even fooling myself this time. How the hell do you think I am? I'm married to a lunatic and my life is a living hell. But I'm paralysed because I love her, or maybe I just think I love her. So, you still think I'm lacking self-awareness? I've filed away twenty years of therapy for moments like this.' Only much later would Dudley decide this was an addiction rather than love.

'Wow!' I said, stunned by his statement, and almost relieved. 'Now what?'

'I shall have to divorce her. This is no secret. We all know it. And I shall have to pay more alimony. And have a steaming shitload of problems . . . I don't know how to do this. I should just die. It would be a lot easier, wouldn't it?'

I stood up. He was looking in the mirror. Staring. Fixing his hair.

'I don't look bad,' he said.

'You look great.'

'That's how I can tell things are terrible inside. The worse I feel, the better I look . . . and vice versa. Why do you suppose that is?'

'Five minutes to curtain.' The Voice of God echoed over a loud-speaker in the dressing room.

'Fifteen minutes for us, then. Coffee?' Dudley asked.

'I think it might make me tense.'

'*Coffee* might make you tense?!' We both laughed. 'I hope these pianos have no ducks in the swan,' he said.

By now, we were so comfortable with *Carnival* that we allowed all kinds of spontaneous things to happen. Dudley added more Nash quotes and ad-libbed better. We added historical facts – sometimes straight out of the encyclopedia – which caused laughter, Dudley's mock erudite readings contrasting with both the music and the Nash verses. Once, before playing the movement entitled 'Turtles', I gave him a gift-wrapped wooden turtle that I had picked up in a local craft shop. Both Dudley and the audience cracked up.

A few weeks earlier, we had added a gag that Dudley loved. Just before playing, and after the orchestra tuned, we mock-tuned the pianos. Simultaneously, he played an A and I played an A-flat. It looked very serious, and Dudley reached under his piano bench to reveal the largest tuning wrench in creation. It had been custom-made for us by a piano tuner with a good sense of humour. The wrench was attached to a wooden handle that was an additional foot longer than the standard wrench.

'That was the visual portion of the programme,' Dudley would usually say after we tuned.

The tour orchestra had watched the gag patiently night after night. This particular evening, as luck would have it, the orchestra wanted to get in on the act. As Dudley picked up the wrench to hand it to me (normally we met centre stage and I collected the wrench and returned to my piano), he saw a note attached to it. He opened the note and couldn't control his laughter. The orchestra members all knew that one of them had written 'for proctological exams only' on it, and they began laughing too. So did the conductor, Stephen Stein. Dudley was in a jam. He couldn't read it to the audience, but the audience knew there was something going on and laughed along with everyone on stage. We tuned and started playing.

Dudley jumped right into the music, and showed no signs of the incident in the hotel room a couple of hours earlier. He always ended the programme with an encore group that included several of his parodies, and the final one was slightly shaky that evening, but there were no other signs of his distress.

After the blow-up in the afternoon, I had resigned myself to the possibility that the performance would be a complete disaster. Nobody could perform with such tension, and Dudley would be unable to focus. I was wrong. I had forgotten that, no matter what was going on, Dudley's real world was music.

We went straight back to the hotel after the performance. Barbra wasn't sure it was a good idea to stay, but figured she would at least see if Nicole, whose behaviour was often erratic, might have calmed down. She got her answer quickly. Nicole was waiting for her. The incident had been simmering during our absence and Nicole's condition was worse, not better. As soon as we reached the first floor where our rooms were located, Nicole came out of the door and lunged at Barbra. She was completely out of control.

'I'm going to kill you. I'm going to throw you over the balcony,' she screeched, chasing after Barbra. Nicole grabbed Barbra and was trying to pull her back towards the balcony, gripping Barbra's long hair and bashing her head against the wall.

By that point, other hotel guests had heard the screams and gathered outside on the lower level, looking up in an effort to see what was going on.

'Get out of here,' I snapped at Nicole. 'Leave her alone.

Somebody has called security,' I said, not knowing for sure, but assuming it was a safe bet.

Dudley was staring at Nicole, frozen and unable to take any action, but with an expression on his face that I had never seen before. A cold, hard look of anger and hatred that I was sure nobody could ever have seen in Dudley. He was almost in a trance.

Nicole lashed out at Barbra again as several hotel security guards arrived. It took more than one to loosen Nicole's grip on Barbra and bring the attack to a close. The guards asked for an account of what had happened. Her instability was clear as she described Barbra as the intruder in her marriage. Barbra gave her account. I gave mine.

Dudley's troubled marriage to Nicole had progressed one notch further and could not be saved. Barbra had head and neck injuries, and suffered from the incident for years, much later being diagnosed with post-traumatic stress disorder resulting from the attack. The combined emotional and physical effects of the attack caused a serious interruption to her career that lasted several years.

The hotel's security, assessing the situation accurately and seeing who they were dealing with, quickly found a room for Barbra, and asked what other help we needed. Barbra wanted to call the police and press charges. Dudley spoke privately with her, and asked her not to do it, for his sake. 'I don't want her going to jail,' he said. 'I know she's crazy, but she's the mother of my son. And I don't want everybody finding out about this.'

Against her better judgement, Barbra agreed. She was very fond of Dudley, and didn't want to upset him further. Later, a lesson learned the hard way, she realised she should have pressed charges. A few months afterwards, Dudley acknowledged that Barbra should, indeed, have called the police. But it was too late. The incident leaked out anyway and was reported in all the local papers the next day, and around the country in subsequent days. Dudley paid Barbra's medical expenses for many months of treatment for her injuries, and when Barbra was unable to work, he paid her six months' lost income and living expenses. Things got even uglier after Barbra's book was published and Nicole sued both Dudley (while they were still married) and Barbra for $10 million, later dropping the suit. As Dudley's marriage to Nicole was dissolving, he told people that Nicole had tried to kill Barbra. When Nicole heard about this and became more enraged, Dudley advised Barbra to leave the country as Nicole had renewed her threats against her.

The next morning, Barbra drove home and Dudley and I took a limousine to the sound booth in the concert hall to record a short promotional piece Dudley had agreed to do for an upcoming performance. When I knocked on his door at the agreed time, Dudley was accompanied by Nicole and Charles. Dudley looked quiet and nervous. I spoke only to him, and we all got in the back of the limousine to take the short ride.

'Don't think you're off the hook,' were Nicole's first words to me. 'I don't trust you with my husband either.'

'Don't threaten me, Nicole,' I said. And the car proceeded. There was no other conversation.

I sat with Dudley in the sound booth, and Nicole and Charles wandered around the hall, watching every move we made. We had one more performance before the tour was over. Nicole and her group left before we did and I travelled back with Dudley.

I gave him the only ultimatum of our entire partnership.

'I can't live like this. You might be able to, but I can't. It's lucky we got through this tour. But I won't ever perform with you if Nicole comes along. If she is there, I will leave.'

'I know,' he said. That was it. She was never there again. Not in a rehearsal, not on tour, not in the audience. I didn't have to say it twice. He knew there was no room to negotiate.

The episode was finally over. We were at the airport in Palm Springs, awaiting our flight back to LA. Dudley and I were standing and looking out of a large window, removed from the rest of the passengers. I was still very upset about the events of the previous two days, and I knew Dudley was obsessing on things, wondering what he could do to make his life more liveable.

I had already asked Dudley why Charles Cleveland, Nicole's ex-husband, was living with them.

'He keeps her out of my hair. She needs a lot of attention. They go out driving in the convertible and playing loud music. I don't like to do that. And two of the kids are his. He helps with them. Where else could he go when he's not in jail?'

It would have sounded like a bad joke, but it was true. Charles had a significant arrest record and had been in and out of jail on drug-possession, burglary and other charges. Dudley had admitted on more than one occasion that he was scared of Charles, but then he would add, 'He's pleasant enough when he's around. I don't dislike him. He's helpful.' Indeed, Charles was friendly and cordial, although Dudley knew that Charles had taken and sold some of his possessions, and didn't want to tangle with him over any serious issues. Jewellery was missing, and larger items, including cameras and recording equipment. Yet Dudley had taken responsibility for

Charles, paid for his trips, bought items he requested. Dudley had even bailed Charles out of jail. Dudley had told Suzy Kendall that he (Dudley) was 'mixed up with a perfidious element'.

Nicole's threat of going to the tabloids with stories of Dudley hiring hookers was weighing on my mind, although it had only been mentioned once. It was the first I had heard of this, and I wondered what would happen if I brought it up. I braved the topic.

'Was that true about hookers?' I asked. He bristled. This was clearly off limits. Normally, no topic was off limits in my conversations with Dudley.

'It was never *my* idea. Nicki hired them.'

'Let me get this straight. Nicki . . . your wife . . . hired hookers for you. I'll remember that if my marriage ever gets dull. Did she pay, then?'

'Of course not. She has no money of her own. I paid.' I was surprised to hear he sometimes paid by cheque. 'But generally they just took their clothes off, and danced.'

'Then why would she care if she thought you were having an affair with Barbra?'

'Because she wouldn't have set it up. She wouldn't have controlled it.'

It was hard for me to get my brain around this. OK, he lived in California, where things were just a little different – that much I knew – but this one was way off the charts, and he knew it. He had hoped that nobody, especially me, would find out about this, but he had forgotten that Nicki always employed threats of informing the tabloid press about the most intimate and embarrassing details of their lives. It was how she kept him in line. I was sure he was caught in something that was scaring him and would drag him down.

'She thought it would make me happy. Nicki wasn't turning me on. She thought this would be a loving thing to do for me.'

'Ughh.' I did not hide my disgust, and we were dangerously close to being overheard. I lowered my voice. 'Maybe you weren't feeling anything for Nicole because she belittles you, insults you, puts you down.'

'Not all the time. Sometimes she is really sweet,' he said.

'Why would you have gone along with it? You could have plenty of women. Why pay for sex?'

'Why should I be discussing with you what arouses me, if you aren't a participant?'

I had no idea what to do with this conversation. Music was a much easier subject, but I kept wondering how Dudley and I could have so much in common, could think alike, be on the identical musical wavelength, and yet be worlds apart in this area. 'What would you know about such things? You've been married to one person your whole life, since you were practically a child.'

'I was twenty-one.'

'As I said, practically a child. You were completely naïve about the world. You still are, as a matter of fact. But at least you're connected to someone — I've never had that. I don't even know what that feels like. I don't know what love is. I'm just trying to survive, to feel good for a few minutes once in a while.'

I didn't object to being called naïve. He was probably right. I thought it was somewhere midway between a compliment and an insult — I wasn't entirely sure which way it was tipped, but decided I would take it as a compliment.

'Hold on. Wait a minute,' I said. 'What about Suzy? You said you loved her. You still do.'

'Of course I do, but I messed that up. Neither of us knew enough to make it work. But it's *much* better as a friendship than it was as a marriage. Perhaps I should have stayed, insisted on making it work.'

I knew I was making things worse, forcing him to look inside himself, at his mistakes, but I was worried he was on a dangerous path in his life. Even with the crude language of the infamous *Derek and Clive* tapes, and Dudley's reputation with women, he had managed to maintain a clean image with the American public. He was still 'Cuddly Dudley', and the public kept forgiving his mistakes, his weaknesses. But reports of abuse – and now, threats of the media learning about hookers, even if they were only stripping, dancing hookers – this would change things, his image would be ruined. It wasn't long before Nicole made good on her threats and sordid bedroom details circled the world's tabloids.

Dudley was right about my life. Brian and I had passed our twenty-fifth anniversary a couple of years earlier, and had worked hard to have a strong and stable marriage. We had a family and a long history. We were very close, close enough for Brian not to feel threatened by my friendship with Dudley.

I had pushed Dudley a little too far, and he was upset that his secret had been revealed.

'Why are you challenging me like this?' he said, his tone close to angry. 'I do what I do.' I felt sad that Dudley had such a big void to fill. It wasn't even about sex, I thought. Dudley, more than anyone, knew he was searching for some inner peace he might never find.

'You're so clean, so . . . respectable,' he added. 'You will go to Heaven if such a place exists, which I *truly doubt*. You probably have some horrible secrets. I find it difficult to believe your head is only filled with pure thoughts.' He leaned in and whispered, 'So all this effort is for nothing, possibly.' He stopped for a moment, looking me firmly in the eye, 'But you shouldn't be asking me such . . . personal questions . . . about my sexual tastes, and so forth, unless . . .'

'Unless what?'

'Just unless.' Typical Dudley. Whenever things were rough in his life he would deflect, turn to humour or bizarre statements. Provoke. It was all banter, half-truths couched in off-colour humour. Suddenly he was two people. 'An honourable wench, this one.' 'Ay,' the other one replied, 'and she'll 'ave nothin' t' do wi' the likes o' thee.' The subtleties of the dialect were lost on me. It was something out of a Shakespeare play I'd missed, I thought, or some Pete and Dud episode I hadn't yet seen.

'Is there oxygen on your pedestal?' he carried on, grabbing his throat and pretending to gasp. A small audience in the departure lounge was straining to hear. I had no idea how to respond, and I was almost sorry I had brought up the subject. I knew *he* was, even though he was now getting some mileage out of it. I felt so . . . conservative. Our plane was boarding. 'To be continued,' he said, picking up his briefcase. 'Take your ludicrous wheels. Let's go.' For some inexplicable reason, Dudley despised the luggage wheels that attached to my carry-on bag, ultimately to be replaced by little bags that had their own built-in wheels. Sometimes he felt obliged to wheel the contraption, as if it meant he were polite, chivalrous – but complaining the entire time down the gangplank. Now, I felt conspicuous and uncomfortable with my wheels. I never liked being watched, offstage, and that afternoon it felt like all eyes were on us. One of my wheels chose that very moment to develop a squeak. I might as well have been naked, I thought.

'If it's carry-on baggage, you ought to be able to *carry it on*,'

Dudley had to add. I thought he was hung up on being literal – that if the airlines had labelled it 'wheel-on baggage' he wouldn't have said a word. He could barely lift his large black leather briefcase, worn at the edges and filled with cholesterol pills, eye drops, several large toenail clippers, which he kept buying in every city, and music, pens and paper, spare socks and underwear and whatever else had fallen in. He hadn't cleared it out in years. But he pretended to lift it effortlessly. The muscles in his right arm told a different story.

'Are you the pot? Am I the kettle?' I said. He tried not to laugh, and offered me a small piece of wrapped chocolate that I knew had been sitting in his jacket pocket for weeks, probably having melted and solidified more than once. The awkwardness of the moment evaporated. He ate the remaining piece; it was misshapen and had a slightly greyish colour to it. Strange for a connoisseur of fine chocolates, I thought.

A big-breasted young blonde was walking quickly towards Dudley, a disposable camera in her hand. 'Oh, pleeeze, could I take my picture with you? I just *love* you!' She handed me the camera, probably purchased after she spotted Dudley, I thought to myself. He stared at her cleavage.

'Of course,' he said, putting his arm round her waist. I snapped twice. I was always the resident photographer. Usually the pictures would have one blonde on each side of him. She slipped a note into his jacket pocket and took back the camera, still smiling.

Finally seated on the plane, he pulled out the note, read it and handed it to me. It had her name, address, a Los Angeles phone number and the words, 'Please call me – anytime. All my love, xxxooo'. I gave it back to him. 'It's your lucky day,' I said.

'I've got enough trouble,' he said, crumpling up the note and tossing it on the floor. I knew that a few years earlier he would prob-ably have made the phone call.

I didn't feel critical of Dudley, just sad that sex seemed to have lost its meaning for him. It was an impulse, not really connected to feelings of love. I thought that, in many ways, he was the naïve one. He needed constant affirmation of his sex appeal, and it had gone too far. I suspected that, despite his always overactive drive for con-quest, he had only in recent years somehow completely disconnected sex from emotion. He knew it, but didn't know how to turn back, how to regain that part of himself that he had lost.

I pulled out the newspaper I had bought to read on the plane. As if destined to be the topic *du jour*, the headline on the first page of the Living section read, 'Keeping the Spark in Your Marriage'. Dudley was holding the right-hand page of the paper, half reading with me. There were enough sparks in his, I thought, to ignite an explosion.

'So do you and Brian still . . . do it?'

'When I was eleven, we used to say the word "it" and giggle, my two best friends and I. Which reminds me of the only terrible juve-nile joke I used to know. A nun went to her Mother Superior, informing her she wanted to become a prostitute. Mother Superior reacted with shock and horror, grabbing her heart. The nun repeated that she wanted to become a prostitute. "Oh, praise the Lord!" said Mother Superior. "I thought you said you wanted to become a *Protestant*."

'My friends and I had to look up "prostitute" in the dictionary!' I added.

'Good joke, very . . . *apropos*. But that's the *best* job of avoidance I've ever heard. Top prize in the "avoidance" category goes to . . .' – opening an imaginary envelope – 'Rena Fruchter! What a surprise.

The question was: do you and Brian still have *sexual intercourse?*'

'Well, of course we do.'

'Are you lying to me?' he asked. This was now our favourite 'in-joke'. It was often hard to peel away enough of the layers with Dudley to get to the truth about something. Sometimes if his answer to a question was suspect, I would say, 'Are you lying to me?' and he would answer an emphatic, 'Yes!' Then we would start all over again, until we got to the *real* truth.

'I'm not lying,' I said, almost laughing. 'Why do you want to know?' I knew he didn't really care, and I wasn't bothered by his attempt to get back at me for challenging him.

'I've known you for the better part of a decade, and I've wondered from time to time, in my idle moments, as any good and concerned friend would. But twenty-five years or so . . . with the *same person?* What's left to do? How can you stand it? I admire your . . . what's the word I'm searching for . . . perseverance?' An old lady on the other side of the aisle was listening intently. She choked on a sip of coffee.

I turned a few pages of the newspaper, reading just the headlines. There was a small item about the incident in Palm Springs. Dudley groaned.

When we landed we were met by a photographer with a huge lens, always a clue it was a tabloid. 'Mr Moore, we heard there was a huge blow-up in Palm Springs. Are you OK? Were you hurt? Can you tell us anything?'

'I'm *fine*,' he replied. 'Everything is . . . *fine*.'

9

CAUGHT BETWEEN THE MOON
AND NEW YORK CITY

IT HAD BEEN A rough couple of years. The solidly successful
years were now clearly in the past. Dudley's personal life was turbulent, and his professional life was rocky. On the surface, it appeared
as though he was continuing to function, to get offers, but some of it
was smoke and mirrors. By 1996, he had moved to and from Corona
del Mar and Telluride, and back to his home in Marina del Rey. He
had failed at the attempt to renew his film career, and had two failed
television series – *Dudley* and *Daddy's Girls*. But he had also completed
two very successful narrative series – *Oscar's Orchestra* and National
Geographic's *Really Wild Animals*, and there had been a string of
orchestral concerts around the country that had gone reasonably
well.

When Dudley's New York agent excitedly told Dudley that he
had been invited to join Liza Minnelli on tour in July, Dudley was
not thrilled. In fact, he groaned and said he wasn't sure he wanted to

do it. At the time the offer was made, he was in New York preparing for a Carnegie Hall gala for Music For All Seasons.

Liza had planned a 'mini-tour' on the East Coast of the United States – just five performance dates, and Dudley would be a late addition to a programme that had been set up months earlier without him. Clearly, he was not being offered equal billing with Liza. Although nobody had actually said it, Dudley knew this was another effort on the part of his management to save his career.

'What's wrong?' I asked, when we had a few minutes alone to discuss it later that day. We had gone back to the St Regis Hotel, where he was staying, for lunch. He looked miserable and was staring at the lukewarm fish on his plate.

'I don't want to be her warm-up act. I don't want to do this.' Dudley hadn't been given a choice about whether or not to accept the engagement. He had been strongly advised to do the tour and his management treated his approval as a formality.

'Can't your management do something about this so you won't be in second place?' I asked. He wasn't really listening. He was very seriously moving mashed potatoes from one part of his plate to another, as though he were on an important mashed-potato mission.

'I don't have a good relationship with her any more. I just don't see the point in doing this. Her audience isn't the same as my audience. They won't *get it*.'

Dudley didn't much like the fact that he was so strongly associated with his role in *Arthur* that people on the street would still call him Arthur, but he knew it was inevitable. It was the film that had solidified his Hollywood career. He had no mixed feelings about having made the film or anything connected with it, except that he didn't like being typecast as Arthur in real life. Nearly two decades later, when PSP caused his speech to become slurred, he would say, 'I'm doomed to become Arthur in real life.' But he had only the most positive feelings about the movie, one of the two films that established him as a major film star.

'I loved filming that movie, and I could have spent my life sitting at the table with Linda (Liza's character), eating meatloaf.' The scene he most loved was when Arthur is standing with his fiancée's father in the living room of their mansion, looking at a huge moose head over the mantle. No matter how often he recited his line, 'You must have hated this moose,' it was always followed by his huge Arthur-style cackle.

Co-star Jill Eikenberry, who played his fiancée, remembered Dudley's high energy in the film, a young cast 'all on the upswing. But I was the "up and comer", and Dudley was totally supportive – he was fabulous. We first met in the restaurant scene – one of my favourites.'

When Dudley learned that Jill played the piano, he encouraged her to play on the set. Like several of his co-stars, Eikenberry said that Dudley was an inspiration and she learned a lot from being in the same cast with him.

In a similar way to 10, in which Dudley had been a last-minute replacement for George Segal, several other actors had been more seriously under consideration for the role of Arthur. Paramount had been developing the script, and Orion (which had produced 10) took it over. Both Richard Dreyfus and Ryan O'Neal had been top choices. O'Neal turned it down. When Dudley's name was suggested by Orion executive Mike Medavoy, there was a major debate among the various partners as to his suitability for the role, in part over the issue of an Englishman playing an American character.

Lou Pitt read the *Arthur* script, loved it and handed it to Dudley. 'Who would I have to sleep with to get this role?' Dudley asked Lou, calling him every fifteen minutes the day he read the script. 'You would have to sleep with too many bodies — you would get confused,' Lou had replied. For several weeks, no decisions were made.

Dudley waited impatiently to learn the fate of the film and ended up doing another movie while waiting — *Wholly Moses*, by all accounts a flop, and a mistake for Dudley to have accepted. But Dudley was paid $1 million for his role — at that time a high fee, and contrasting noticeably with the $100,000 he was paid for *10* and $300,000 for *Arthur*.

Dudley, who was realistic about all his films, wrote openly about them in many of his letters to friends. He had only the highest praise for *Arthur*. However, he described *Wholly Moses* in one letter as 'very drab. The material was very bad in that film . . . it is a piece of crap, but I thought mistakenly that it would have been fun to do.'

Dudley had fond memories of his work with Liza in both of the *Arthur* films, particularly the original one. They had developed a solid friendship while filming *Arthur* in 1980 and, although they spoke infrequently, there was a bond and a sense of equality they shared on screen. Liza was definitely on the short list of his friends. In 1988 Warner Brothers produced the sequel, *Arthur 2: On the Rocks*, and Dudley and Liza found it easy to pick up the friendship where it had left off eight years earlier.

Liza's super-stardom had increased during the 1980s and 1990s. She surpassed Dudley, and it created an imbalance that Dudley didn't like. Now, playing second fiddle on this tour was an open wound for Dudley.

Dudley knew that he should have been more aggressive about his career, and should have been willing to take a stronger stand on issues that were important to him. But his excuse was that his father had been a very passive man, so it was in his genes. It was the same explanation he offered for his own weak skills as a father. 'My father was passive, detached. No wonder I'm like this. It's inevitable.' As far as Dudley's career was concerned, he didn't really have a plan; he let things take their course and hoped there would be a positive outcome.

As was increasingly the case these days, Dudley let others make important decisions for him. He never told his agent and business manager what he really thought, or more importantly how he *felt*, about Liza's tour. He left them alone to decide for him and to work out the details. They made a few demands to Liza's group about equal billing, which were granted in the contract but, with her huge entourage and extravagantly staged production, did not substantially alter the situation. The final plan was for Dudley to open the show by himself and for the rest of the evening to belong to Liza. He would join her for a couple of numbers during the second portion of the show, but the main show was, still, hers.

The first rehearsal in New York City was a disaster. Dudley, who never did well in second place, couldn't focus on the music. Liza was agitated and paid almost no attention to him. Dudley found her behaviour strange and erratic. He was angry and distracted, and people in turn thought he had been drinking. I came in halfway through the rehearsal, amazed when I felt the frenetic pace of everything going on. Musicians having their own rehearsals in corners of the room, Liza looking over the sheet music, Dudley practising the piano and trying to get Liza's attention.

'Liza,' he said to her, music in hand.

'Just a minute, sweetheart,' she said to him, dismissively. He continued, not used to being ignored; not even hearing it.

'Liza, what do you want to do in this spot?' he asked, pointing to a passage in the music.

'I'll be there in a minute,' she snapped.

Dudley was fuming. At that moment he switched off whatever was left of his friendship with Liza. In his personal life he allowed a lot of leeway. Professionally, there was none. He required the kind of consideration Liza was unable to provide during that rehearsal. Nothing in their relationship would ever be the same.

Liza had an entourage that filled the rehearsal space, and Dudley was lost in the crowd. Used to being the centre of attention in most situations, he reacted more and more negatively to the setting. Dudley and Liza had barely agreed on what pieces they would perform together. Some of the orchestra parts had been ordered but had not yet arrived; there was no way to rehearse effectively without them. After about an hour of accomplishing very little, he decided he was finished with the rehearsal, picked up his music and headed for the door.

We went back to the hotel and up to his room, where he immediately picked up the phone to call room service. 'What would you like?' he asked me, the room service operator already on the phone. He didn't identify himself, although the St Regis operator addressed him by name, as the operators did with every guest at the hotel. It didn't occur to him that he could have looked at the menu first. He heard my involuntary chuckle. 'What are you laughing at?' he asked.

It was hard to explain. Dudley had to do things the minute he thought of them. There was no logical order, and I knew I was under lunch pressure. Still, it was a relief from the chaotic setting we had just left. Dudley seemed to have tuned out the experience, at least for the moment.

'I don't know. You order. I'll look at the menu.' By the time he had finished ordering a five-course lunch, and carefully selected a glass of Chardonnay, fifteen minutes had passed, and I was well prepared for my moment in the spotlight. 'I'd like grilled chicken, fruit salad and coffee.'

'Whipped cream? Ice cream?' said Dudley.

'No thanks,' I replied. I was on a diet, as usual.

'Is that all? What about some dessert? Pie? Salad?' I was sure I could feel the pain on the other end of the phone line, the room service operator wondering if it would ever end.

But she was patient. He was, after all, Dudley Moore, and if he took twenty-five minutes to order lunch, instead of everyone else's five minutes, that was OK with her. 'Thank you very much,' he said. 'Now, how long do you think it will take to get here?' With that, he let out a guffaw. The operator had a sense of humour. 'Not quite as long as it took to order it, sir,' she had replied.

He looked at the music he had dumped on the table, and it brought him back to the reality of his situation.

'I don't know why I agreed to do this,' he said. 'I'm sure it was just for the money, but that was possibly the wrong reason.' Still, he didn't want to drop out. He felt it would look bad and the word would get around that he couldn't handle performing a simple programme with Liza Minnelli.

The tour opened at the Garden State Arts Center in New Jersey on 3 July 1996. The sold-out concert was billed as a pre-July 4 extravaganza. In keeping with what I eventually learned was his unbreakable habit, repeated before nearly every performance, Dudley had forgotten half of his tuxedo and had to rent one. Usually it was a cummerbund or bow tie (he had collected dozens, but they were rarely in his suitcase), sometimes the tux shirt, or the cufflinks, but this time he had no trousers. Good for a couple of jokes, but he really needed trousers to play the tour.

On the morning of the first performance, he called for a limo and went alone to a well-known New York establishment for a tuxedo fitting. In the dressing room, he began to feel dizzy, and halfway through the fitting, he vomited. Later, the owner of the store reported to someone glad to have (and spread) some juicy celebrity gossip that Dudley had been drunk. But he hadn't. Back at the hotel, he phoned me at home in New Jersey and said he felt really ill. His stomach was hurting and the room was spinning. 'I've got a virus.'

'You need to see a doctor,' I said. 'Do you think you should cancel tonight?'

For a moment I wondered if it was the stress of the situation, his feeling unprepared and not ready to go on in second place, but I quickly dismissed the thought when he sounded genuinely ill.

'I've never in my life cancelled a performance,' he said. 'And I can't start now. I can get through this. And I don't need a doctor telling me to cancel.'

'What if you throw up onstage?' I asked, believing it could happen.

'Then the audience would have a surprise. Or they would think I didn't like working with Liza. But I can do this. I'm not in a position to start cancelling. Once you do, you are never the same profession-ally – never dependable.' He was adamant, and there was no talking him out of his decision, even if he felt ill, and no matter how much he would rather have avoided being onstage with Liza.

The rest of the afternoon, I couldn't stop thinking about Dudley's plight, wondering if we could have seen this in the crystal ball in April when he'd been asked to take part. He should have said no to the tour. I took a long walk, feeling a sense of doom about the evening's performance.

The Arts Center was just a few miles from my New Jersey home, and Dudley had arranged tickets for the members of my family who were able to attend – Brian and two of our daughters and our son-in-law. We all went backstage before the concert. Dudley appeared shaky, but pretended to be fine. We were concerned about what was to happen, and my daughters tried to cheer him up. We tried out some new dirty jokes and offered words of support, vitamins and remedies for an upset stomach.

Finally, we took our seats in the auditorium, a 5,000-seat arena with a roof and open sides. When Dudley came onstage, there was little doubt that he was the warm-up act for Liza Minnelli and her entourage. He couldn't switch on his onstage persona, as he had always been able to do. He was driving a train uphill and it was slip-ping backwards. Those of us who were close to him could feel his ambiguity, even his hostility, bursting through his failing attempts to be both humorous in his spoken words and bright in his musical selections.

'What's going on?' someone in the row ahead asked. 'He's not funny at all.' The audience applauded politely, but it wasn't the response he would have received just a few months earlier. The next day, Dudley briefly considered dropping out, making any excuse he could, but his code of honour as a veteran performer prevented it.

He continued – dragging himself to Saratoga Springs in New York, to the Oakdale Theatre in Wallingford, Connecticut, and finally to Boston, Massachusetts – the one performance that was better than the rest. I attended the Connecticut performance, and the rest of the week heard many complaints in his several daily phone calls. Dudley said he disliked the halls, the weather, the food, the hotels and, always, the concerts. Eventually things improved, but he summarised the experience as 'demoralising', and he was determined never again to perform on the same stage with Liza. It was years before they would speak again.

10

CHASING KANGAROOS

DUDLEY LIKED AUSTRALIANS, WHO he said were 'a good blend of British and American qualities'. For several months during the spring and summer of 1996, there had been talk of a possible Australian tour. Dudley hadn't performed there in twenty-five years and had very happy memories of the previous visit, with his jazz trio.

For a while, we had been working on the creation of a show entitled *Dudley Moore at the Piano*, assembled through our production company. It was a narrative and musical journey through his life, seen largely through the music he had written, and featuring a two-piano segment as the central core of the programme.

Getting the Australian project off the ground was not easy for Dudley's management, ICM Artists, to arrange. As much as we both wanted to go to Australia, we were resigned to the fact that it might never happen. Just as everything was set, it looked like it would all fall apart with one final thud. It wasn't until we were well into the tour that we learned that the finances had still been threatening to dissolve while we were on the plane out.

Dudley's agent, Lou Pitt, scheduled a Los Angeles try-out the night before we left. Dudley was excited, and believed he had a good chance to pull his career back together. He had renewed energy, and pushed us both to practise. For this tour Dudley took over the role of resident perfectionist and slave-driver for our duo.

Dudley resisted the idea of a script for the show, saying he could 'wing it', but Lou insisted that Dudley needed prepared material, jokes and stories that would be written but could feel spontaneous. Dudley finally agreed, and Lou contacted Dudley's old friend and colleague Peter Bellwood, a friend since the early days of Dudley's career in Britain. Like many of his formerly close friends, Peter had been cut out of Dudley's life once he began living with Nicole.

Peter was warm and very forgiving, with a slightly resentful edge over Dudley's neglect of their friendship, but he was happy to be hired to work with Dudley on the script. Peter had won over Dudley's confidence with one joke – which eventually became Dudley's infamous trademark Sheep Joke, and night after night drew the longest laugh of the evening. It was the perfect vehicle for an Australian audience. Dudley told it in a slightly intoxicated tone of voice, reminiscent of his Arthur character.

A man was arrested for having sexual intercourse with a sheep. He was brought before a jury of his peers for a trial.

The prosecutor said to him, 'So, Mr McPherson, you were arrested for having sexual intercourse with a sheep.'

'Yes, that's right. I had sexual intercourse with a sheep.'

'And can you tell the jury what happened next?'

'As I was withdrawing from the sheep . . . (at this point the roar of laughter was always deafening). As I was withdrawing from the sheep, the sheep turned round and, with his front paw, he tickled me under the testicles.'

The foreman of the jury turned to the woman sitting next to him and said . . . (*long pause*) 'A good sheep will do that.'

We were scheduled to play the try-out programme for L'Ermitage Foundation in Los Angeles the night before going to Phoenix for an orchestral concert; then we were to fly out for a five-week tour that zig-zagged across Australia and New Zealand, followed by performances in Hong Kong and Hawaii.

We had repeated the entire show many times. 'From the top,' Dudley would say with an air of authority, and we would go straight through the programme from start to finish, several times a day. 'We've earned a break,' he would say at the end, opening a small decorative 'applause box' that broke into thunderous applause as the lid was lifted, making him laugh every single time it was opened. The box had been a gift to me from an old friend, but I had given it to Dudley, as his need for it seemed ever so slightly greater than mine. I was sure that he opened the box repeatedly for an extra ego boost when he was alone.

I was already checked into the Windham Belage Hotel, where the programme was to take place, when Dudley arrived. He appeared shaken, not responding properly, not greeting me with a quick hug as he normally would have and certainly not ready to perform – he was worse than I had ever seen him.

As soon as Dudley began his opening monologue, everyone knew something was wrong. This was more than an off-night. I stood offstage and out of view and cringed as he struggled to move from one line to the next. I felt like I was in the middle of a strange and disturbing dream. This couldn't really be Dudley having so much trouble with the material he had known so well only a few days earlier.

The audience included people Dudley knew and many prominent members of the Los Angeles community, and they seemed puzzled and concerned for him. Dudley was struggling to remember the order of the programme, even with his written notes on his music rack. I was seated at the other piano, facing him, for the second half of the programme, and he seemed relieved not to be solo any longer – to be able to share this burden. The audience was relieved as well, and the Gershwin two-piano arrangement of *An American in Paris*, which we had practised for months until we could have played each other's parts, went reasonably well. I looked across the piano at him and he smiled. We engaged in a very brief and impromptu dialogue that made the audience laugh, and there seemed to be some hope of rescue. I had always assumed that Dudley, the veteran comedian, would do all the talking, but the moment of unexpected dialogue that he initiated seemed to help.

It wasn't until the end of the evening that I learned that Nicole had physically and verbally attacked him earlier in the day. As Dudley removed his tuxedo shirt to put on his dressing gown, I noticed a bruise on his arm. He winced as the robe rubbed across his skin. I didn't have to ask him what happened.

'She slammed the car door on my arm.'

'How *could* she?' I asked, furious, worried, wondering how much worse their relationship would have to become before he could leave.

'It's not her fault. She just doesn't understand that I have to leave, to work. She wants me to retire.'

'And do *what*?'

'Stay home with her and the kids. I would go crazy. This is what we're fighting about. She wants me to give up everything.'

'What do *you* want?'

'I want to give *her* up. But I can't. I don't know how. I'm at the end of my life. I need somebody to be with me. I know it would be better if it weren't Nicole. I know I need to get out of this situation.'

He admitted that during the programme we had just played, the scene of fighting and violence had replayed itself over and over, that his arm hurt, that he couldn't concentrate. That he had been on the verge of tears once in the middle of the Gershwin.

He was completely exhausted. I had doubts about the tour, but it also seemed like his only chance now. Dudley had so many inner conflicts that I didn't know how he could pull himself out of the murky, depressed place he had fallen into. I hugged him. He held on for a long time, and exhaled deeply. 'Thank you,' he said. 'I can't wait to get out of this country.'

At the end of the evening, he took an extra dose of the strong sedative Ativan, which was becoming more and more his habit, and went to sleep.

Over breakfast the next morning, Lou Pitt, who had been at the concert the previous night and had spoken to people he knew in the audience, wanted us to cancel the tour. Dudley flatly refused. He said he would be better on the tour. He had just had a bad night, he added. Once again, a lot was at stake. Dudley was heavily in debt and needed the money. He was worried that his career was seriously in trouble. There were no film offers. Not one. He wanted to play the piano, but he was distracted by his private life.

Dudley didn't tell Lou about his fight with Nicole the previous afternoon. He should have, but he didn't want to use it as an excuse. Dudley already knew Lou's strong views on the situation, and he didn't want to hear the lecture one more time. He could have recited it back to Lou, word for word: 'You've got to get out of this marriage before it kills you . . . and ruins what's left of your career. She doesn't care about you – just your money.'

Lou was more than Dudley's agent; he had been Dudley's close friend for many years and through many relationships. Lou was one of the few people whom Dudley trusted with the truth of his life, his feelings, his troubles. He let Lou know him the way only a few people did. Lou was devastated by what he saw happening to Dudley, and had tried reasoning with him many times. But he knew that this relationship with Nicole was different – it was a bizarre addiction that nobody could understand.

Lou was very fond of Brogan Lane, Dudley's third wife, and never understood why Dudley had to end a marriage to someone who obviously cared for him so deeply. Lou was angry about Nicole, but more than that he was scared for Dudley's safety. He wanted Dudley to go on the tour for his reputation, and equally to get him away from Nicole. But at the same time, he didn't want the performances to go badly and finish off what was left of Dudley's flagging career.

We both believed that, away from Los Angeles, Dudley had a better chance of forgetting the chaos in his life and that he would rise to the occasion. I promised to keep in touch with Lou frequently. And we were on our way, halfway around the world.

The trip from Los Angeles to Melbourne was about seventeen hours long, and after the events of the previous week seemed even longer. But it provided a good buffer between the emotional stresses of Los Angeles and the promise of a new start in Australia. On the plane trip, Dudley survived by eating large and frequent meals, watching film after film, and sleeping as much as he could. And he drank his traditional solitary Bloody Mary.

We played one game of Scrabble — my idea, as I had brought along a miniature travel set. But we had dissolved into fits of laughter at the words he wanted to place on the board — mostly rude words. The set was so tiny that it was hard not to lose the pieces between the seats. 'Do you want to stop?' I finally asked, after he had violated every rule with a series of well-placed words that included 'fuck', 'shit', 'cunt' and 'arsehole'.

'I don't want to play this stupid game. I'm humouring you,' he said, annoyed. 'But we'll keep playing.' He didn't seem bothered that my score was higher, with legitimate non-scatological words, but we played for an hour and a half, and then he said I was driving him nuts worrying about the microscopically small Scrabble pieces, which we kept dropping, so we stopped.

By the time we landed in Australia, the press was ready for him. They had arrived with cameras — both still and video. And Dudley was ready for the attention — he was craving it — and began the trip with all the optimism he could muster. Knowing he would be filmed in the act, he somehow managed to stage a spontaneous-looking fall onto the luggage carousel as he reached for his suitcase, which got away. Dudley was on his back on top of somebody else's suitcase, his legs in the air, and had to be rescued by an airline attendant before disappearing outside the building.

About a hundred people who were waiting for their luggage saw it happen, and it was a perfect and endearing way for him to start the trip in Australia, where the public adored him and didn't care what the tabloids were saying about his private life. The press didn't care if his carousel spill was accidental or staged; they made the most of it. They also mentioned that Dudley had stepped off the plane wearing a sticker that read 'Wake me for meals', a sticker that remained on his jacket for five weeks.

With Dudley appearing in Australia for the first time in twenty-five years, arrangements had been made for ABC-TV in Melbourne to tape the first pair of concerts for broadcast, and to give the tape to our production company after airing it a few times. Mark Smith, a representative from ICM in New York, had flown over to offer support and wanted to be sure that the tour would start off well.

The day after our arrival, the theatre had arranged a major press conference, and Dudley miraculously held his own with a roomful of reporters. The next day, another miracle, he was the guest speaker at a luncheon where he answered questions in a witty and entertaining style I hadn't seen in months. A couple of the most important publications were allowed time with Dudley in private, with the stipulation that the interviews focus on his music and his career. There was a ban on discussing his personal life, which had recently been a major tabloid topic.

I was appointed police force by Dudley, who seemed unable to say, 'This topic is off limits.' Since most of the press wanted to interview me as well, Dudley and I had agreed that if they asked about his personal life, I would spare him the evil deed and say, 'Dudley' management would like me to remind you to focus on Dudley' music and career.' We rehearsed, so I would learn to say it charmingly. With his coaching, I learned my part well.

Most of the reporters tried to push for personal details. Dudley tried everything he could think of to make me laugh and disconcert me, and sometimes had to confess to the reporter what was so amusing. One reporter wrote that Dudley's personal life was 'off limits' but that Dudley was forthcoming on all other subjects.

Just as one interview was about to begin, Dudley got a phone call from Nicole, who was on the warpath after learning the content of Barbra Paskin's biography, about to be serialised in the London press. As it was an authorised biography, Nicole held him totally responsible for negative things that had been written about her behaviour, including her drug use, her relationship with her previous husband, Charles, who lived with them when he wasn't in jail, and other unsavoury details of their private life.

'I can't talk to you now. I have an interview about to start,' he told her.

'I don't give a fuck,' she shrieked so loud she could be heard through the phone receiver.

I had just opened the door to the reporter, and was stalling him in the outer foyer of the suite. My hands were shaking, as I heard Dudley's voice taking on the same tone it had had a few days earlier in Los Angeles. And my heart was pounding. The interview was an important one; Dudley had to do well. This was no time for a setback.

'Have a seat. Let me see if he's ready,' I said. Fortunately the suite had an exterior room. Dudley was in the living room, still on the phone.

'What's going on?' I asked.

'She's blaming me for everything that's in the book. She says I should have defended her. How could I? It's all true.' He had his hand over the mouthpiece and was whispering to me. He was scared. Nicole was screaming. He held the phone away from his ear. 'I'm going to fucking blow up your house, you asshole. You wait and see. Don't try and stop me. You've ruined my life.'

'I can't talk to you. I have to do an interview. I'll call you later.' His hands were shaking as he replaced the receiver. 'What should I do? Will you talk to her?'

I could see the strain in his eyes, and the fear. His miserable home life had followed him all the way to Australia; it had jumped right out of the phone into his hotel room. I sat down on the couch next to him, and took his hand.

'She won't blow up your house. She's just threatening. I'll try to calm her down.'

I showed the reporter in, and Dudley made an excuse for the delay. I thought he would probably not be able to keep the incident to himself and was hesitant about leaving him at that moment. But I believed Nicole might do some real damage and that was more critical than whatever he might say to the reporter. Later, he said he remembered the ban and only remarked that he was having trouble with his wife. No details. The reporter had said, 'I've heard that's off limits, so let's talk about your music.' A lucky break.

While Dudley was being interviewed, I went into another room and dialled Nicole's number. At that point, despite the Palm Springs incident, she was still willing to talk to me. She was furious with Dudley, and continued to issue threats. She had seen an advance copy of the story about to be published, and she knew that Dudley's beloved beach house in Marina del Rey was the best ammunition she had.

I spent nearly an hour on the phone with her, using all the psychology I knew. I was no expert in handling her crises, but I managed to talk her out of doing anything violent. She promised to hold off on carrying out her threat to blow up his house, and I promised her I would tell Dudley all her concerns, discuss them with him and have him call her back later. 'You have to stay on the line when he calls, so you'll hear how he always lies to me,' she said. At the end of the conversation, I was completely drained, said goodbye and went into the living room where Dudley, having finished the interview, was at the piano playing one of his own 'Songs without Words'. I sat on the couch without saying a word. He had trusted me to handle it, and knew that I had.

Dudley was concerned about the opening night as he had not performed on camera in a while. He had not for a moment forgotten how much trouble he had faced in the Los Angeles try-out. He was feeling better, but still tired and pushing himself to function. I had done some reading on the subject of Ativan and had begun to wonder if part of his physical problem had to do with the prescription drug, a strong sedative, which he had been taking for several years. He was using it to help him sleep, but he wasn't sleeping. He had increased the dose himself in an effort to sleep more.

I suggested he try to cut down, and he was willing to do anything that had half a chance of helping him to feel better. I had come prepared with all the vitamins I knew might help – large doses of B complex, in particular. He appeared to have more energy, and more humour, as he cut the Ativan in half and took more vitamins. But I wasn't completely sure if it was the reduction in sedatives, or gaining some distance from the crisis back home.

The pair of opening performances in Melbourne were surprisingly good. Dudley loved being onstage with cameras filming every word, every note. On the opening night, Mark Smith and I stood offstage as the first concert began, barely breathing. 'Please,' I thought. 'Let this go well.' The audience cheered as he stepped onto the stage, and he bonded with the crowd immediately. Their support carried him forward. Ten minutes into the show, Mark and I looked at each other. We should have both passed out by then from lack of oxygen, but finally drew a pair of breaths. 'It's going well,' he said.

The trip continued to be a roller-coaster ride, professionally and personally. The reviews were just as varied, starting with one that called his performance 'brilliant' and a '10', and another whose headline wondered if Dudley was drunk onstage. Dudley continued to deal with his personal crisis on his own terms and in the way he usually handled crises – he obsessed on it, discussed it in all its possible ramifications, blamed himself for more than half the trouble, looked for solutions and, finally, wondered if or how he would survive. In one interview, he spoke of death and said he was at the end of his life. But the minute he touched the piano, he seemed to forget all the rest. The rehearsals were wonderful and hilarious. We practised many hours, and he pushed hard to make sure everything would be perfect.

After the Melbourne concerts, we went to Canberra and were met by Bill Miller and Simon Wellings, an unlikely pair of entrepreneurs who had somehow managed against all the odds to finance their portion of the tour, and were happy to make it clear they had pulled it off by the skin of their teeth. They were with us for the next two weeks. Dudley took an immediate liking to both Bill and

Simon, and the feeling was mutual. They had already described themselves, quite aptly, as 'a couple of cowboys', and Dudley joked endlessly with them. But later it became clear that the cowboys had put their own personal finances on the line for the tour, including Bill's house as collateral. Dudley became more and more determined to make it work. He felt responsible to the pair; he was touched by their devotion.

We became a touring quartet, and the better they got to know Dudley, the dirtier all their jokes became, always apologising to me in advance for what I was about to hear. We were followed by the press, viewed as some sort of bizarre side show. One afternoon, Dudley had stayed behind in the hotel, while the rest of us went exploring. Over dinner, Simon asked Dudley, 'Well, how was your afternoon? What were you doing, anyway?' Looking out of the corner of his eye to make sure somebody would be within earshot, he turned to Simon and said, as innocently as he could, 'I spent the afternoon wanking,' much to the dismay of an elderly couple at the next table, who never realised it was purely for their benefit.

In each city we acquired more luggage. Dudley didn't like the idea that people carrying his luggage might be lifting too many pounds. 'Why should they be suffering on my behalf?' he asked. So he bought two new suitcases and divided his belongings. We would go walking in the afternoon, and on more than one occasion came back to the hotel wheeling new, empty luggage so Dudley could make his suitcases lighter and I could carry around interesting gifts I had found to take home. We started out from LA with four suitcases. By midway through the Australia tour, we had eight suitcases, and four smaller bags with music that had to go as carry-on luggage.

Finally, they had to send one car for us, and one car for the luggage – one of the more embarrassing moments of realisation that no, indeed, we were not travelling light. At one Australian airport, the press turned out with video cameras to film the arrival of our now famous luggage. I believe we made the 6 p.m. news that night.

Dudley spent some time searching for kangaroos, and wanted to drive around until we found them. But, as he said to the concierge at a Perth hotel, 'None were forthcoming. Do you know where we might find kangaroos?'

'At the zoo,' the concierge replied drily. Off we went, without a moment's delay, to the nearest 'nature sanctuary', with Dudley insisting on getting as close as possible to the animals. He was very fond of a koala he met there, eager to hold it, and surprised to learn how heavy it was.

He was thrilled to enter the area where the kangaroos were housed, but as he approached the kangaroos, they took off in another direction. I had brought along my video camera, and one of my all-time favourite shots was Dudley chasing, as fast as he could, after a kangaroo.

In Adelaide Dudley agreed to meet with a young boy whose story was all too familiar. Bill Miller remembered it as 'one of the most moving moments on the tour'. The youngster, about ten years old, was a talented pianist and had a deformed foot. He was being bullied and ridiculed at school, and his mother brought him to the concert and sent a note backstage asking if Dudley would meet the boy. At the end of the concert, while his fans waited outside, Dudley spoke privately with the child for about fifteen minutes, 'and probably changed that kid's life for ever,' Bill added.

In Sydney, the last stop on the Australian tour, and Bill Miller's hometown, we were staying in an exquisite hotel. Dudley was tired, and struggling to keep his energy up. He tried to be charming in a never-ending series of parties and receptions; the strain was showing and the Sydney performance suffered. The following morning, I opened the front door of the suite to discover a newspaper with a review of the previous night's concert, implying that Dudley was drunk onstage. Dudley had carefully read a wide variety of good and bad reviews since the start of the tour, but for the first time ever, I hid this one from him. He could handle a bad review, but he couldn't deal with people thinking he was drunk, particularly onstage.

A little later, in New Zealand, Dudley began having trouble with one finger that wasn't responding properly, and was very depressed about it. He kept looking at the finger, unable to believe it wouldn't respond the way it always had. Now we know that this was his neurological condition beginning to manifest, but then it was just another mystery.

There were only a few concerts left on the tour, and Dudley had the strength to make one important decision. He was not going back to Nicole, or to Los Angeles. He was going to London.

11

AUSTRALIA TO ENGLAND

DUDLEY WAS ATTACHED TO England by a very long umbilical bungee cord. He didn't want to return to live there, but he needed to go back frequently – to see Suzy and other friends and family, and to remind himself of his roots. Wherever he lived, certain British products lived in his kitchen – Dundee orange marmalade, for example, and jars of blended malt and cod liver oil, which he would consume by the spoonful.

Dudley liked the American lack of reserve. 'I can say anything I like, and it's OK here.' He liked being able to discuss personal and psychological issues with perfect strangers, and never feeling like it was inappropriate. But if there was one thing keeping him in California, besides the obvious career advantages of living near Hollywood, it was the weather. Dudley often spoke about the sunshine. It was a buffer to his depressive tendencies. And he adored never having to wear an overcoat.

Dudley could be outrageous, and say outrageous things, but he was at the same time a very private person. He was often quoted as having said 'sex and Chinese food' were what life was about. And Dudley had taken a lot of flack for an off-the-cuff interview comment favouring 'meaningful one-night stands'. It was his way of avoiding intimacy, which he sought but found frightening.

Dudley was in another transitional period in his life. Dealing with another failed marriage and asking himself the same questions about what to do next, what to do to make his life better. It made perfect sense that he would go back to England to further ponder these issues and search for answers.

We returned to Los Angeles a couple of days before Thanksgiving, both exhausted from the long plane trip and five weeks on the road. I was eager to go back home to see Brian and the family. Dudley was still firm in his decision to go to England. With his tendency to waver in his decisions, particularly anything involving Nicole, there was no guarantee that he would really get on the plane and go to London. We were set to ride to the airport together the next morning. I would fly to New Jersey and he would, hopefully, board a plane to London.

We had been speaking to Suzy Kendall by phone while in Australia, and she understood the urgent need for Dudley to have a place to go where he would have the support of friends and be able to recover from the turbulence of his marriage. Although Suzy and I had never met, we had begun to develop a bond through our many phone conversations during the five weeks of the tour.

Suzy was very protective of Dudley, and she had been frightened and concerned by what she was hearing. There was a lot of bad press about Dudley's marriage to Nicole, some of it painting Dudley in a negative light, as neglectful and abusive. Suzy was worried, and Dudley had confided in her that he needed to escape from his situation. Dudley's friendship with Suzy had outlived their marriage, and Dudley had made it clear he wished their marriage had not broken up, that his life would have been different had he understood what he might have done to save the marriage.

Dudley was articulate, if fatalistic, on the subject of why each of his marriages had ended, and now he had to face the fact that his marriage to Nicole was doomed. Each marriage had tapped into a different part of his personality, but they all had in common the fact that Dudley felt trapped – that some negative feeling, stemming from his childhood, was triggered every time. 'It's as though I sign the paper, and they put the chains on me. There's an extra step in the marriage ceremony. You may kiss the bride. Here are your *chains*.'

Dudley liked to sum up in a few words what had gone wrong in each marriage. Suzy and Dudley had argued over having a child, and they were better as friends than spouses. Tuesday had been 'difficult and irrational'. Brogan and Dudley argued over Dudley's need for freedom and Brogan's concerns that his finances were not being managed well. And now he simply described his marriage to Nicole as 'insane'.

Watching his own parents live out their days in what he described as an unhappy, dead-end marriage, watching each other get older and ultimately waiting to die – that was Dudley's view of marriage. The last words Dudley's father ever spoke to him were these: 'Don't let it pass you by.' Each of his four marriage licences was an affirmation of Dudley's death sentence. Twenty years of therapy couldn't change it, although he understood it all pretty well and was ready to give anyone who would listen his full dissertation on the institution of marriage.

Suzy had wanted children at a time when Dudley, as he later said, hadn't been ready for fatherhood. They had planned to have a child at the time they got married, but Dudley kept changing his mind from week to week, a factor distressing for Suzy, who initiated their divorce. Suzy began her career as a model and became an actress. Practical, intelligent, a beautiful blonde with a good sense of humour, Suzy remained grounded and, after divorcing Dudley, retired from acting to raise a family a few years later with her new husband, Sandy Harper.

Dudley went from his marriage to Suzy, whom he continued to adore as his friend, to a stormy marriage to the actress Tuesday Weld, with whom he fathered his son Patrick. Tuesday had been a child star with a major American television career at an early age. Beautiful, hot-tempered, funny and quick-witted, as a young adult Tuesday was a free spirit not bound by anybody else's rules. Tuesday and Dudley fought constantly, but it took them a couple of years to end their marriage even after making the decision to get a divorce.

Dudley was closer to Suzy's daughter from her marriage to Sandy Harper than he was to either of his own sons. He doted on Elodie Harper, helping her with her Latin and music homework when he visited, and spending many hours with her as she grew up.

When Elodie was ready for college, Dudley wanted to write a letter to help her get into Oxford. When she refused the help, insisting she needed to get in on her own merits or not at all, he confessed that he was particularly proud of her. Despite his own precarious financial situation at that point, he insisted on contributing financially to her education. Dudley was linked to Suzy, and occasionally referred to her as his wife, no matter who else he was married to at the time. In his mind, it seemed, she had been his one real wife.

Dudley knew he could count on Suzy to protect him from his difficult situation in Los Angeles, and he was also comfortable with her husband Sandy. Sandy was happy enough to have Dudley visit any time. Suzy had invited him to visit after the tour, and we both urged him to avoid going home first. Dudley knew he was too vulnerable to return to Nicole.

By phone from Australia to London, Suzy and I had also discussed Dudley's use of Ativan. She was knowledgeable about the drug and worried about its negative effects on Dudley. And Suzy was supportive of my attempts to reduce his use of the medication. She was also surprised to learn of Dudley's recent use of non-prescription drugs, as he had been very opposed to drug use in his earlier days. By the end of the tour, his use of Ativan had been reduced by two-thirds, and he was more alert and functioning better.

Dudley had several phone conversations with his business manager, Hugh Robertson, who was supportive of the decision to go to England. Dudley told Hugh he wanted to be sure that Nicole and the children had enough money to live on, and he told Hugh that he was finished with her, and planned to file for divorce. It wasn't the first time he had said it, but it was as though he needed to say it aloud a few times to remind himself of the decision.

Dudley and I had been together for five weeks and we didn't like the idea of being on two separate continents, but there seemed little choice at that moment. Our friendship had strengthened, and we enjoyed our musical partnership. It was a critical time in his life, and I was concerned for the future.

When we landed in Los Angeles we went straight to one of the airport hotels. It was obvious that Dudley would change his mind about going on to London if he spent even ten minutes in his own house. It was a surprise when he stood firm in his decision to keep his location a secret from Nicole.

The next day, he was met at the terminal by an airport representative assigned to help him get through to the first-class departure lounge as quickly as possible, and providing some degree of reassurance he would not change his mind. My flight was an hour later from a different terminal. I got out of the car to say goodbye while all his suitcases – still four of them from the Australia trip – were being loaded onto a cart. We had one last chuckle about the luggage. 'At least in this country we and our luggage can fit into the same vehicle,' he said. He looked at the stretch limousine, which had luggage on the seats and in the boot. He was holding his briefcase, which he didn't like anyone else to carry. He set it down for a moment. We embraced and he frowned. 'When will I see you again?' he asked.

'Probably sooner than you think. I'll miss you,' I said.

'Me, too. I mean, I'll miss you too.' He turned and started walking, looking back until he bumped into somebody. Then he laughed. 'I've never mastered this,' he said.

I waved and got back into the car, heading for my terminal.

Dudley did arrive in London. He called the next day to say that he was *fine* and the trip had been OK. 'I was sitting next to someone who kept talking about my films. I'll stop short of saying it was boring. A good ego boost,' he said, 'but no chance to sleep.' Suzy was relieved that he hadn't changed his mind before boarding the plane. But she hadn't seen him in a while and she sounded concerned that he didn't seem quite like himself. And it took only a couple of days for Dudley's Ativan use to increase again. He couldn't sleep and somehow believed that would be the answer to his troubles. After seventeen years, Dudley had difficulty leaving the drug behind. He wouldn't accept the idea that he had built up a resistance, and that it took more and more to get the results he expected. It was no longer helping him to sleep, and he was becoming more tired during the day.

A few days went by and Suzy phoned me. She was worried. Dudley was troubled, physically and mentally out of sorts, just not quite right. She had arranged for him to check into a small private clinic in central London, well known for treating addictions to pre-scription and non-prescription drugs, and offering the counselling to go along with it. 'I think you are doing the right thing,' I said, reassuring her. 'That will give him a chance to improve.' But I had doubts and I knew that Suzy did too. Something didn't feel right, and we were grasping at straws, hoping this was the right path, but not entirely sure.

Dudley and I spoke nearly every day by phone through the end of November and early in December. Although only two weeks had passed, I was more concerned than ever. He sounded terrible. We had become very attached during the Australia tour and he wanted me to visit him in London. He said he felt lost, and wasn't sure he could manage being in a UK hospital, with so many childhood memories and his strong fear of abandonment, which had surfaced again recently. 'This is bringing back everything I feared as a child,' he confessed. 'I hate the idea, but if you and Suzy both think it will help, I'll try to do it.'

He clearly felt the need to address some of the childhood

memories, and I believed that being separated after five comfortable weeks on tour, when he had felt secure and close in our
friendship, had triggered a new sense of abandonment. I felt guilty,
almost responsible, and wondered if I should have invited him to
come to New Jersey instead of encouraging him to go to England.
But it had seemed the best solution at the time, and Suzy was eager
to help. I knew we would miss each other, but it hadn't occurred to
me that Dudley might feel rejected.

I encouraged Dudley to follow Suzy's suggestion and go into the
clinic for an evaluation and whatever treatment they might be able
to offer. He reluctantly agreed, but asked if I would come to visit as
soon as possible. 'It's cold and drizzly. We need to rehearse for the
March concerts. Suzy says she wants to meet you. Can you perhaps
come over for a quick visit – a couple of days?' I hesitated, remembering that New York to London was never an easy weekend trip,
but I felt sure he wouldn't have asked if it hadn't been important.
He certainly wouldn't have said 'perhaps'. I hesitantly broached the
subject with Brian.

'You just got home,' he said. 'Is it important for you to go now?'

'I think so,' I replied. But I was torn. I had been away for weeks
and thought I should stay at home. Yet Dudley's situation was feeling like another crisis. I knew Brian would be understanding, but I
was trying his patience.

'If it would help for you to go there, I don't mind,' Brian said.
'Just make it as short a trip as you can.'

I arrived in London on a bone-chilling, drizzly December morning,
going straight from the airport to the clinic, where I visited Dudley.
He was relieved to see me, and we embraced for a long time, but

was concerned to see that he had deteriorated in just a few weeks. The symptoms that had begun in Australia and New Zealand were a little worse, but it was hard to be specific about them, and this was baffling to the doctors. Dudley seemed confused by what he was experiencing. His balance was unsteady. He felt dizzy. It wasn't until several years later that we learned Dudley also suffered badly from what one doctor finally termed 'hospital dementia', caused by fear and lack of control over the daily routine in one's life.

After a few days in the clinic, Dudley was becoming a difficult patient. He was refusing to wear clothes – a dressing gown when he was walking around, but nothing more, and he was restless and impatient, looking at his watch frequently, as though he expected his mysterious condition to improve in a few hours. As a rule, Dudley never wore pyjamas, but the nurses and doctors at the clinic didn't think this was acceptable for a patient there. 'I just want everyone to leave me alone,' he said emphatically.

He refused to participate in any of the group sessions or treatment programmes that were offered to him. He wanted to listen to music, and he kept asking what was happening to him, hoping that someone would explain what was wrong. I had never seen him in such bad shape. He was better off with short visits, so both Suzy and I would come and go during the day. He was on his best behaviour when Suzy was visiting, and she wisely knew that Dudley would do well with fifteen-minute visits, and had a good sense of when to leave.

On one break, I took a long walk to Madame Tussaud's. It was the first time I had been there, but what a depressing journey it turned out to be. I discovered a figure of Dudley seated at the piano, looking many years younger and very fit. I stood and stared for a long time, as young girls in pairs photographed each other standing next to his wax likeness. Backstage after concerts, Dudley was always being photographed between two women, arms around both, all faces beaming. Just the same with his wax likeness, only this time it was teenage girls, giggling, one on either side of the not-quite-perfect wax figure.

A strange and morose sensation came over me as I was struck by the irony of Dudley being just a few blocks away, in hospital and suffering from a mysterious condition that would take another two years to diagnose. If only those young girls knew the truth. I continued my walk through the museum, but the image was burned into my brain. The contrast between the two pictures, Dudley in wax at the piano and Dudley lying in a hospital bed, wearing only a sheet and wondering what was wrong with him, would never leave me.

The next afternoon, I purchased a fax machine for my father-in-law, who lived near Brighton. I was planning to take a train down to the south coast that evening, so I left the machine in Dudley's room for a few hours. Dudley was at first amused when I told him I would carry a fax machine from London to Brighton by train, which seemed perfectly logical to me.

'Don't you think that's a little *nuts*?' he finally said, a slight edge to his voice. 'I'm sure they sell fax machines in Brighton. Why are you taking it from here to there?'

'Because I found it here. I would just like to arrive by train and visit them, fax machine in hand!'

I was relieved that Dudley was willing to argue about this. It was a good sign. He could be very stubborn and would obsess about insignificant things, picking on little details as though they were deep and important intellectual issues. And he would dig in his heels and insist that things would make more sense *his* way.

'Well, I should arrange a car for you then, if you have to take this heavy box.'

'It's not heavy,' I insisted. 'It was the lightest one I could find.'

'We'll get a car for you.'

I wasn't sure who was included in the 'we'. I suspected it was just for effect, as though an extra person would provide additional ammunition for his argument.

'Thanks, Dudley.' I kissed him on the cheek. 'That's such a nice offer. But I'm happy with the train, and it's quicker. If you get a car for the fax machine, that will double the cost of the fax machine.'

'Ughh. You are so *stubborn*,' he said.

I thought that would be the end of it. He sighed and paused, waiting for me to continue the argument. I didn't, which annoyed him. He wasn't thinking about his condition. He was obsessing over my fax machine.

'Well, where are you going to put it on the train? What if all the seats are taken?'

'Under my feet, or on my lap, or on somebody else's lap.'

'Well, you seem to have thought of everything. So I can't change your mind about this?'

'Nope.'

'Good then. Why did you say you were doing this?'

'Fred is deaf. He needs it to communicate, and he probably won't get one for himself.'

My 78-year-old father-in-law, who had become progressively more deaf following a war injury, was thrilled with the gift. I stayed overnight in Brighton. The next day, when I went back to visit Dudley, he wanted to hear all about Fred's reaction.

'It was nice that you took it for him,' he said. 'I wish I could have seen his face.'

Before I went home, Suzy and I met privately with one of the primary physicians treating Dudley at the clinic. He escorted us into his small office and sat us down in two chairs opposite him. He was seated behind a large desk, looking very official. 'I'm sorry to tell you this,' he said. 'We've done a lot of tests, and we're not sure exactly what is wrong with Dudley.' He said Dudley's use of Ativan and other drugs had probably caused his problems, and we would have to come to terms with the fact that there was no hope he would ever return to performing and functioning at a high level. He was impaired.

Suzy and I were shocked to hear what he had to say. We knew he was well-meaning and trying to prepare us for the worst. We knew something was wrong, but we were sure there had to be a better explanation. We both left the hospital depressed and fearful.

At Suzy's home in Hampstead, we spent a long time talking about what her life with Dudley had been like, and how their friendship had deepened over the years. Suzy and I spoke easily and, perhaps because of our mutual concern for Dudley's life and condition, it was easy for us to be open.

Dudley had been in hospital for just a few days, and not registered under his own name, when the staff reported receiving a call in the middle of the night from someone claiming to be Dudley's wife. They were under strict instructions not to give out any information, but Nicole assumed from their reaction that she had found the correct place, and the next morning the press turned up in front of the building, reporting without confirmation that Dudley was in a small London clinic receiving treatment for drug addiction. The news circled the globe, while Dudley stayed in his room, continuing to refuse the treatment that was offered.

At the end of a long and difficult weekend, I returned home and continued to keep in touch by phone. After Dudley had been in the clinic for about two weeks, the doctors felt he was not going to benefit from anything they had to offer and he was discharged. He returned to Suzy's home and tried to regain his strength, which had declined from two weeks of inactivity. We resumed our daily phone conversations. Dudley was restless. He began to talk about staying in London, and moved up to the second floor of Suzy's home, which he called his 'flat'. He started practising the piano, as there were concerts scheduled in the spring. He tried socialising with friends – his agent Dennis Sellinger, from ICM in London, his singer friend Barbara Moore, and a small circle of other friends from his past life in London.

Dudley was fond of saying that life, and his career, had just happened to him – a number of very lucky breaks and 'the proverbial being in the right place at the right time'. Others observed that he had worked hard, but Dudley never felt that he had.

Throughout his life he struggled with the feeling that he didn't deserve his success. Dudley grew up in a working-class family in Dagenham, living in council housing – row upon row of identical-looking homes. The family's first house was hit by a bomb in 1941 (luckily unexploded) and they had to move. Dudley's schoolmate Jim Johnson recalled first meeting Dudley at Kingsley Hall, a church-based community centre that still uses the Cramer piano Dudley played there. In one extraordinary confession, Dudley told

Jim about his big secret — 'He said that he had a disgusting foot.' Their mentor Russell Sherman, a teacher in Dagenham County High School, devoted himself to identifying talented youngsters. He took Dudley to get special boots, encouraged his musical and acting abilities, and helped him to rise to his potential.

Dudley's first taste of a more elegant life occurred at Oxford University. 'When I first went there, I thought I had died and gone to heaven,' Dudley said. 'I found myself in the most beautiful place I could imagine.' His mother Ada, whom he had so often described as distant, was jubilant over her son's opportunity. 'She ran into the street screaming, "My son is going to university!"' Dudley remembered her exuberant reaction fondly. It went a long way towards affirming the support he had so often doubted.

At first, though, Dudley also felt very uncomfortable at Magdalen College, and thoroughly aware of class differences. In later years he laughed at his efforts to get rid of his tell-tale Dagenham accent and adopt one more suitable to the new status afforded by attending Oxford. Yet class differences were disturbing to him throughout his life. He fought for the underdog; in his daily life he showed the same respect for people in every occupation or social class.

Dudley earned a Bachelor of Arts degree in music in 1958 and stayed an extra year to complete a Bachelor of Music degree in composition. At Magdalen, he had played violin, piano and organ, and was in the choir. And he had begun to come into his own when he joined a college theatrical revue performing comedy.

At the same time, he was playing jazz piano, inspired by Erroll Garner's style. One evening, as John Dankworth tells the story, the Dankworth Band and Cleo Laine were performing for a Magdalen College Commemorative Ball. 'Incidentally, one of the support bands that night was a new, still struggling Rolling Stones,' Dankworth said.

At the end of the evening, they were listening to jazz piano sounds coming informally from another room. 'The sound we heard was not "student jazz". It was mature, impressive and expertly executed, but it was above all BIG. So we were not a little surprised when we got round the upright piano and there was the source – a diminutive Dudley. We had a chat, and told him that if he was ever in need of a job to let me know.' Dudley did call upon Dankworth, but not for more than a year.

Once he overcame his social discomfort at Oxford, Dudley had an active social life, but no real involvements with women. He recalled his early encounters as a teenager – 'The idea of intercourse was completely frightening,' he said, adding, 'I fondly recall the first breast I ever fondled. The girl wasn't even attractive, but I stood on some bricks to reach her. I felt this *thing*, as though I'd put my hand on a sheep's eye.'

Fascinated by sex, Dudley had many flirtations but claimed that, 'technically, I actually lost my virginity at 23', in a one-night stand with a young woman whose name he couldn't remember. 'After that, I began making up for lost time,' he said, an account confirmed by friends and colleagues who could hardly believe the parade of women in and out of Dudley's dressing rooms in the early years of his career. Dudley recalled with combined amusement and embarrassment a time when he was late for his entrance in a *Beyond the Fringe* sketch because he had been occupied with a female acquaintance in his dressing room. As soon as he rushed onstage, his fellow Fringers knew exactly what he had been doing.

Now back in Hampstead with Suzy and her family after his hospital stay, Dudley was grappling with strange symptoms but still thinking he would somehow regain his strength quickly.

The transition was difficult for Suzy. She was accustomed to worrying about Dudley, but not ready for the problems he was facing on a daily basis. And with Dudley and Suzy under the same roof for an extended period of time, it was hard not to make mental comparisons between life now and life as it had been in the same house thirty years earlier.

Suzy recalled their life together as a young couple, and said they had had a very simple lifestyle. 'In England he didn't have the huge fame or money that America brought him. He was in many respects an innocent. When I first met him he didn't have a home, but rented a room in a friend's house,' Suzy said.

With Dudley back in her Hampstead home, there nevertheless remained an undercurrent of fear on Suzy's part that he might return to California. The tabloids on both sides of the Atlantic showed a steady interest in Dudley's whereabouts, periodically turning up on Suzy's doorstep, fuelled by Nicole's claims that he had abandoned her and their son and was resuming his relationship with Suzy.

Although his financial support of Nicole and Nicholas (as well as Nicole's children by Charles) never lapsed, Nicole portrayed him as cold, detached and neglectful.

In preparation for concerts in Arizona and Illinois in March 1997, and in New York in April, I made one more trip to London to rehearse with Dudley. For weeks ahead, he had been telling me about his difficulties in practising and playing the piano. 'My hands feel like strangers,' he said. I tried to be encouraging, reminding him that he had been under a lot of stress and that he needed to give it time. In February, a few weeks before the next round of concerts, I flew to London. It was a relief to see that Dudley was doing better. He had more spirit and energy. He wanted to go out to restaurants. We did the rounds of all his favourite Indian restaurants. We went to the cinema and saw the movie *Shine*, which Dudley wanted to see – a film about Australian concert pianist David Helfgott, who has an emotional breakdown at the beginning of a major career. Watching the film was a moving experience for Dudley, who was grappling with so many problems in his own life.

One morning, we went to Chappell's Music Store in the West End. Dudley eagerly selected almost everything they had for two pianos, and one-piano four-hands. The sales staff smiled as we carried huge armfuls of music to the counter. It was a purchase that seemed to represent more his enthusiasm for the piano than his actual musical tastes. We went straight from the shop to the Steinway Piano Company, where Dudley had arranged several hours of practise time, interrupted only by the inevitable lunch, that day at Langan's Brasserie. Dudley liked the food there and appreciated the chance to introduce me to 'bubble and squeak'.

'You know, I couldn't come back to this place until the owner died. I was banned from coming here.' He told it with an air of the *enfant terrible*, proud that he could have elicited such a response from Peter Langan, owner then of the famous restaurant.

'Langan invited me in because he wanted me to invest in the restaurant. He was sure I would just say yes.' But, in fact, Dudley had refused. Not only was he kicked out on the spot, he said, but barred from returning to the restaurant in the future. Dudley had been simultaneously horrified and amused.

'Now that he is dead, though – nothing to stop me from coming back.' The staff that day had no knowledge of Dudley's history with the place, and he was the honoured guest that lunchtime.

We went back to Steinway and continued reading through some of the new music. Dudley was right. He was having trouble playing. 'You haven't had much of a chance to practise lately,' I said.

'That never made a difference in the past.'

It was true. Dudley had managed to keep his technique at a reasonably high level just by playing a little bit every day. He had never over-practised. He had always been able to sight-read difficult works. His old friend Bobby Mann, retired first violinist of the Juilliard String Quartet, had said often that 'he had the greatest sight-reading ability of any musician I've known'.

Dudley's fingers had never failed to respond, and he was facing something new, something mysterious. And something truly frightening to him. What had started three months earlier on our tour as a problem with one finger was spreading to the others. We were in a practice room at Steinway with a mountain of music on the side of the piano rack. Dudley turned page after page, trying out passages to see if the problem persisted. His right hand was unpredictable. 'My fingers feel like sausages. What is this? What is happening?'

We went back to practising the familiar pieces for the spring concerts, and things began to improve a little. Over the next few days, the rehearsals improved enough so that when I returned to New Jersey I thought the March concerts would go well.

Dudley said he would come to New Jersey before the North Carolina concert, and would stay at my home for the next month. There were several concerts coming up, including our third one at Carnegie Hall in New York – this time on his birthday, 19 April, with a big celebration planned. Dudley asked Suzy and Elodie to come to New York for the concert, for which he would narrate *Peter and the Wolf*. He would also compose an orchestral fanfare, called *Funfare*, that would have its world premiere at the concert. Did we dare to hope, once again, that things were improving?

12

PETER AND THE WOLVES

AS AN ADULT, EVERY hospital stay for Dudley was traumatic. Staying at the clinic for two weeks was more than he could tolerate. He was tortured by every aspect of the stay, despite the promise of a positive outcome. And despite the fact that he had agreed to go, he felt imprisoned.

The fact that he had no more information after his stay at the clinic than before, and that there was only a marginal improvement in his condition, was disturbing to Dudley. But there were concerts coming up and he was determined to keep his career going.

Suzy was hoping that he would stay in England, as far away from Los Angeles as possible, and allow himself to heal after the abusive situation he had finally left for good, or so everyone hoped. Suzy helped him to set up the living space he called his flat on the second floor of the house they had shared during their marriage, in which she still lived with her husband Sandy Harper and their daughter Elodie.

A few weeks before the concerts scheduled in the spring, including the Carnegie Hall concert on Dudley's sixty-second birthday, he flew to New Jersey, as planned, and stayed with my family, intending to return to London the following month.

Dudley began composing *Funfare*, a short orchestral piece with which to open the Carnegie Hall concert, a Music For All Seasons programme. And he began preparing the narration for *Peter and the Wolf*, with Larry Gelbart's witty, updated version of the classic story. But the composition went slowly, a major contrast with his previous experiences of working to deadline. Dudley also noticed that he was feeling slightly dizzy and developing a balance problem. Occasionally he would fall for no apparent reason. In the aisle of an airplane, even while the plane was on the ground, he would invariably lean to one side or the other, and sometimes topple right over. People would help him up, laugh and assume he was drunk. Occasionally he couldn't help overhearing snide comments.

'I think it must be my club foot coming home to roost,' he said drily. Or maybe it was an inner ear problem, he thought. 'Could be a virus.' And there were problems with his eyes. He had them checked frequently but his prescription remained the same.

'I feel strange,' he said. 'My eyes feel . . . funny. I can't describe it . . . just funny. Not funny ha-ha, though.' Dudley tried to make light of the situation, but a lot of little things were going wrong.

'Everyone in my family starts disintegrating at age sixty. My sister had a stroke. It's to be expected.' He would use one of his many voices, a high one we knew had belonged to an elderly aunt. 'So you're a Moore, are you? Your time to fall apart. Bits and pieces of you must go now. Which bit or piece will it be today?'

He could never remain too serious for very long. 'I've been

meaning to ask you,' he said. 'What happens if you use up all your odds and ends except one?'

'I've *no idea*,' I said, imitating the way he always said it. 'What?'

'I've no idea either. I was hoping *you* would know.'

As much as Dudley disliked hospitals, he enjoyed visiting doctors. With all the mysterious things going wrong, and still no clue as to the possible explanation, he responded to suggestions from several friends that a complete neurological examination was the logical next step. Check for small strokes, do a brain scan and other routine neurological tests, as well as blood tests of every description.

Dudley was beginning to believe, as one doctor had suggested, that he might have had a series of small strokes, too small to show up on most of the tests. He believed it for a while, and announced to other people he was sure that's what it was. He said it made sense because his sister had suffered from a stroke. But people generally recover from small strokes, and Dudley was getting slowly worse.

He was a challenge for any doctor to examine.

'Well, Mr Moore, how are you?'

'I'm *fine*, thank you. How are you?'

'Pretty well, but why are *you* here?'

'Oh, I'm not sure. I feel funny. Well, I know I'm supposed to *be* funny. People *expect* me to be funny. But I suppose they don't expect me to *feel* funny. Well, that's why I'm here.'

Then he would stop as though he had explained it all. He always looked surprised when the doctor would continue with more questions.

'What about your *symptoms*?' the doctor might ask. It wouldn't matter which doctor he was visiting. The conversations were usually about the same.

'Everyone in my family starts disintegrating when they turn sixt
My sister had a stroke, so I guess I may have had a stroke, or some
thing like a stroke. Is there anything else that's *like* a stroke? And m
father, well, he used to stare above your head, and I find I do that
I start above your head and then lower my head until I'm looking i
your eyes. I'm beginning to believe this is hereditary.'

'Anything more . . . specific . . . than that?'

At that point in the conversation, the doctor would generall
look over at me in a hopeful way. Of course, I did have the informa
tion, from discussing Dudley's medical minutiae with him for hour
on end, but I had invariably hoped that I wouldn't have to speak fo
Dudley. He was very specific and detailed at home in spelling out a
the things that were bothering him. And on many other subjects, a
least those about which he felt strongly, he was outspoken, stub
bornly so. But in a doctor's office, he needed help. He wante
somebody else to speak for him, to provide the answers, to say ho
he felt. He wanted to be protected in any medical situation.

Eventually we solved this problem by making a list of his symp
toms at home and carrying the list to the doctor's office, along wit
the list of his medications.

In April 1997, a new hospital date was set for the Monday follow
ing his birthday concert. At the doctor's urging, he agreed, onc
again, to a hospital stay for evaluation. This time, in New York Cit
at NYU Medical Center.

Five days hooked up to electrodes measuring brain waves, alon
with a series of other tests, and non-stop visits from friends to kee
him from experiencing his usual problems with hospitalisation. A
the end of the stay, Dudley was informed that he had calciu
deposits in the basal ganglia of his brain, probably causing mino

ut irreversible frontal lobe damage, the centre of the brain that ontrols rational thinking. It seemed logical to him, 'although I've ever been as rational as some people,' he said. The diagnosis pro- ided an entertaining explanation when friends asked for the results f his tests.

'I've got calcium in my brain. Could be some teeth that grew in he wrong place. I shall be giving up milk immediately. And cheese. s well as *all* attempts at rational thinking.' But a few months later nother highly respected neurologist pointed out that many people ithout any symptoms at all have calcium deposits in their brains. pparently it didn't explain much about Dudley's condition.

He was becoming more and more frustrated. His balance was oticeably more unstable. One time he fell backwards. 'Need a big ign here' – pointing to the air above his head – 'Bumps in the Air. id you see that? I tripped backwards . . . over air.' But it didn't appen again for a very long time, so he thought nothing more bout it. He didn't know that falling backwards was a tell-tale sign f PSP, and a symptom that distinguished Progressive Supranuclear alsy from Parkinson's disease.

Years earlier, Dudley had been diagnosed with the warning signs f glaucoma. Eye drops were prescribed, and he used them faithfully. This little bottle – it's all that stands between me and blindness.' lis vision remained clear, and the pressure indicating possible glau- oma remained in the normal range, but one doctor began to vonder if the eye drops, or the pre-glaucoma condition itself, were ausing his mysterious symptoms. The brand of eye drops was hanged, but nothing improved. He didn't know that eye symptoms re used to diagnose PSP. So far, none of the doctors Dudley visited ad made that connection.

At one of his performances, another *Peter and the Wolf* narration, he did what for Dudley had been the unthinkable – he used a large armchair onstage. The audience took it as a stage prop – he was seated to tell the story – but for Dudley it was one more bit of proof that he was in trouble. It was another small defeat. He knew he would have been in danger of falling during the 25-minute narration, and he couldn't take the chance. That would have given the audience further proof he'd been drinking. He knew that's what people were thinking, and it disturbed him greatly.

Dudley said that one of the reasons his partnership with Peter Cook had dissolved was because of Peter's drinking. Dudley couldn't tolerate the fact that Peter had been drunk onstage. Dudley also felt unfairly penalised for having played the role of Arthur so well, and subsequently having been typecast by the public.

Occasionally, on his list of mysterious symptoms would be that some of his words sounded slurred. It was unpredictable, but he found that sometimes on the phone he would be asked to repeat a sentence. He heard this happening, and began to speak more slowly and more distinctly to compensate. Perhaps he was tired, or stressed, he thought. Perhaps he wasn't paying attention to how he was speaking. But it was another tiny little sign that everybody missed. Of the broad range of neurological conditions, PSP (a distant cousin of Parkinson's disease) is one of the most misdiagnosed. Victims of the condition report spending up to six years going from doctor to doctor searching for a diagnosis. Because of the rarity of the condition, most physicians are not familiar with it. In fact, Dudley's condition was diagnosed relatively early, because his problems at the piano caused him to begin the search earlier than might otherwise have been the case.

Dudley was in the process of getting divorced from Nicole, but was still wondering why the relationship had been so disastrous. Wondering about it; then obsessing on it. It only took one phone call from her early in June, and he was on a plane heading for LA.

'She promised it would be different this time,' he said. 'I'm not sure I believe her, but I have to try.' A devastating move for him, as it took only twenty-four hours for him to learn that 'it *is* different this time, as she promised. It's much worse!' While in the middle of this 'reconciliation', Nicole served him with a lawsuit. It was a $10-million lawsuit against Dudley and Barbra Paskin, as well as her publisher and the *Daily Mail*, with a long list of grievances including domestic violence, libel, conspiracy, negligence, invasion of privacy and intentional infliction of emotional distress. Apart from Dudley and Barbra, the other suits were dismissed on grounds of jurisdiction, but Nicole finally dropped the suits against Dudley and Barbra when Dudley was hospitalised the following September for open-heart surgery.

However, much to the shock of friends, they stayed together for a time after Nicole filed suit.

Dudley was trapped again, in the addictive cycle of abuse, remorse and forgiveness. He moved out of her house, then back, then out to an undisclosed location that only three people knew, then back again, and after a few weeks, back to New Jersey.

This pattern was not unfamiliar to Dudley. It had taken him a long time, and many attempts, to leave his marriages to Tuesday Weld and Brogan Lane. The time spent within each marriage was fairly short – two years on average – but leaving the marriage could be another two years of break-ups and reconciliations. He and Tuesday broke up more than a dozen times, and well after his marriage to Brogan had ended they travelled together. His highly publicised romance with Susan Anton, which ended in 1984, was, at four years, longer than most of his marriages (a lot of the column inches it generated being devoted to the nine-inch difference in their heights). His marriage to Nicole, however, was the only one in which so many people were concerned for his safety.

By this point, every move he made was in the public eye, with reporters stalking both Dudley and Nicole, monitoring their arguments and the progress of their divorce, and frequently publishing photographs. The marriage was ridiculed in the press. During the summer, the fights became more frequent and Dudley was slipping into a deeper depression, taking anti-depressants and coming out of his bedroom less frequently. When Dudley was not working, it had long been his habit to retreat to the quiet of his bedroom. When he was depressed, he spent even more time alone, in his bedroom. We continued talking by phone, but the calls would be interrupted by screaming. He would quickly get off the phone. 'Sorry, stuff going on. I'll call you later.' Usually he would call, but sometimes days would pass and nobody would hear from him.

It was a turbulent summer, another attempt on Dudley's part to give his marriage 'one last try', several times over. Dudley filed and then dropped the divorce. Nicole did the same, then Dudley refiled, hired a bodyguard to protect himself in his home, and petitioned for a restraining order.

I was sitting on the rocks by the ocean in Maine. It was the beginning of August and I had returned from a whirlwind and wonderful mother-and-daughter week in Greece in time to leave for a couple of weeks in Maine and Nova Scotia, which Brian and I had planned months earlier. We were visiting old friends at their summer home in Maine, then going to tour Nova Scotia for the first time. It was a breezy, sunny day in the most peaceful spot imaginable and we were happy to be doing something that seemed so . . . normal . . . after what had felt like a very chaotic few months. Socialising with friends, cooking, touring the area — Brian and I had almost forgotten what this was like. I was sitting on a huge expanse of rocks at the edge of the ocean, but on the other end of my mobile phone, and inside my head, everything was still in turmoil.

During the difficult weeks of that summer, Dudley's friends were having trouble reaching him. We were all talking to each other, wondering what could be done to help him. Else was very worried. Lou said Dudley had called him and didn't sound right. Hugh Robertson, his business manager, felt this was not the time for confidentiality, and wanted to set up a telephone conference call that included the four of us.

The time was set and it only remained to be seen whether there would be any signal on the rocks in Maine. I was quite surprised when the call came and the signal was as clear as it could have been, in strong contrast with the dark and cloudy issues being discussed.

Dudley was not part of the phone call. By that point, the information we all had was that Nicole was insisting, as proof of his love and devotion, that Dudley should sign over half of everything to her. Half the house, half his total assets. We were appalled. Dudley had said he was tired of fighting. He wanted to give in. It seemed he had lost his mind, and we all discussed, in his absence, how to protect him . . . from himself.

The conversation lasted nearly half an hour, but no conclusions were reached. However, we all agreed to phone Dudley and try talking him out of such an insane and devastating financial move. Nobody could imagine how it would all end up, but he seemed on a path to self-destruction.

I hung up the phone and joined the others, who were by now far out on the rocks overlooking the ocean. They could tell I was worried, but I couldn't talk to Brian about it in front of our friends. It seemed too crazy to put into words.

Later that evening I phoned Dudley. 'We really need to talk,' I said. 'About what you are doing and what's happening to you. About Nicole. Tell me what's going on.'

'She wants half of everything. She says it's not about money, and that if I really love her I'll give her half of everything to prove it.'

'What do *you* think?' I asked.

'I think it's about the money,' he replied without a moment's hesitation. He was not crazy. He was completely rational and he knew exactly what was going on. He saw it for what it was.

'I think it's about the money and not about love,' he added.

'What do you want to do, Dudley?'

'I want to give her half of everything. Then I want to die as quickly as possible. I want this to be over. All of it. I'm tired of fighting. Can't live with her. Can't live without her. But mostly can't live *with* her. She's sweet, but evil. And she wants everything I've got. She wants blood. So I'll just give it to her, and then I can kill myself, if I have the guts to do it.'

It wasn't the first time he had spoken of wanting to die, especially feeling trapped in his relationship with Nicole. But it was the strongest, most serious I had ever heard him sounding on the subject of his own death.

'What are you thinking? How serious are you?'

'I don't know. That's where I'm stuck – *how* to do it. When I play the scene in my mind, I get all the way through it. All the way to the point where I've made the decision to die.' It seemed odd, but slightly reassuring, that he had two separate images of his impending suicide. In one, he was talking directly to me about it. In the other, he was describing the scene that was playing in his mind. He continued with the scene. 'At that moment where I say to myself – OK, it's time *now*, I'm completely paralysed by it. Totally undecided. Would I take pills? Slit my wrists? I don't know. If I slit my wrists and didn't do it right, I would have trouble playing the piano. I can't take that chance. I'm sure I would have to take sleeping pills. I've got them stockpiled just in case . . . two whole bottles.'

'Oh, Dudley, this is terrible. There has to be another way out of this. Why don't you come back to New Jersey?'

'I will . . . I will. I just need to sort this out first.'

I really didn't think he would kill himself. He had carried the thought process further, or perhaps he was simply explaining it better. But he was stuck, and scared, and not sure he could do it successfully. He could handle a concert not going well, or a failed film, but Dudley didn't want to be a failure at committing suicide. He thought he wouldn't have the skills it would take. He was very squeamish about blood. I knew he wasn't making up the stockpiled sleeping pills, but it still seemed more like he was expressing his feelings than forming a plan. Despite his words, I believed he had a strong will to live and the hope that things would somehow get better.

'Do just one thing,' I said.

'What's that?' he asked.

'Don't kill yourself. And don't give her half of everything you've worked your entire life to achieve. Nobody in the world has a right to ask you for that.' (At that point we didn't know that half of everything would have included half of Dudley's nearly $2 million debt.)

'That's two things,' he said. 'Is it one thing, or two things, you are asking me to do? And, by the way, I should remind you that you said, "Do just one thing".'

'Yes, I did say that.'

'But you are really asking me to *not* do one thing, but two things,' he said.

I exhaled. There was hope. I wasn't sure, but I thought it unlikely that anyone had ever committed suicide while worrying about grammar. I believed Dudley's life was about to be saved by the God of Grammar, to whom he obviously said his nightly prayers.

'I know that we are really discussing two things. I'll rephrase this: Please do *not* do either of the two things we have been discussing. Don't kill yourself, and don't give away half of everything you own.'

'OK,' he said. It was that simple. OK.

A few days later, there was another big blow-up. Dudley told Nicole he knew it was all about money, and he wasn't going to give her half of anything. He began making plans to come back to New Jersey in September to record the works of Gershwin.

13

GERSHWIN TO MAYO

DUDLEY HAD ALWAYS LOVED the music of Gershwin. The centenary in 1998 of Gershwin's birth was the perfect opportunity for Dudley to celebrate Gershwin's music and simultaneously spearhead the production of a new CD.

After a long couple of weeks following the latest big blow-up, Dudley turned up at Newark Airport on 1 September 1997, and we started work on the music of Gershwin. His combined jazz and classical backgrounds made him an ideal pianist for Gershwin's style, and he showed unusual warmth and insight into the luscious harmonies and melodies.

We began in the small Morristown, New Jersey recording studio of Skipp Tullen, a fine recording engineer and a close friend. Dudley liked Skipp, respected his work and felt comfortable being in his studio.

But as soon as Dudley started playing the first of the preludes, something was far more troubling than it had been the last time I had heard him play. The first phrase was beautiful, but the second one fell apart right in the middle. He started again and this time he stumbled through the first passage and the second one was good. Something would go wrong in a different spot each time he tried. He was frustrated and unhappy. He kept stopping, holding up his hands and looking at them, totally mystified by what was happening.

After an hour of repeated failures, he stopped and said he wanted to practise more and try again the next day. We went back home and there was a slight improvement; once again he was optimistic. He assumed it had just been a bad morning.

The second day in the recording studio started out better. But within half an hour, the problems of the previous day were back, full force. Dudley tried for about two hours, but in the end he was close to tears.

'I think we'll have to abandon the whole Gershwin project,' he said. 'I can't record sounding like this.'

We had intended to finish the solo pieces first, and had set aside several days to rehearse and record in a two-piano studio in Manhattan. But instead we went home and made a phone call cancelling the New York dates, although the word 'cancel' was not used. It would have been too final. Dudley felt crushed. He was beginning to believe he was witnessing the end of his dream of spending his later years playing the piano.

'Something is really wrong with me. I know it. 'I've never thought my playing would be so affected by . . . whatever this is,' he said, looking at his hands over and over, as though they were some-one else's. 'What should I do?' It was a tough question. There was no doubt that something had to be done – something that would, finally, uncover the mystery of what was wrong with Dudley.

There were days of doing research on the internet and talking by phone to all the doctors we knew, searching for a good medical institution that could do the right kind of complete evaluation and come up with definitive answers while at the same respecting Dudley's privacy and confidentiality. It was a tall order. Around that time Dudley only needed to blink and it was reported by the international press.

The Mayo Clinic in Rochester, Minnesota appeared the likely candidate, and we scheduled a visit that would take an estimated three to five days of outpatient testing. On a date originally set aside to record Gershwin in New York, Dudley and I flew to Minnesota, checking into a large suite in an old and well-known hotel not far from the clinic – a hotel used to dealing with confidential, high-profile situations. Dudley was not registered under his own name. We settled in to prepare for what looked a gruelling three days of tests – physical, neurological and psychological.

A kind and overly friendly representative from the public relations department of the clinic was assigned to make sure that Dudley could get to and from all of his appointments and tests without being kept in waiting rooms or walking through the busiest corridors. If he was occasionally recognised, people kept their recognition to a hushed and respectful whisper.

It took only two days of testing to discover that Dudley had a hiatus hernia (a common condition causing heartburn), a minor problem that can easily be controlled with medication. Next, the cardiac department discovered a small hole in his heart (*paten foramen ovale*). Dudley liked being able to rattle off the Latin term for his condition. It sounded impressive and more serious than it really was. Doctors said the tiny hole had probably been there for many

years, not causing much trouble, but that they could repair it surgi-
cally with a simple procedure. Finally, they discovered that one
artery had significant blockage. Although there was no immediate
danger, several heart specialists who examined Dudley believed it
could account for some of the symptoms – certainly his depression
and lack of energy, they told him.

They recommended immediate but non-emergency surgery,
stating that, without it, a year down the road Dudley could be a
prime candidate for a heart attack. At that point, Dudley would
have said yes to anything giving him half a chance to return to his
previous levels of energy and health. He immediately agreed to the
surgery.

Dudley was calm, but the small group of family and close friends
who heard about the upcoming surgery were all in a panic. Dudley
had been scheduled to do a Christmas pantomime in England,
although he had never been enthusiastic about it. He had met a representative from the theatre; flyers and posters were already
prepared for the production, advertising Dudley in the role of
Buttons. The production, Cinderella, was to be at the Mayflower
Theatre in Southampton. Dudley was relieved that now he had a
legitimate medical excuse to cancel.

In discussions among Dudley, me, Lou Pitt, Dudley's publicist
Michelle Bega and the public relations department at Mayo, a joint
decision was made to issue a simple statement immediately following the surgery. Only a few people were informed of the surgery in
advance, and a statement was prepared, and approved by Dudley, to
be issued once the operation was successfully completed and recovery under way. The surgery was deemed straightforward, and the
physician discussed with Dudley how he would make the scar as

small as possible so that it wouldn't be seen onscreen in future films.

One of the evenings before surgery, we were having dinner in an amusingly pretentious restaurant where a violin and piano duo were playing background music – some light classical and popular selections.

In the middle of one selection, Dudley looked up at them. 'They are *dreadful*, aren't they?' he said. 'Bad enough to cause indigestion.' Dudley had ordered a large rare steak (it was unusual for him to order beef) and garlic mashed potatoes.

'They are pretty bad,' I said. 'But it's probably not much fun playing while people are eating and dishes are crashing.'

'Crashing. That would be *well deserved*. OUCH – what on earth was that note?'

'A C–C sharp–D – that's the widest vibrato I've ever heard!' I said.

'A suicidal vibrato.' Dudley began laughing. Quality was important to him. It didn't matter what the circumstances were. If somebody was playing on a street corner, he expected it to be good. Sometimes it would be, and then he was happy enough to stop on the street and listen. Dudley had a broad range of musical tastes, but one major requirement. If he had to listen to music, it should be of the highest quality.

He continued working on the steak, which filled a large plate. 'Do you think they'll take a break soon?' he asked.

'Probably after we're done,' I said.

A few minutes passed, and the duo did take a break. They came directly to our table.

'You *are* Mr Moore, right?'

'It appears that I am,' Dudley replied. 'Nice to meet you.'

'We're so honoured to meet you,' one of the men said. 'We saw you, and you made us just a little nervous. We're not usually that bad.'

'Well, I should hope not,' Dudley answered lightly, smiling. They didn't know he was serious. Both men asked for his autograph.

Dudley ordered a very rich dessert. He was anticipating weeks of post-surgical jelly, 'flavour: red – I love that. Doesn't matter if it's strawberry or cherry or raspberry – the flavour is *red*.' He knew it would be a while before he could order Death by Chocolate again – a frozen ball of chocolate fudge and walnuts covered in whipped cream and drizzled with chocolate and raspberry syrup in fancy patterns. And the inevitable espresso. It seemed a challenge to keep the round dessert on a flat plate. I expected it to go flying across the room at any moment. That had happened to me once at a formal dinner, and I was laughing just thinking about it.

'Think of it as my last supper. In case anything goes wrong – if they forget to put my heart back in, for example – and people ask you, what did he have for his last supper, you are the only witness.' I interrupted him only long enough to ponder the question of whether that would really be everyone's first question.

He paid no attention and ploughed right on. 'You can tell them – a big, rare, juicy, artery-clogging steak, and this thing, whatever it's called. Look at this thing. It's massive. And hard as a rock,' he said, trying to chip through his dessert with a knife and fork. 'Would you like to try it?'

'I'll wait until it softens up a bit,' I replied. 'It looks too dangerous.'

'*As the actress said to the Bishop.* What an interesting conversation, if somebody was only *hearing* it!' He started laughing, but stopped abruptly. 'You don't think I'll die, do you?'

'Of course not! Heart surgery is practically routine these days. Easier than pulling the teeth out of your brain.'

'Oh good. That helps a little. I've got a lot left to do – as soon as I'm back to normal.' I looked at him. I didn't have to say it. 'Oh, right. I almost forgot. The whole business about being normal.' It was a point of honour with Dudley not to be considered too 'normal'; if he was in any such danger he would do or say something outrageous. 'As soon as I'm back to . . . whatever I'm supposed to be back to. How's that?'

'Much better.'

'It's interesting how society conditions us to think there is such a thing as *normal*. What is that? Do you know anyone who is normal?'

'I do know one person,' I said. He never asked who it was.

'Can you even define normal? When I think normal, I think boring. I would remove the word from the dictionary. Both words. Normal and boring, as I detest both – emphatically,' he added, emphatically. I found it amusing that my one 'normal' person, my calm and happy niece, was somebody he liked very much, and found interesting.

I had planned to return home after the few days of tests, as there was an organisation to run, and Brian was on his way to Nova Scotia to sign the papers for a property we had purchased during the summer, more or less on a whim, and without really stopping long enough to think exactly what it would mean to live in New Jersey and have a summer cottage in Nova Scotia. It was an action totally out of character for both Brian and me. We had stretched our finances to do it. Everyone who knew us thought we were nuts, except for Dudley, who said, 'I should expect nothing less of musicians masquerading as pioneers.'

Once again, although Dudley had agreed to the surgery, he was becoming more and more frightened by the idea, and by the thought of another hospital stay. I said I would stay through the first few days, the most difficult time. But it wasn't only his medical condition that needed attention. Dudley was incredibly depressed, and Dr Michael Palmen, the psychiatrist who had met him during the days of evaluation, felt Dudley needed several weeks of inpatient therapy after the surgery. He wanted Dudley to have intensive therapy privately, and to participate in an outpatient group programme while actually living in the hospital.

Dudley was hesitant. He wanted his life to improve, but he was worried about what it would involve. He didn't like the idea of being in a group therapy programme, though he'd done it before, many years earlier. He said he would consider it but not make a decision until after the surgery.

On 25 September 1997, Dudley underwent open-heart surgery that lasted about three hours. By all reports it was uneventful. It was early afternoon by the time I was allowed into the recovery room. Dudley was still under sedation, hooked up to machines and intravenous fluids, and connected to a ventilator, with a tube in his throat. I was told that the surgery had been a complete success, but the first time seeing him was an enormous shock. He looked so helpless lying there, with a machine helping him to breathe. It was too soon to know how well he would come out from anaesthesia.

The previous day I had purchased a tape player and a dozen tapes of works by Bach, Mozart, Mahler and others – works and performers Dudley liked best – as well as some comedy tapes. If there was one thing we knew from our work at Music For All Seasons, it was

he healing power of music. And there was plenty of documented
vidence about the healing power of laughter.

I put on a Mozart piano concerto, played by Alicia de Larrocha.
Within half an hour Dudley opened his eyes. The anaesthetic was
wearing off. Although the tube made it impossible for him to speak,
he was alert. He squeezed my hand, and was able to respond to
questions by squeezing once for yes and twice for no. Two squeezes;
he was not in pain. One squeeze for Mozart; two for Mahler. It was
the very beginning of a long recovery from surgery. There was a
twinkle in his eye as I told him I had cleaned out the bargain bin at
the music store. For some inexplicable reason, the bin had been
heavy on the Ms. Mozart, Mahler, Mendelssohn, Milhaud.

The next day he was able to get up, with help, and was moved
into a room where he remained for a few days while regaining his
strength.

But after a couple of days he was still confused and disorientated,
and, most frustrating for Dudley, unable to dial the telephone. It
might have been a small glitch for others, but for Dudley it was a
catastrophe. He couldn't get the numbers right, no matter how
many times he tried to dial them. He would get halfway through a
familiar number and make a mistake. He would try again and it
would be a different mistake, just like his attempts to play the piano
a week earlier.

The hospital staff were encouraging, explaining to Dudley that
after any major surgery it was not uncommon for basic tasks to be
very difficult. For Dudley, being unable to dial the phone – his lifeline – was frightening. He did not accept their explanation, nor did
he want anyone else dialling for him.

After a few days I went back to New Jersey. Dudley agreed to

stay for the intensive programme, on the condition that I would
visit regularly, and I arranged to be back for a visit a fortnight later. I
was relieved he had agreed to participate in the programme.

Dudley had, of course, participated in a group therapy programme many years before, in California, early in his career. He had
been in a high-profile Hollywood group that met weekly under the
leadership of a psychotherapist and dealt with a broad range of
emotional issues. It was where he met director Blake Edwards and
got his first big Hollywood 'break' in the film 10. At the Mayo
Clinic more than a quarter of a century later, the circumstances in
his life were entirely different. He needed time to recover slowly,
and to start physical rehabilitation under supervision. He also
needed to deal with his depression, and with the major problems in
his life.

All of his medical records continued under a pseudonym he had
carefully chosen (he had several of them ready for different situations) and the hospital protected his confidentiality well. I was
given several points of contact – and a password to prove it was me
on the phone – to get information, as well as a direct line to Dudley.
The staff and doctors were so aware of security issues that his real
name was not used once during the several weeks of his stay – in
reports, in person or on the phone. When Dudley began recovering,
he found this amusing. It was as though he was playing a role, and he
waited to see who else would play along, and who would insist on
challenging his fake identity.

On one of my visits, he reported a conversation with someone in
the outpatient group he was attending.

'I know you are not really "Dick",' the woman had said. 'I believe you are actually Dudley Moore. You look like Dudley Moore. You sound like him too.'

'Well, I might be,' Dudley had replied. 'But I'm not sure. I woke up one day and everyone was calling me "Dick", so I must be "Dick".'

Everyone in the group had signed a confidentiality agreement. Whatever happened in the group stayed in the group, and it was an honourable group. Proof positive was the fact that no member of the press ever learned of his eight-week therapy programme until several years later when he spoke about it.

At the end of his time there, Dudley finally 'admitted' his true identity and the night before he left held a pizza party and Dudley Moore film festival at the home of one of the group participants. For a year or more, he continued to receive letters from some of the other group members, always addressed to his assumed name.

A short time into the private portion of the therapy programme, Dudley was diagnosed as having an addictive relationship to Nicole, and the Mayo Clinic staff began working with him on a regular basis to help him understand that he was a victim of abuse, and that he was showing all the classic symptoms of an abuse victim in an addictive relationship.

Dudley could see it when it was explained to him by Ann Koranda, a kind and down-to-earth therapist, a specialist in treating addiction. He liked talking to her. She presented ideas as carefully as possible, and waited for him to comment or ask questions, or to challenge her. As with most of the medical staff at Mayo, she had been well briefed and was unaffected by Dudley's celebrity status, only trying to help him understand the syndrome, why he had fallen into such a destructive pattern, and how he could find the strength and skills to recover from it.

Dudley invited me to attend one of the sessions when I was visiting. The therapist gave him a series of charts and diagrams showing the stages in the pattern, all very familiar to Dudley.

First the honeymoon stage, she said, where everything seems wonderful. Then the build-up of tensions. Eventually a violent blow-up. Then remorse on the part of the attacker. Apologising, saying it will be better next time. Finally, forgiveness on the part of the victim. Then the cycle starts all over again. It could be a cycle of days, weeks or months. Dudley looked at the graphs and said he could track when the blow-ups were likely to happen.

But it wasn't enough for Dudley to hear it once or twice. They spent weeks covering the same territory, over and over, in more and more depth. And looking at why Dudley's childhood and feelings of low self-esteem made him a prime candidate for such abuse. He didn't feel worthy. He wasn't sure he really deserved good treatment, and he was ready to take the blame for things that weren't his fault. As with most similar cases, all the good qualities he knew he had did not help him to feel deserving.

He was benefiting from the therapy and the group sessions, but it was a slow and uphill battle. He felt he should have been making quicker progress. He was beginning to feel less depressed, but he was impatient for his energy to return and that wasn't happening.

From the end of September until he left hospital in mid-November, I visited Dudley every other weekend, sometimes arriving on a Friday afternoon and joining him for some of the sessions, or for meetings with the staff presenting their progress report. Dudley was involved in the cardiac rehabilitation programme, but still using a walker, and having some trouble giving it up until midway through his time there.

On the weekends, I was permitted to sign Dudley out for various activities. A member of the staff would accompany us, like a strict schoolmistress, to my rented car and make sure he was safely installed with his seatbelt fastened, then off we'd go. Dudley didn't mind – he said it made him feel safe and protected. When we returned, we would call ahead and be met at the back door and he would be escorted back to his room.

We had dinners in one of two restaurants he liked, went to the movies, theatre, concerts, or shopping for clothes. One evening I turned on the car radio to hear that one of the local radio stations had started a 'Spot Dudley Moore' contest, offering prizes. Dudley thought it was flattering and started laughing. 'How much did they say they were offering? Hmm. Well, where should we go to be spotted, then?' The Mayo Clinic's staff, however, had heard the same broadcast and was *not* pleased to learn of the contest. Although Dudley wasn't even registered under his own name, they used their managerial clout to put an immediate stop to the contest.

In a restaurant, when Dudley found a dish that he liked, he would order it over and over and over again, until he finally got tired of it. Then onto a new dish. There were some dishes that would continue indefinitely. While living and performing in New York during the 1970s, he reportedly ordered the same meal at Barbetta day after day for more than a year – gazpacho, fettuccini and chocolate mousse. In one little restaurant near the clinic, he became attached to a lamb dish made with mango salsa, and said he would dream about it between visits.

And we talked, for hours and hours, about his therapy, about how he would put into practice the skills he was learning. How he would learn to identify the difference between what he wanted and what other people wanted of him.

'Rationally, yes, I know I'm a good person. Rationally, I know I'm intelligent, talented, a good musician, a good actor. I know I can make people feel good and laugh. I'm sensitive, generous. But emotionally, I'm a small boy from Dagenham with a club foot. Everybody is trying to persuade me to think differently about it. How can I absorb the changes? How can I apply what I know to be the truth? How can I make myself *feel* differently? That's my challenge.'

It was hard for Dudley to change. But he did come to understand that since he had begun his involvement in an addictive and abusive relationship, he had progressed deeper and deeper into depression. Everything in his life was affected by it.

'This is like any other addiction,' Koranda had explained. 'You cannot pick up one cigarette if you were a smoker. In this case, you cannot speak with her, write to her, take her letters or phone calls, or see her, or you will be right back where you were.'

'I can understand what you are saying,' Dudley said. 'I didn't like being in that place of abuse, but I never really knew how I got there. Now I do.' He smiled. It was a small but important step for Dudley. Getting out of his 'place of abuse' physically was one thing. Getting out of it mentally another matter entirely. But he didn't want to be hurt any more. He was tired. He wanted to feel safe.

By mid-November, Dudley was feeling better, walking without assistance, thinking more clearly and ready to be discharged from the hospital. It had been an experience unlike any other for him, and he left with a commitment to continue physical and psychological therapy. He was told that, while the initial recovery from open-heart surgery was usually completed in six to eight weeks, it could take six months or more to fully recover.

It had been nearly two months since Dudley had experienced 'freedom', and he said that he couldn't wait to get back to 'civilian life'. It was a few days before Thanksgiving, and Brian and I were eager to go to Nova Scotia to experience our new cabin in the woods. We knew that Dudley was tired, and it was an unlikely trip for him so soon after his discharge from the clinic. But the doctors declared him well enough to travel and Dudley declared himself well enough to take the two-hour flight from New Jersey to Nova Scotia.

'I'm coming along, and there's no point in arguing with me,' he said. That was true. Decisions were difficult for him, and it was rarely productive to argue with Dudley if he was firm in a decision. 'I've been cooped up long enough in the snow. I need to get out and do something different.' He had no idea *how* different.

'It's a cabin in the woods, by the beach,' I said. 'The beach will be cold. There's no presidential suite.'

'You must really think I'm a spoiled brat. Don't forget where I've been the past eight weeks. A shack in the woods will be comparative luxury. I promise not to complain.'

'It's not winterised. There's no insulation. It may be cold.'

'I'm from England, remember? Well, if you and Brian don't want me to come along, just tell me. I'm tough . . . a little tough.'

'No, that's not it. Of course we do. We both do. I just don't want you to be disappointed, and cold, and wonder why we dragged you from a hospital in a snowy town to a cold cabin in the woods. We think we're pioneers, but I will be the first to confess — we don't know what the hell we are doing. This is new for us. I don't even know how to light a wood stove, and that's our main source of heat there. Something about a flue and kindling wood, but more complicated than turning the dial on a thermostat, I think.'

There was a long silence. 'OK, I can see you are concerned for my well-being, and not trying to exclude me. That's a relief, because I'm not really as tough as I pretend to be.' He laughed. He suddenly realised that nobody would ever think of him as tough. 'I would have felt *very* rejected if you really didn't want me to come along, although I would understand you might like some time alone with your husband. Speaking of which, is Brian angry with me . . . yet?'

'Why should he be angry with you?'

'For taking up your time. For my taking advantage of your kindness. This is different from being away on tour. That was professional. This is personal. He could have said, "Just let him *rot* in that hospital".'

'He cares about you, just as I do—'

'Because I don't want to cause *too* much trouble for you. But does Brian know that I appreciate this . . . that I appreciate you? Does he know how close we are? Does he know I might not have pulled through this otherwise? And if I were Brian I could be resentful, perhaps.'

'I think he knows you appreciate my help, and his too. Some people think he's tough, just because he's big.' It was always a sight to see Brian and Dudley together. Brian, at six foot four and 280 pounds, and Dudley at five foot two and a half, and 135. Funnier still when they would sing English folksongs together, including one of their favourites – 'I've Got a Lovely Bunch of Coconuts'.

When our daughter Karen was in law school, she worked part-time in an Irish Pub in New Jersey. We would have dinner there occasionally. On the way home, Brian and Dudley would invariably become Irish for the duration of the half-hour drive, singing Irish songs and telling bawdy Irish jokes. It would only take one beer.

Dudley was obviously thinking of what our friendship meant, and concerned that he was being intrusive. Our friendship, and his place in my family and in our lives, was evolving. He had concerns I hadn't known about. I was glad he had brought it up, but not sure I had all the answers. My other friendships tended to be more distant, external to the family unit. Dudley was right in the middle of everything. Our lives were already intertwined. I hadn't yet made the connection that we had, as he knew, crossed over from professional into personal.

'Brian is like you in some ways. He's very sensitive; he's not afraid to cry. He doesn't see real friendship as something superficial, with artificial limits when things are difficult. And I think he respects the way I am.'

'Obviously I don't know Brian the way I know you — I never will — but I really want him to like me, to trust me.'

Brian didn't like my leaving for weekends, but knowing Dudley's need for support, had not objected at all. He knew Dudley was in a difficult situation, and we all thought he would heal from the surgery, complete his therapy and recover. It never occurred to any of us that his health would continue its downward path. We had no plan ready for what was to come.

By the time we had left Rochester, Minnesota, snow had been on the ground for weeks. It was cold, dark and dreary. Dudley had arrived there in September with his summer clothes, and we left with a winter jacket purchased from the one shopping mall with which we had become very familiar.

It was a big production moving Dudley out of hospital, getting him packed (he had somehow accumulated a lot of possessions in his two months there, and gifts people had sent, including teddy bears and gourmet foods). The morning of our trip back, we piled many bags into the car and headed for the airport. Two months earlier, Dudley had left me in charge of his wallet and $600 in cash, and was glad to have them back in his pocket, as though it were the final proof that life was returning to 'whatever it is supposed to be – you know, what other people might refer to as, heaven protect us – "*normal*".' He whispered the word 'normal' in my ear. It was as dirty a word as any he knew.

Dudley was glad to be back in New Jersey and equally ready to head for Nova Scotia a couple of days later, having determined that he was truly welcome on the trip. We had arranged a short trip, only three nights away, with a flight back to New Jersey on Thanksgiving morning, in time for Thanksgiving dinner with the extended family.

Dudley was comfortable travelling first class, but he could be equally comfortable – sometimes it appeared more so – without the trappings of luxury. The little planes that flew from Newark to Halifax had no first-class section, and our first flight on that route was packed.

When we landed and collected a rental car, we discovered it had been snowing in Halifax, virtually the same weather we had happily left behind in Minnesota, but we didn't mind the two-hour drive past miles of snow-covered trees. Dudley had no second thoughts about this trip. He was thrilled to be anywhere that wasn't a medical institution, and he quickly regained his spirit of adventure.

We arrived at the cabin to discover, as we had anticipated, that it was freezing cold. It was still in the condition I remembered from my previous visit months earlier, before Brian and I had become the proud owners. Only the main living area had finished floors. The bedrooms were a mess, and the previous owners had left everything there, as though they had been picked up by an alien spaceship. Books filled the shelves, some written by the owner's father. Three years later, we were to learn that our theories about their departure hadn't been far from the truth. They had seen a panther (a very rare sight in Nova Scotia) walking through the field, a few feet from the kitchen window, and that was enough for them.

Dudley's room, which eventually was decorated to his liking in a bright yellow colour that everyone else disliked, was small, with a high bed and old rickety furniture that we discarded and replaced in time for our stay the following summer.

But on that first November trip, we all felt like pioneers in the wilderness. Despite the ridicule of friends and family who thought we had bought a place in the arctic tundra, we knew that Nova Scotia had warm weather in the summer. But we had no idea how cold an uninsulated cabin could be in the winter. We had a couple of wood stoves, electric blankets and some electric heat, and it took nearly twenty-four hours to get the temperature in the cabin up to 68 degrees Fahrenheit. The nearest supermarket was twenty minutes away. We bought some food at the general store, and found the one local restaurant that was open for lunch and dinner.

There followed an incident that Dudley took great pleasure in recounting, to my embarrassment, for several years. We were shocked to discover that, once the heat was on, the dormant flies in the cabin came to life. Luckily, this never happened again, but on that first visit we were tormented by the buzzing insects. 'This must be a Hitchcock movie,' Dudley said. '*The Flies!*'

Brian didn't waste a minute. He drove to the general store and asked for some insect spray and flypaper. 'Turned your heat on, eh?' the storekeeper said. Other locals were ready with advice. He came back to the cabin feeling like an expert. Dudley and I had fly-swatters in both hands and had made quite a killing during Brian's fifteen-minute absence.

Dudley would tell this story at all types of gatherings, particularly at elegant dinner parties. Anywhere he could have an impact. After the first few times, I took him aside. 'Dudley, you make it seem like our cabin is in some horrible slum. It embarrasses me.' He didn't want to stop telling the story, even though he knew it annoyed me every time. It was always good for shock value, and the more elegant the setting, the more he would embellish the story, adding thousands of flies, piled up on the window sills, falling into our (imaginary) soup or coffee. Brushing them aside to eat our sandwiches. (That never happened, but it would make his tuxedoed listeners cringe – he would then give me a triumphant smile.) Eventually I made my objections stronger, and only had to give him one dirty glance and he would cut the story short, but only after telling some choice part of it.

Finally I came to the conclusion that I was just too concerned with what people thought. This was part of Dudley's lesson. I was too uptight. Who cared if my summer haven appeared to others to be a fly-infested dump?

I stopped objecting. Apparently my reaction had been at least three-quarters of the fun for Dudley. No longer able to irritate me

TOP: John (Jock) Moore, Dudley, Ada Moore.

ABOVE: Dudley as a baby with sister Barbara and Mum, 1936.

RIGHT: 'I started life as a choir boy -- I know some of you find that hard to believe.'

ABOVE: Dudley and 'fellow soldiers' in play by Jean Anouilh (Oxford production and tour).

BELOW: Dudley and Peter Cook with director Bryan Forbes (center) on the set of Dudley's first film, *The Wrong Box*, 1966.

OPPOSITE: Dudley with Peter Cook and Stanley Donen *Bedazzled* by Raquel Welch.

ABOVE: Dudley and Suzy
Kendall in 1970.

LEFT: Dudley and son Patric
1984.

BELOW: 'Uncle Dudley' hold
newborn Dvorah Southland
two hours old, March 29, 19

COURTESY OF PATRICK MOORE

ABOVE: Dudley and Bo ...ek, sharing a moment ...ou's party, 1999.

ABOVE: 'Lunch, my favourite meal!' – Dudley, Rena, Brian, Nova Scotia, 1998.

ABOVE: Sarah Bellwood, Lou Pitt, Peter Bellwood, Dudley, Brogan Lane, Parker Stevenson, Berta Pitt, Kirstey Alley – an atypical Hollywood outing.

ABOVE: Dudley backstage at Carnegie Hall on his birthday, 19 April 1997 with Rena, Lauren Bacall, Susie Dullea, Roberta Peters, Keir Dullea, Brian Dallow, David Alan Miller, Peter Bellwood.

ABOVE: Karen Dallow, Jasmine the cat, ...dley, Elise Dallow – his favourite pose.

ABOVE: Birthday kiss from Else Blangsted, 1998 – 'I'm turning how old today?'

ABOVE: Mixing harmonies with the waves – 'What happened to my house? I thought my house was on the beach.'

RIGHT: 'Anxiety,' excerpt from Dudley's first composition, age eleven – 'I suppose it was a precursor of things to come.'

BELOW: Dudley and Rena in Carnegie Hall. Christopher Seaman conducting the New Jersey Symphony Orchestra, April 1996.

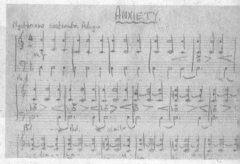

ABOVE: November 16, 2001 – Dudley and
Prince Charles at Buckingham Palace, a
proud moment as he receives the CBE.

BELOW: Dudley and Julie Andrews,
good friends sharing a moment after a
Philadelphia performance together.

LEFT: Dudley in a
pensive moment.

ABOVE: Rena and Dudley
studying the score. 'What do
you think of this tempo?'

ABOVE: 'Why am I holding these
flowers? And what can be done
for this tulip?' Australia, 1996.

by telling the story, the thrill was gone. He stopped. I had raised four children and survived their adolescence; I should have remembered the psychology.

By the middle of the first summer, with some new furniture, a coat of paint, new floors and window blinds, the cabin underwent a major transformation. It had graduated to a 'cottage', and even Dudley had to admit that the change was remarkable. 'And no more flies. I am suitably impressed,' he said. But that first visit, we only survived two nights in the cabin. The third night, we drove nearly two hours east to Halifax and checked into a five-star hotel. Dudley insisted it was his treat. We had reserved two rooms in Brian's name. They took one look at Dudley and immediately upgraded us to the Presidential Suite. We had dinner served in the immense dining room of the suite.

Perhaps we could not have settled in the Wild West, but we had bonded with our cabin and were ready to go home. The following morning we flew back to New Jersey. The adventure had been good for all of us. For Dudley it was a particularly good transition from hospital life back to civilian life. His road to recovery seemed a little less daunting.

14

YOU LOOK JUST LIKE
DUDLEY MOORE

FOR THE NEXT FEW months, Dudley took part in a vigorous series of programmes designed to bring him back to energetic good health. Using another assumed name, he joined the cardiac rehabilitation programme of our local hospital in New Jersey. Some years earlier, in an attempt to become physically fit, Dudley had installed a gymnasium in his California house. State-of-the-art exercise equipment, a television suspended from the ceiling to help pass the torture time, carefully chosen works of art on the walls and a complete sound system.

Dudley's 'health kick' lasted only a short time, and the gym became a showplace for guests, who would dutifully get on the bicycle and try lifting the weights, and report how impressed they were. He got more mileage from the off-colour invitation. 'Would you like to come upstairs and see my equipment?' he would ask anyone who hadn't previously been to the house. If they were repeat

...ould say, 'I've expanded my equipment. Allow me to show you.' The joke never wore off for Dudley.

Now in New Jersey, he thought he should buy a treadmill, highly recommended by the cardiac rehabilitation department. It would go into one of the spare bedrooms in our house. Off we went dutifully to the nearest Sears store. Dudley, Brian and me.

In the past, it had been Dudley's habit to shop quickly, pick out the best item (sometimes just the highest-priced item, figuring it had to be the best) and bring the sale to a conclusion as quickly as possible. With no professional work on the horizon, and hints of financial troubles, Dudley was beginning to learn that there were other ways to shop.

He was intrigued by the choice of treadmills in a wide range of styles and prices. He began speaking with a young salesman, who seemed to recognise Dudley.

'What are the specific functions of all these buttons?' Dudley asked. 'And what makes this machine cost twice as much as that one?'

The salesman's explanation was detailed, and lengthy. After a few moments, Dudley lost interest. He was pretending to pay attention, nodding his head, but it was easy to see that he had already tuned out. He was looking to see which treadmill had the most stream-lined design and shiniest metal parts. He asked Brian and me for our opinions.

After Dudley announced his choice, the salesman said, 'You look just like Dudley Moore. There's an amazing resemblance.'

'Yes, there certainly is,' Dudley said. 'I've noticed that in the mirror.'

We never knew how Dudley would respond. It was different

every time. It depended a lot on the person doing the recognising, and how much Dudley could amuse himself.

'And your accent. It's a lot like his too.'

'That's right,' Dudley said. He took out his credit card to pay, figuring that would put an end to the speculation, as it generally did. But much to our amazement, the salesman said, 'My goodness. Your credit card says Dudley Moore too. Is this just a coincidence, or did you change your name to be the same as his?'

Dudley could barely control his laughter. At that moment, the young man's supervisor, who had been listening, came over to the cash register.

'You *idiot*,' she said quietly. 'That *is* Dudley Moore.'

Nobody expected to find a celebrity like Dudley living in suburban New Jersey, and the variety of reactions surprised Dudley, who thought he had already experienced the entire bizarre range. He loved using his credit card, as it was his ticket to entertainment of a different sort than the ads had promised, such as in a restaurant, paying for a meal:

Waitress: This credit card – it says Dudley Moore.

Dudley: Yes, that's right.

Waitress: So, you're Dudley Moore?

Dudley: Yes, as a matter of fact, I am.

Waitress: Wow! – long reflective pause – Are you sure?

Dudley's room was on the first floor of our New Jersey home, a large three-storey Tudor-style house built in 1927 by an English architect. He felt very comfortable in our quiet neighbourhood, saying it was 'beautiful and verdant'.

Dudley had brought along the possessions that seemed most important to him, and left everything else behind in Los Angeles, wavering over what to do about the house. He believed it was worth about $4 million, and that it would provide for his retirement if he sold it. Dudley didn't yet know that, with his broad power of attorney, his business manager had borrowed heavily against the equity in the house, and Dudley's expenses were being paid from this loan. And if the house had once been worth $4 million, property values had declined. The house was not nearly the security he thought it would be.

Earlier, while Dudley was bringing in a steady income, he hadn't needed to worry about his retirement. Now, there were film royalties but no new sources of income. Hugh Robertson told him he needed to be careful about spending. Dudley had never heard that before, and it was an unpleasant surprise to him.

Brian and I had agreed that Dudley would stay with us while he was recovering from surgery and getting himself ready to resume working. We weren't yet discussing how long that might be. Dudley was thinking less and less about ever going back to live in Los Angeles. He toyed with the idea of living in England. He also thought about living half the time in New Jersey and the other half in London. Dudley usually had trouble with decisions, and this was a big one for him. It was also a waiting game to see how quickly he would progress back to full health. It was clear that he needed a lot of support to do this, without having to worry about where he would be living.

Apart from his medical expenses, alimony and child support, Dudley's daily expenses were small. He wanted to pay 'rent' for staying in our house, but Brian and I refused.

'I don't want money mixed up in our friendship. Brian and I both feel very strongly about this,' I explained to him.

He wasn't happy at all about that. Dudley liked to show his appreciation with money, and thought it was 'strange' (translation: 'really dreadful') that we didn't feel the same way he did.

Finding another solution was new and difficult for him, but we needed to arrive at some sort of compromise. We discussed the whole issue in depth for only one day – an unusually short time to discuss a serious matter with Dudley – until it was resolved, and then we never discussed it again.

'It's not right. You have expenses,' he said.

'In principle, I agree with you. But Brian and I both earn respectable salaries. It would be different if we needed the money.'

'But I'll be using electricity, water, other things.'

'How much electricity can you use? How much water? It could only be a few dollars a month, and you are our guest here. I think it's rude to let a guest pay for these things.'

'But I have more money than you do.'

'I'm sure that's true. But so what? That doesn't change how I feel about this.' I was having trouble getting the point across. People were always asking him for money and he was used to it. He was comfortable 'lending' it or giving it away. He would get letters from strangers telling him their troubles and asking for money. Usually he did not give money to strangers, unless it was a specific charitable organisation and he believed in the cause.

'We're Children of the Sixties,' I said. 'Liberals. From the generation that believed our conventional parents had it all wrong.'

Finally, he understood. 'Oh, you mean the "money is evil" generation – until you discover that you have to buy a house and feed your starving children. *Triplets* must have changed your thinking a little!'

'Well, I suppose, yes, we did learn that we had to make enough money to feed our starving children, but this doesn't have anything to do with our friendship. You can't pay us rent, or it will make us feel like bad hosts.'

'Then how will you know I appreciate what you and Brian are doing?'

'You can tell us once in a while. Or not. You can give us a hug, or keep an eye on the chicken roasting while we are out. Little things are fine.'

'Watch the chicken?'

'Why not?'

'That sounds revolutionary, but fun. I can probably do that.'

Since fish and chicken were top of his list, it was a safe bet, but I had really only meant it as a joke, and he was serious. We knew his cooking skills to be just a little erratic. Dudley had told Brian the story of a Christmas turkey cooked for him by his housekeeper. All Dudley had to do was to remove the turkey from the oven and let it cool for fifteen minutes before serving his guests. He had removed the turkey and put it in the garden, just outside the back door of his LA home. After cooling it for fifteen minutes, he opened the door to discover the entire turkey covered in ants. I figured that was a mistake he wouldn't make twice.

We also knew that sometimes, when filming in a cold climate, he would carry his lunch wrapped in tin foil and ready to cook slowly – on top of the heater. When the studio smelled strongly of his infamous trout, he explained, he knew lunch was ready. Other members of the cast had protested; this novel cooking technique was apparently short-lived.

'I don't know how *well* I can watch the chicken, but I think I can do it . . . Well, one thing then. A very, very important thing for me. Can I pay for lunch when we are out?' he asked cautiously.

'Yes.'

'And what about for Pat?' Pat Bruno cleaned the house once a week. We paid her $75.

'That too.' And that was it. We had resolved the issue. We were all happy with the resolution. We thought that we had defined the very essence of compromise and drank a Pellegrino toast 'to our magnificent skills at conflict resolution', as Dudley described them.

'Do you know the definition of compromise?' he said.

'Probably not, if this is a joke.'

'The wife gets what she wants and the husband is miserable.'

I wondered if that was his definition of marriage, not compromise.

We nearly had to take Pat to hospital the first time she came to clean the house and found Dudley there. Nobody had thought to warn her. Dudley immediately gave her a raise, and it didn't take long for Pat to get used to seeing Dudley in the house without reacting. Later, when he lived in the adjacent house and needed more care, Pat became his cook and housekeeper.

I suspected we ate lunch out all too often so that Dudley could exercise his part of the bargain. It was a daily ritual. It only took a few weeks to identify a few restaurants that we rotated. They were selected according to the dishes Dudley liked and the restaurant's discretion. Dudley continued to get stuck on a single dish and order it for months. One year, it was chicken quesadillas. Several restaurants were quickly eliminated after clippings appeared in the local newspapers, with quotes from the owners stating exactly what

Dudley had eaten for lunch, and who was with him. Usually they got both wrong.

After going to a restaurant a few times, one of us would call pretending to be a reporter. One time Dudley made the call, with an American accent, and trying hard not to laugh. This was Dudley being tolerant of my reluctance to have our daily lunch reported by the media. I knew he didn't really care about the intrusion.

The only glitch in his phone call was that Dudley always pronounced the word 'restaurant' in the French manner, complete with silent 't'. It had to be a dead giveaway. 'We've heard that Dudley Moore is in the area,' he said, covering the receiver long enough to laugh, 'and we'd like to know if he has eaten in your restau*ran*.'

'Yes, he comes in here once or twice a week,' was the most frequent reply. Generally they exaggerated the frequency of the visits.

Three restaurants replied, 'We don't disclose who our patrons might be,', and those became Dudley's three top choices. Once inside the restaurant, he was always happy to be recognised.

On one occasion, we were having dinner with a group of family and friends – ten in total. Halfway through the meal, an elderly woman came over to the table and said to me, 'Oh, my goodness, aren't you *Rena Fruchter*, the pianist? I heard you play a couple of years ago, and you were wonderful. I'm so happy to meet you.'

'Yes, I am. Thank you!' After she left the table, everyone else reacted by laughing – except for Dudley. She hadn't noticed him.

Dudley developed 'superior skills as a late-afternoon roasting-chicken watcher', he reported one day. We only called upon him once every few weeks to do this important job. He would phone me at the office to report. He was proud of his new skill, and happy that t was a non-financial way to show he was a participating member of he family.

'This chicken, it's beige and looking fine.' In this context the word 'fine' had a Southern accent, more like 'faaan', to distinguish it from his ordinary use of the word to convey how he was feeling, no matter how was *was* feeling. 'I'll baste it and call you again in thirty minutes,' he would say. 'But one of the wings is slightly darker than he other. It's mysterious.' He was very precise in his analysis. And he call would come exactly thirty minutes later, to the second.

'It's slightly brown and smells good. I'm putting salt on it.'

That was scary. Dudley loved salt and oversalted everything. He was told to cut out salt after the surgery, but he told one of his doc-ors he would rather die than live without salt. Since his blood pressure was low with the medication, he was allowed to reintro-duce salt into his diet, in moderation. 'Would you mind defining "moderation"?' he had said. That seemed to explain a lot about Dudley.

Or: 'I'll continue watching and call you in thirty minutes.' Once I found a chair in front of the oven. I believed he had pulled a chair into the kitchen and was really watching through the oven's little window, but I decided not to ask. It was also possible he was having a meeting with Alexander, our dog.

Next call: 'It's done. The little plastic thing has popped out and he wings look perfect. I'm turning the oven off. Are you coming home to do the rest of this dinner? I'm *starving*.'

Dudley was focused almost entirely on the process of recovery, attending all the various therapies that were scheduled and meeting with psychologists – several in a row until he found one he liked.

And when his balance continued to get worse, and the complaint about the funny feeling in his eyes returned, there was the inevitabl parade of neurologists.

It was becoming clear that he had recovered well from his open heart surgery, but still had exactly the same symptoms that had sen him to the Mayo Clinic in the first place, only now the symptom were worse. We all began to believe that the blocked artery ha never been the cause of his symptoms. He was spending more an more time lying down, 'because I feel *safer* in this position'.

And he was feeling dizzy. He was playing the piano a little ever day, but not to his satisfaction. His hands were working less effec tively. He was beginning to drop things occasionally. Sometimes cup he was holding would go flying. We put the liquids in a covere cup. If he poured his morning cereal from the box into the bow most of it would be on the floor. He thought he was clumsy, or care less, but he refused help with these small tasks.

One day, all of these things happened to him in the course of few hours, and he finally asked for help. His breakfast had ended uj mostly on the floor. He was trying to play the piano – a piece that h had written years earlier and performed hundreds of times. But hi fingers wouldn't move around the keys. He was getting stuck, play ing wrong notes. He went into the kitchen to pour some apple juic from a container he had handled many times before. This time, i slipped out of his hands and spilled all over the floor.

He was upset to have caused such a mess, and reached for a towe He was frowning. 'I don't know why this is happening. I'm so care ful, but things just fall out of my hands.'

'It looks like a coordination problem,' I said. 'And it's not you fault. You're not careless – I've seen how careful you are.'

He sat down on a chair, looking puzzled.

'I don't know. I thought the surgery would fix my troubles, but I really do think it's something else. I'm getting worse. I can't work. I feel like I'm never going to improve.'

It was time to resume the search for a diagnosis. First, to doctors in New Jersey and New York. Next, a visit to another well-known institution – Johns Hopkins Medical Center in Baltimore, Maryland. It was a four-hour trip from New Jersey, but seemed worth the effort. All the signs were pointing to a neurological problem that doctors at the Mayo Clinic may have missed. We knew there were renowned neurologists at Johns Hopkins. Dudley met with one of the chief neurologists there, Dr Stephen Reich, whom we later learned was a specialist in PSP. He put Dudley through a battery of tests, and said he wasn't sure exactly what was wrong. He suggested another appointment in a few months, and never mentioned PSP. He didn't even suspect it during that first visit.

In many respects this was the worst time for Dudley – not knowing what was happening to him. Once he knew the truth, as bad as it was, he could deal with it, begin to move forward, make decisions about his life, his work. But for many months, every day was troublesome and puzzling. He was craving answers, and wondering if there would ever be a real explanation for his problems.

Continuing his quest, Dudley saw another series of doctors. One said he had 'multiple system atrophy', a condition as dreadful as it sounds. Another doctor went back to the earlier theory and said Dudley may have experienced minor strokes. A third said he could have any one of a dozen rare neurological conditions that are difficult to diagnose, and an answer might never be found. Another said he was probably recovering slowly from his surgery and should 'wait it out'.

He repeated the standard neurological tests a dozen times – walking slowly with one foot in front of the other, closing his eyes and touching the tip of his nose with his forefinger (this test always made him laugh), touching each finger to the thumb of the same hand as quickly as possible, and remembering a series of words and numbers in a particular order, then repeating them back.

The 'I'm fine, thank you. How are you?' conversation was repeated over and over with every doctor, and he was asked for his complete medical history, he said, 'at least 250 times. This one is number 251.' He always said it cheerfully, and the number was always 251; he wanted to get across the point that he was a little tired of the same old thing.

Finally, one of Dudley's physical therapists referred him to a young and highly respected neurologist at JFK Medical Center in Edison, New Jersey. Dr Martin Gizzi took one look at Dudley's eyes, which were exhibiting slowed horizontal movement, and said there was no doubt that Dudley had Progressive Supranuclear Palsy. Dudley didn't react. He had already heard that he had a dozen other dreadful conditions. What made this diagnosis any more reliable than the rest?

Later that day, I spoke by phone to Dr Gizzi. He was very clear about the diagnosis. 'It's a degenerative neurological condition. A syndrome. All of Dudley's symptoms fit this syndrome. There is no cure. Eventually he will be in a wheelchair. There are some medications that may help to control the symptoms, but there's nothing that will cure this.'

Dr Gizzi was very clear, and kind. Dudley had liked him very much.

'But there's one thing that's puzzling to me,' Dr Gizzi said over the phone. 'When I gave Dudley the diagnosis, he didn't react at all.

Most people would react with surprise or shock, or at least ask questions.'

I said, 'Dudley has already been diagnosed with everything under the sun. He may not have believed you.'

Dr Gizzi followed up with tests that confirmed his diagnosis, including a rotary chair test he had designed, he explained, 'examining eye movements generated in response to moving visual targets, and in response to movements of the head. Miniature infrared video cameras track the speed and accuracy of eye movements', and the measurements show if the brain is processing the information properly. With this proof, Dr Gizzi was certain of the diagnosis.

Still, Dudley added this diagnosis to all the others, and didn't accept it until more than a year later, when his symptoms were more defined and it was confirmed by two more doctors, including Dr Reich. Then he went back to Dr Gizzi for treatment, and was, for different periods of time, under the care of both Dr Gizzi and Dr Lawrence Golbe, then president of the PSP Society, and with his finger on the pulse of all the medical trials that were taking place around the world.

The same evening he had first visited Dr Gizzi, Dudley began talking about his condition. 'I've been told so many different things. What Dr Gizzi said may be true, but how do I know what to believe? If this is the real diagnosis, there's no hope for me. No hope at all, and I'm going to die from this.'

Dr Gizzi had not actually said that to Dudley. But he had heard and absorbed the diagnosis very well, and read between the lines of Dr Gizzi's gentle manner. His gut feeling was that this could be the true diagnosis. But he chose to postpone his own acceptance of this devastating diagnosis as long as he could.

'I want to keep searching before I accept this fate. If this is true, I'll function less and less, until I'm in a wheelchair. Then I'll die. And this means I'll never play another concert.' Then he laughed at the way it had come out. 'Of course I'll never play another concert if I'm *dead*. No, this is an impossible diagnosis for me. I don't like it at all.'

15

CATS IN THE CAR

('THIS TRIP IS *HOW LONG?*')

THE SUMMER OF 1998 was the first time we would all go to Nova Scotia for a long stretch. Dudley wanted to spend our six-week summer stay there with us, and despite *The Flies*, he couldn't wait to go back. His suitcases were packed days in advance. It didn't take long for Nova Scotia to become one of his favourite spots in the world. We learned the hard way, though, that the route from New Jersey to Nova Scotia was a route we would fly, not drive, with Dudley!

On the appointed day in June, we got up at 5 a.m. The cars had been packed the night before, and the plan was for Brian to lead the way in the van packed with all the big items and Alexander, our ten-year-old Golden Retriever. Dudley and I would take the Honda, filled with as much as we could fit (Dudley and I were already known for our inability to pack lightly, and this was, after all, a six-week trip) and all three cats – Vicious, a sweet-tempered calico cat,

233

and her two adult offspring: Bear, a large, male black cat who looked very macho, for a cat, but was afraid of everything including bananas (during the summer we were all surprised to learn that he was not afraid of mice, but a very good mouser indeed); and Malkin, a small female with the appearance of a big calico fur-ball.

Dudley loved all three cats and did not mind sharing the car with them; they were in individual cat carriers for the entire trip, in accordance with veterinary instructions. Until that day, the felines had not travelled anywhere except to and from the animal hospital for their periodic check-ups. Those visits called for only ten minutes in the car. These suburban cats were not prepared for the ordeal they were about to face. Neither was Dudley. As soon as we were fifteen minutes into the trip, one of the cats started to howl. Then a second joined in. Finally all three were engaged in a deafening chorus of cat howling.

Dudley and I had brought music along, and several complete Shakespeare plays on tape, on the off chance that we would run out of things to talk about. We were trying to have a conversation about his childhood – about his earliest memories of piano lessons, and piano technique, and after a few minutes we were shouting.

'WHAT DID YOU SAY ABOUT SCALES?' I asked him.

'I SAID I HATED THEM'– loud meowing in the background – 'I PRACTISED THEM BUT I HATED THEM. I SHOULD HAVE PRACTISED THEM MORE. MY TECHNIQUE WOULD PROBABLY BE BETTER NOW.'

We tried to continue, but the noise was making it impossible to hear each other, and Bear was rattling his cage.

'WHAT THE HELL DO THEY WANT?' Dudley asked, finally losing patience.

'WHAT DO YOU THINK THEY WANT? THEY WANT TO GET OUT OF THEIR CAGES, AND GO HOME, AND POOP IN THEIR LITTER BOXES.'

'WELL SO DO I,' Dudley said, his momentary anger diffusing into fits of laughter.

We were only an hour into the trip, and I could not imagine how we would get through the next nine hours. Of the three possible ways to get from New Jersey to Nova Scotia, we had decided to take the longer of the two land routes, to Bar Harbor, Maine, leading to the shorter boat ride (three hours rather than overnight) – a route we never duplicated after that summer.

The veterinary doctor had provided very specific travel instructions for cats, as though he had the ultimate feline travel manual. Feed them in the morning, put them in their cages and don't let them out. 'They will sleep for most of the trip,' he had assured me. He did not advise tranquillisers because of the medical risks. Another hour into the trip, and the cats were still at it. I had a headache. Dudley was beginning to lose his sense of humour. Then we both noticed a terrible smell.

'Did you do that?' Dudley asked.

'No, did you?' I replied.

Slowly, he turned around. 'Must have been one of YOU,' he said, scowling at all three cats. 'That's disgusting. Who trained you?'

'That would have been Vicious, their mother,' I told him.

'Well, I shall be having a little talk with her IF WE EVER FINISH THIS GODDAMN FUCKING TRIP.'

'Getting a little *irritable?*' I snapped back at him. Two hours, I had just learned, never to forget, was the limit of time Dudley could sit in a car. And we had eight hours left.

'It must be time for lunch,' I said.

It was not quite 8 a.m., and I pulled out my mobile phone to call Brian in the car ahead to tell him it was time for whatever meal we should have after being on the road for three hours. Brian was not happy. Our travelling styles were very different. Brian's habit was to drive until his bladder was bursting. I preferred stopping to check out all the rest areas along the way and do a comparative study of Roadside Coffees I Have Tasted. Dudley wanted to be anaesthetised for the trip. There was no meeting of minds here.

We saw a sign for a restaurant that we didn't yet know was famous for miles around – a restaurant that doubled as a bookstore and gave every patron a chance to take home free used books that had been donated by other people as they were passing through. We pulled off the highway and were relieved to get out of the smelly car. We made a wise decision to have breakfast first and deal afterwards with whatever catastrophe the cats had caused. Calling it a 'catastrophe' momentarily tickled Dudley's funny bone.

A cup of coffee and breakfast brought about a noticeable improvement in Dudley's mood. He ordered his usual restaurant breakfast: scrambled egg substitute (because he was watching his cholesterol), along with ham, bacon and sausages, fried potatoes and toast, butter and marmalade. It was an order that usually made the servers smile. And black coffee with as much sugar as he could dissolve in it, along with two little packages of artificial sweetener (because he was watching his weight).

We took as long as we could to eat breakfast. Brian was ready to get back in the car quickly and start driving again. Dudley was not. We also had the cat clean-up to look forward to. We identified Bear, the fearful cat, as the culprit. They were all quiet when we came out of the bookstore/restaurant, carrying books that we squeezed into the available inches of space left in the two cars.

Carefully, we lifted Bear's cage out of its secure position and moved it so that we could open the little door and remove the soiled towel, replacing it with newspapers. Dudley helped to hold him in place so he wouldn't escape, talking to him the whole time.

'It's OK, Bear, I know exactly how you feel. I'm not enjoying this trip any more than you are. I would poop in the car if I could. It's not really your fault. It's her fault,' he said, pointing to me. 'Only another eight hours and we'll be on the boat.'

As soon as we got back onto the highway, Vicious started to howl, then Malkin, and finally Bear. We turned on the CD player – Mozart symphonies, very loud, and after another two hours they all went to sleep. Dudley did not, however. He stared outside for a while. Then we were able to talk again. Only another two hours and it would be time for lunch.

That was the only really long car trip Dudley and I ever took. Until that summer, it hadn't sunk in that Dudley's absolute limit for most non-musical activities was two hours, total. I might have realised that we were headed for trouble if I had remembered a 1992 tour, when I had watched him insist to concert promoters in Minnesota that if it was a three-hour ride from one concert location to the next, they would have to arrange a flight. Never mind that, in that instance, the three-hour limousine ride would have been the quickest route. Dudley said he couldn't stand three hours in a car and wasn't about to discuss it any further. There was no public airport that would make it any closer. An alternate plan was proposed. They could arrange a ride for him to a small airport: an hour and a half. Waiting for private jet to arrive: 30 minutes. Taking private jet to small airport close to the new city: 1 hour. Limousine ride to new hotel: 45 minutes. Total: 3 hours, 45 minutes. The promoters thought logic would prevail and Dudley would accept the three-hour limousine ride. Dudley was much happier with the complicated flight plan, so they arranged it for him.

Finally arriving after the interminable trip, we drove down a long gravel driveway opening onto a small meadow with a house, set in a dozen acres of woodland. We had been there a few months earlier in cold November, but in the summer the lush green gave it a different kind of appeal. Down a short path through the woods and we were on a white sand beach. Although Dudley's Los Angeles house was right on the beach, he almost never set foot on it. There were too many people, he said, and it took too long to get to the edge of the water.

Our first summer morning in Nova Scotia, Dudley wanted to go to the beach. Using his cane for support, he walked carefully down the path, over the moss-covered rocks and stepped out onto an exquisite beach with an impressive rocky central point. The water had gentle waves and was shallow enough that he could walk a long distance before it became deep. And nobody else was there.

Before leaving New Jersey, Dudley confessed that he did not own swimming trunks. 'I know it sounds strange, but I never went on the beach in California,' he said. Part of it was still his hesitation over publicly revealing his club foot and his small, thin left leg. While buying some things he needed for the trip, I picked up two dark blue swimming trunks so he would be prepared. When he realised that he was safe, and that nobody else would see him, he was ready to go in the ocean, and went in about as far as he could go and remain standing.

After only a few hours in the cottage, we all realised that something important was missing. A piano. Suddenly the idea of spending six weeks without a piano seemed impossible. Our little village has a general store, a small church and a community hall. The nearest large town is Liverpool (like in England, it is set on the Mersey River), and while there is a supermarket and a main street filled with small shops, there is nowhere to rent or buy a piano. Brian, Dudley and I began looking in the newspaper ads for used pianos, and I was appointed to head the research team. They would then join me for the final phase.

On the chosen day, I made arrangements to try three pianos, all being sold by individuals living in and near Halifax, a large city two hours away. Only the third piano was good enough to remain on the list. I gave a $50 deposit and promised the owner, a music teacher who had one piano too many, that I would return the following afternoon with two more experts. She thought it a little strange, but as nobody else was rushing to buy the instrument, she was willing to have her piano undergo the necessary scrutiny.

The next afternoon, we all drove to Halifax. Luckily for Dudley, the trip was just *under* two hours. Arriving at the home of the music teacher, we each proceeded in turn to play the pale green, no-name upright piano. 'My goodness, you *all* play well,' she said, as we each pronounced the piano's action good, even, easy to play and nice to the touch.

Dudley played jazz. We all stepped back to listen to each other, to be sure we could live with the instrument, at least for six weeks.

We declared it sold, went into the kitchen, where I pulled out the remaining $300 Canadian (about £100) from my purse and our gracious hostess made us tea. Dudley was seated opposite her at the tiny kitchen table. 'And what do you do?' she asked. She had already asked Brian and me.

'I'm a musician, and an actor,' he said.

'You look very familiar. Have we met before?'

'Oh, I don't think so,' Dudley said. 'It's my first time here.'

'Hey, wait a minute. You're not . . . No, you couldn't be, not here in my kitchen, could you?'

'Yes, I could be,' Dudley said, beaming.

Two days later, the green piano arrived on our doorstep, and it was well used that summer. We were certain that it could not survive the Nova Scotia winters in an unheated cottage with no insulation. But when we returned the following summer, the green piano not only worked perfectly but was still in tune. And the following summer as well. To date, it has been tuned just once and is still going strong.

Going to museums was not high on Dudley's list of activities, unless there was a special exhibit of an artist he particularly liked. But he did enjoy museums dealing with the methods and history of transportation. He was fascinated by a huge railroad museum we visited in Lancaster, Pennsylvania. In Halifax we went to the Maritime Museum of the Atlantic, which had as one of its exhibits a well-known hydrographic survey ship built in 1913 by the British firm of Swan, Hunter & Wigham Richardson, and 'retired' from the seas in 1969. Despite having to go up and down stairs and through narrow hallways and staircases, Dudley was fascinated by the ship's history and eager to explore the vessel.

A shy young woman in charge of the tour addressed a group of about twenty tourists seated in a small room on the ship. Dudley was in the first row, and she noticed him but said nothing. She kept trying to speak, but was losing her words and coughing; stopping, saying excuse me, and starting over again. The tour continued around the entire ship, the young woman continuing to have big problems with her presentation. At the end of the tour, we all thanked her and left the ship.

'She seemed affected by my presence,' Dudley whispered. I had never seen anyone so paralysed by coming into contact with Dudley. But it hadn't surprised him, and it was a reaction he hadn't minded at all.

A week later, Dudley and I were returning from the 45-minute drive to the nearest town with a movie theatre. Although Brian didn't mind a 12-hour car trip, a 45-minute drive to see a movie seemed intolerably long, and he stayed at home to read a book. On the way back Dudley noticed the declining petrol gauge – he had previously appointed himself as Petrol Police inside my car – and said we had to stop. We pulled into a station. I filled the tank and he stepped inside to pay with his credit card. As he got back into the car, I started the engine and we heard the young female cashier pick up the phone and shriek, 'Oh my God, you will never in a million years guess who just bought gas here. I have his credit card receipt in my hand. DUDLEY MOORE. I'm holding his autograph. I just touched his hand. I can't believe it.'

I looked at him. 'Well, that was some reaction!'

He smiled. A certain smile he used only after a very nice boost to his ego.

Around that time, Dudley had taken a step back to look at his life, and was learning to accept the fact that his performing career would never be the same again. He was depressed about it, but beginning to take stock of what he had achieved and how many people had been positively affected by his work. That summer he was quietly appreciative of the attention he received. His warm relationship with the public had always been important to him, and meant a lot to him. He had always answered his fan mail personally, for as long as he could continue to do it. He loved reading the letters, or hearing them read to him. Now, more than ever, he cherished every personal example of the devotion of his fans.

Travelling to Nova Scotia with Dudley was a bittersweet annual event. He loved being there, but it was the place we could most clearly see the progression of his condition. At home in New Jersey, the decline was so slow and so gradual that we barely noticed it. But come June or July, we would open the door to the cottage, and Dudley's decline from the previous year would hit us all squarely in the face – his increasing difficulty in walking down the hall, trouble turning the corner and heading from one room to another, getting in and out of bed – it was easy to remember where we had left off ten months earlier, and hard to face the fact that each year brought Dudley a few steps further along the slow walk to the end of his life.

That first summer in Nova Scotia, Dudley was still in relatively good condition, and he joined us in enthusiastically exploring the area. The local community was at first stunned to have a celebrity in its midst, but contrary to the more outgoing American approach, people in Nova Scotia whispered but kept their distance.

Dudley was always very aware of their reaction, and wanted to be sure people knew he was there. But a part of him responded well to a public that was quietly, unobtrusively impressed by his presence, and extremely proud that Dudley had chosen their place to spend his summers.

And they were fiercely protective of his privacy. Everyone knew where our spot was, and once the word was out, the press were eager to find Dudley. But nobody was saying a word. A tourist had reported to the *Chronicle-Herald*, the primary Nova Scotia newspaper, that Dudley had been seen in a little restaurant called Seascape, and it was big news in the next day's paper. But the locals, we later learned, who knew exactly where we were, came up with a variety of stories if asked by the press. One said they knew Dudley had been on a yacht but had left the area. Whatever it took to protect this celebrated new community member.

Brian and Dudley went to the Grub and Grog one afternoon. The place was completely empty when they arrived. Brian noticed that the owner was on the phone after taking their order. Gradually, people arrived and sat down at the tables. Within half an hour, the place was filled. Everyone looked, and smiled. But nobody bothered Dudley. They were just happy to be in the same pub as him.

It was a summer of visitors, with all our friends and family coming to see what a crazy thing we had done, getting a summer place in a strange, faraway land that had arctic weather, or so they all thought. The first brave visitors were my sister Felice and brother-in-law Jay Platt. Dudley already knew them well, and enjoyed their company.

Our entertainment in Nova Scotia was a little different from the theatre, movies and concerts we generally attended at home. The local community in Nova Scotia would turn out in full force to attend farm fairs and fish festivals and, much to our surprise, a boat sinking. We learned that an artificial reef was being created off a nearby island, in order to attract both fishes and human tourist divers. Curious, we all piled into the car on a hot, sunny day and found the nearest parking spot to get a good view from a hilltop overlooking the water. We had been told that it would take about a hour to sink the boat. We brought all the necessary equipment Bottles of water, sunscreen, snacks, hats, cameras, binoculars. Abou forty people – most of the town – came to watch, and we claimed good spot with an excellent view of the boat. I was a little surprise to learn that we were in front of somebody's house, but none of th rules of being intrusive applied for special events like a boat sinkin

We sat on a picnic bench that belonged to the owners of th house on top of the hill. Eyes glued to the boat, not wanting to mi the big moment, we watched. And watched . . . and watched. For a hour. Conversation flowed freely, so we didn't notice it had been a hour and a half. After nearly two hours, we realised that they wer having problems sinking the boat. People were starting to leave.

'I think we should go home and watch the bread rise,' Dudle said. He didn't like being out in the sun for a long time. He had bee a good sport, but we were dangerously close to his two-hour limi We left the spot and went out to dinner, on the way coming wit a good list of alternative, but comparable, forms of entertainmen Watching each other sleep. Watching tomatoes grow. Watching bee ferment. The next day it was reported that the old boat, which ha been built too well to sink, had taken about eight hours to go dow Holes had to be blown in the bottom of it to help things alon Nobody had stayed to the bitter end.

Once again, Dudley had been spotted but not bothered Eventually, people came to know that Dudley would be seen regu larly in the supermarket buying fish, or in the video store (it was te feet square, and under a roof that incorporated a delicatessen, a appliance store and a general store) renting armloads of movies an

...ying chocolate. Word got round that they could actually speak to ...udley and he would enjoy having conversations with them. But in ...ve years there, nobody revealed to an outsider exactly where to ...nd Dudley. We knew that almost anywhere else he would have ...een given up in exchange for a small bribe, but not in this magical ...ot.

Dudley liked the fact that our little town had a population of 60 ...ar-round and 120 in the summer. He found himself constantly ...mused by the mispronunciation of one of the local towns — Port ...Iouton, so-named because a seventeenth-century sheep fell over-...oard there. The locals call it Port 'Matoon', presumably because of ...me 'issues' with the French. Dudley knew French well, and ...mphasised the proper pronunciation every time we passed a road ...gn with the name on it.

...eturning to New Jersey at the end of the summer, Dudley knew we ...ere facing a long trip. When we got into the car in Bar Harbor after ...e ferry ride, Dudley asked how long it would take to get home. ...his time I actually knew the answer, and we had one of only a ...andful of real arguments that occurred during our entire friendship.

'Ten hours, interrupted by staying overnight somewhere,' I ...eplied.

'What do you mean ten hours? You know I hate being in the car ...hat long.'

'Dudley, it's the same trip we did on the way up six weeks ago. ...he same length, the same drive, the same ferry ride.'

'Well, I didn't know it was TEN HOURS IN THE FUCKING ...AR.' The cats, at least, were quiet this time, although I wasn't sure ...hy.

'Well, the route hasn't changed. We went there. We're going
back. It's the same trip.'

'I wouldn't have come in the car if I'd known.'

'What would you have done?'

'I would have flown.'

'And left me to drive all your stuff home?'

'Right.'

'Well, that's really nice of you.' I was fuming. Normally he would
think about how I felt, and try to help. He was blinded by the length
of this trip, and I was facing ten hours in the car, the two of us
annoyed with each other. And Dudley looking at his watch the
whole time.

'Well, we're in Maine. Do you want me to look for an airport
here?'

'Never mind,' he said. He was sullen. I was unsympathetic.

'I still can't believe you would have sent me with half a carload of
your stuff, and flown by yourself. Why would you do that?'

'Because I can.'

He had gone too far.

'This is real life, not a celebrity event. I don't like driving ten
hours either. But it seemed to make sense, so we did it! It seemed
worth it for six good weeks.'

He had enjoyed the summer immensely. I felt hurt that he had to
make such a fuss. There was nothing left to say, and I didn't think he
got the point. We were silent for a very long time.

'I wouldn't really have made you drive home by yourself,' he said
almost inaudibly.

'OK.' It was a strange way to break the ice. I waited to see if more
was coming.

'Oh, God. Sometimes I'm not a very nice person. It was temporary insanity. I'm sorry. I was just ranting, raving too. I hate long drives . . . and I took it out on you. I don't want you to be upset with me.'

'Thanks,' I said. 'I thought I knew that . . . but —'

'Next time we're flying. I'm getting us tickets.'

And we did, from then on. The trips became more and more difficult, but every summer Dudley wanted to return to the place he grew to love.

'Do you think I'm a nice person? I mean, generally, not today specifically; not two hours ago, in particular. I need to know. And you can be honest about this.'

I wasn't sure how he would react, but I told him that '86 per cent' of the time I found him very nice, caring and thoughtful. It might as well have been 85 or 88 per cent, but he took my initial assessment seriously. He appeared relieved to hear it had been so high, after our argument.

'And the other . . . 14 per cent?' he asked cautiously. 'I'm sure 100 per cent would be an achievement, but what am I like the other 14 per cent?'

'Self-absorbed. Egomaniacal. Difficult.'

'I think that's possibly true. But frankly I would have said 49 per cent.'

'49 per cent which?' I asked.

'49 per cent those awful things. But I've been working on this . . . a lot. Years ago . . . many yeaahs agow,' he said in a mock British accent that wasn't his own, as if beginning a long story, 'I wasn't very nice to people, particularly women. I did some things I'm ashamed of.'

'Such as?'

'Oh God, there were many examples. Using women, and discarding them. But the one I was always sorry about . . . *the turning point* . . . I met a French woman somewhere. Spent some time with her. A couple of days in bed. Then I asked her to come to Los Angeles to visit me. She was eager. I bought her a ticket.'

'That sounds nice enough,' I said.

'Oh, there's more. Don't jump to any nice conclusions. When she arrived, she called to let me know where she was staying. And she called again. And a third time. She was in LA for six days, and I never called her back. Never saw her.'

'Why not?'

'I don't know. I had moved on to something else, or somebody else. I wasn't interested any more. I didn't care. I liked being in charge. Perhaps all of the above.'

'She must have been very upset.'

'I never spoke to her again. But it bothered *me*. I think I changed because of that. I thought to myself, I didn't want to be that kind of a guy. I think I'm a nicer person now. Do you think there's hope for me, for the remaining 49 per cent?'

'We could just call it 14 per cent. That's not too bad, 14 per cent.'

16

ONE LAST TRY

DUDLEY WONDERED IF IT would ever be possible to reconnect with some of his old friends. One by one, he had cut his ties during his last marriage; very few of his friendships survived that period. In contrast with his earlier years when he maintained a large number of casual friendships, by the late 1990s he was only keeping in contact with those who wanted nothing from him and could accept his physical decline. He had stopped communicating with a few that he felt guilty about abandoning. Robert and Lucy Mann had always been there for him. Dudley knew they were hurt by his silence but didn't want them to see him in his decline. It took until 2001 for him to reconnect with them.

For Else Blangsted and Suzy Kendall, there was never a lapse in contact. They were with him in spirit at all times, and always at the other end of the phone. He didn't feel self-conscious about allowing them to know his problems. He waited for their phone calls and insisted on seeing them whenever it was possible. Very different personalities, they each knew a different side of Dudley – Suzy from her perspective as Dudley's first wife and close friend, and Else, sixteen years his senior, from a professional friendship that grew into a lifelong personal one. While it seemed possible for him to cut many people out of his life, Dudley established certain ties that could never be broken. They would travel to see him, and he would make the extra effort, however difficult, to visit them.

In the autumn of 1998, it had been a year since his surgery and he was still going for physical therapy. He was finally divorced from Nicole, and feeling very much like his California life was in the past. Plans for a visit to England were under way. Dudley thought he was strong enough to handle one phone call to Nicole to make sure his son Nicholas was doing well. Dudley made the call and reported that he hadn't been affected; there was 'no problem at all'.

The following day, Nicole called him back. An hour later Dudley said he was going to California for Christmas. He said he would stay in his own home, not with Nicole. He would visit Nicholas. He knew he might be vulnerable and would need help, and he asked my daughter Elise and one of his male physical therapists, Bill Marder (the son of our good friends Carol and Herman Marder), to join him for the trip. He planned to make a decision about selling his house, to ship some of his possessions to New Jersey and to decide which items could be shipped at a future date. The trip was to last for one month, after which he would return to New Jersey.

No sooner did he arrive at his Marina del Rey house than Nicole was on the doorstep. By the next day, he was at her house, and Dudley was asking Elise and Bill to drive him back and forth. He had fallen right back into the trap, as predictably as his therapist at the Mayo Clinic had warned him. Soon after his arrival, the tabloid press also learned of the visit and began following Dudley everywhere he went. Reports appeared in several papers incorrectly identifying Elise as his nurse and Bill as his bodyguard.

Dudley was away from New Jersey for the first time in months, and his life was becoming more and more chaotic by the day. There were phone calls from Dudley, and calls from Elise, with her concerns for his safety. There were also calls from Nicole, sometimes in the middle of the night, asking all kinds of questions about his condition.

A few days before Christmas, Dudley asked Elise to take him to the mall to buy a Christmas present for Nicole. Dudley, who had always been so generous to everyone around him, bought Nicole a $20 piece of costume jewellery, and nothing else. It was an unspoken message about their relationship.

Two days before Christmas, Nicole began asking him for money. They had a major blow-up when she asked him for $1000. Dudley called her names, some ugly ones, and said she only wanted his money. He went back to his own house and called me, sounding despondent.

'Everyone was right, but I needed to be reminded how terrible it was. She wants my money – and she doesn't love me. I called her a greedy, disgusting cunt. I probably shouldn't have said that, but that's what I felt at the moment. I'm coming home.'

'Good,' I said.

'Get me on the next flight out of here,' he added. The next day was Christmas Eve, and Dudley, Elise and Bill flew back to New Jersey. A few days later, Brian and I flew to England as planned. Dudley joined us. So did Elise.

That was the last time Dudley ever attempted to contact Nicole. The last time, in fact, that he ever saw her. His relapse could have been disastrous, but it wasn't. It had served to remind Dudley why he had divorced her. It was a quick refresher course and the relationship was, finally, over, the door shut with firmer resolve than ever before. It was, he said simply, 'the end'.

Dudley was still thinking he would buy a flat in London and 'become a bi-continentalist, spending half the year in New Jersey and half the year in London. It seemed like an excellent idea. Suzy liked the idea of having Dudley nearby, but she had already determined that his increasing physical problems would make it almost impossible for him to live on the second floor of her house and negotiate a winding, narrow staircase. She was very concerned about his safety and disappointed that the layout of her house would be difficult for Dudley.

Suzy began searching for flats where Dudley could have a place to live and assistance with daily chores, yet be near enough for her to visit often. When she explained her concerns to Dudley, he was angry. He felt she had gone back on her promise to let him stay in her house. He refused to accept the fact that his physical limitations would be difficult for her, and that the stairs would be dangerous for him. He was fuming about it and had trouble telling her how he felt. Finally, he did. They were both upset, but there was no way Dudley could remain angry with Suzy. There was too much friendship, too much love. Eventually he accepted that her reasons were good ones and the original plan hadn't been as simple as he had assumed.

Suzy had done a lot of research and by the time we all arrived in England, she had brochures and information on many different types of place that Dudley could purchase. He was interested, but when he phoned Hugh Robertson to discuss the various possibilities, his business manager told him that he could not afford to buy a place, and could not afford the cost of private medical care without his American medical insurance, which would not cover him in England. Dudley was also not happy about living on his own, with only professional assistance. The plan was quickly abandoned. Dudley made the decision that he would visit Suzy once a year, and that she and Elodie would come to the United States to visit him once a year.

We began that trip by visiting Brian's father and stepmother in Peacehaven on the south coast. We stayed in the lovely village of Alfriston, and had daily visits with the ageing Fred and Wynne, who were in their eighties. Dudley was fond of them and found them amusing, and Fred treated Dudley with fatherly care. Wynne was an artist and had been a dancer in her youth; she had been surrounded by actors linked to her family. She and Dudley had a lot to talk about. Dudley spent two hours with them every day. When the clock reached the end of the second hour, however, time was up, and we had to drive Dudley and Elise back to Alfriston.

Early in January, Dudley went to London by himself to stay with Suzy. It was during that week he finally realised that Suzy's concerns for his safety had been valid. Dudley still had trouble asking for help. He hated the fact that he could no longer drive – it made him feel weak. He objected to the fact that somebody was always on one side or the other helping him to walk. He wanted to get up and walk anywhere without assistance. Suzy had asked Dudley to call for help, even in the middle of the night, but he wouldn't do it. He didn't want to disturb anyone. He didn't want to be dependent on anyone. So he started down the stairs alone. Everyone in the house was awakened by loud crashing sounds, as Dudley hit the wall and tumbled down the stairs, bruising and scraping his face. He had somehow managed to fall without really injuring himself.

'My years onstage,' he said. 'I know how to fall in a relaxed way.'

But he had scared everyone else, and his face looked battered.

The incident was only two days before we were to leave England, and Dudley was snapped by a press photographer at the airport. There was speculation over what had happened to Dudley. Once again, the assumption was that he had been drinking, and another lot of theories did the rounds, which Dudley found very upsetting.

Until that trip to London, we had assumed Dudley's stay in New Jersey was temporary. Temporary until his condition improved. Temporary until he went back to Los Angeles. Temporary until he went to London. Temporary until he arranged to split his time between London and New Jersey. Temporary until he completed the next round of therapy and was better. As if the fog was lifting while we watched, our arrival in New Jersey after that trip to England left us with the realisation that Dudley wasn't going anywhere else. New Jersey was home.

We had never really discussed this as a possibility, but he had somehow become very comfortable and was thinking of our home as his home. Yet giving up his California residence was going to be a major step. He didn't yet seem ready to make such a decision. He was secure being part of our family. But so many years of his life had been in California. He knew that the Hollywood part of his life was over; but until he was ready to relinquish his California house, the end to that era didn't *have* to become a reality.

'Do you think I could just . . . stay . . . for a while longer?' Dudley asked one day. I could tell he had put a lot of thought into how to phrase this question.

'For how long?' I asked.

'For a good long time,' he said. 'Until we figure it all out.'

'That could be a really long time,' I said, laughing. 'It's OK with me if you stay here.' I added. I was relieved he had felt comfortable enough to ask. But I felt confused, had conflicting emotions. I didn't want Dudley to leave but I knew it would make all our lives more complicated if he stayed. He was so vulnerable, so easily hurt, and now, being sick, he needed the support more than ever.

'But what about Brian? Will it be OK with him?'

'I don't know,' I had to say. 'I would have to talk to him about it.'

'I don't think it would be as OK with him as it might be with you. I should think he would have mixed feelings.'

'What kinds of mixed feelings?'

'I know he likes me. And I like him. We talk about a lot of things. We have a lot in common — you, for one thing. And music, compos-ing, the piano — and our childhoods in England. But I don't think he would like the idea of having me as a permanent house-guest.' He was quiet for a moment, and I didn't know what to say. I didn't think he was finished speaking.

'I think I could be viewed by him, frankly, as more than he really wants to deal with in his life. A nuisance. The straw that might pos-sibly break the camel's already aching back. Sand in his eye. A sharp stick up his arse. A splinter under his toenail. A—'

'Geez! I get the point. You can't possibly think you are *that* much trouble.'

'I'm just a *tiny* bit sensitive about my position in the family. I want to be part of this, but it's all a bit . . . unorthodox. I'm the guy who came to dinner and never left. It's a few years after dinner, and I'm still here. And, well, I would be lying to you if I said I wanted to leave. I'm happy staying here. And' – he whispered – 'I don't generally use words like "happy". So don't quote me or I shall be forced to deny it! It's out of character . . . happy . . . Well, I know I can be a miserable, self-centred misanthrope, but I like it here. I don't think any of us planned this.'

He was so right. Over the past couple of years, he had settled in. Brian would later say that our family was like a big feather pillow for Dudley. He was enveloped and secured by it. But at that moment, I kept trying to take a detached look at the situation, as though from the outside looking in.

'You are right. Who could have planned this?' I said.

'Well, could you intercede on my behalf? In the event that Brian absolutely hates the idea and wants to put my belongings out on the front lawn?'

'I doubt that he would take such a hard line as that.'

Dudley and Brian were good friends, and spent a lot of time together. They talked a lot about music, and Dudley was usually ready to listen to the music Brian was composing and tell Brian his thoughts. This would often lead them into long musical discussions.

We had reached a point where there were two Dudleys – Dudley our family member, and the renowned celebrity Dudley Moore, whom everyone else saw when we were outside. It was becoming increasingly difficult to reconcile the two Dudleys. Our Dudley joined us for almost everything we did. This was new for Dudley, and he loved this aspect of our joined lives. He was part of something big. He felt security all around him. Our friendship, growing closer all the time, was only part of the whole picture. He loved the whole picture.

He loved Sunday brunch with the family. Usually Karen and Elise, with friends or boyfriends. Ruth and our son-in-law Stuart, who had moved back to New Jersey from Las Vegas. Our son Joel and daughter-in-law Mary Ellen and their three children – Cecily, Eric and Jenna. Sometimes my sisters Felice and Dot and Felice's husband Jay. And other friends or family members. Between ten and fourteen people would turn up every week for early afternoon brunches that would last three or four hours.

There was always a lot of laughter, Dudley joining in no matter what had caused it. And it didn't usually matter, as the laughter around the table was often over the silliest things, but always contagious. It only took Karen and Elise looking at each other, and they were off and running. Dudley was next to join in. Brian wondered what could be so funny, and his 'I don't get it' response would touch off another outburst.

Once Dudley caught it, his own outrageous laugh would spur everyone on. One time, it was simply a heavy cut-glass plate, a family heirloom rarely used, with 'light' diet cake on it. Dudley went to lift it, and it was impossible. Someone said, 'Heavy cake, Dud?' He broke into one of his funny accents, followed by a story about his mother having used one Oxo cube for the gravy, instead of two, when Dudley was on a diet.

Although our family included representatives of several religions, we had huge traditional Jewish brunches. Dudley said his mother had informed him he was one-eighth Jewish. 'She looked around the room and whispered it, when she was sure nobody else would hear it. But I believe I'm really a quarter Jewish,' Dudley said.

Sometimes he attended services with us during the High Holidays, happily wearing a yarmulke. In England he went to church with Suzy. 'I'm not religious, but maybe if I cover enough religions they'll find a spot for me somewhere in Heaven – a spot with a piano.'

Dudley liked all the brunch foods, and piled his bagel so high with such an unlikely combination of ingredients not always found on top of each other – lox (smoked salmon) and kosher salami, cream cheese, whitefish salad, lettuce, tomatoes, onions, cucumbers, three kinds of cheese – that it was impossible for him to take the first bite. Invariably things would go flying – the dog was poised under his seat, mouth open. He never learned to put less on the bagel. He blamed it on Elise, or more accurately on a story about Elise. As a teenager she was packing for a short trip and attempting to take more than she could possibly carry.

'Why don't you take less?' I had asked her.

'I don't have less,' she had replied. This was one of Dudley's favourite quotes.

Dudley was thrilled when Ruth and Stuart announced that they were expecting their first child, and he watched Ruth's expanding belly with great anticipation as their unborn child grew. He was immediately dubbed Uncle Dudley. When Ruth went into labour, the women of the family, Karen, Elise and I, were ready to meet Ruth in the labour and delivery room.

Brian would join us after the baby's birth. But Dudley expected to join the parade of women heading out of the door, and was somewhat disheartened to learn that Ruth would probably want only her husband, her mother and sisters to join her. We might have remembered that only a month earlier, Dudley had insisted on staying for Ruth's baby shower rather than going out with the men – thirty-five women and Dudley. He sat patiently as Ruth opened all the baby gifts, chatting comfortably with the guests.

Now Dudley seemed surprised not to be joining us for the birth. 'Oh,' said Dudley, who was rushing to get dressed and had just put on his jacket. He hadn't stopped to think. 'I suppose it could make her feel a little self-conscious. You mean she would rather I come in *afterwards*, not have me watch the whole process?'

'I think that would be better,' I said. I gave him a hug. 'Uncle Dudley – that has a nice ring to it.' We didn't want him to feel left out. But nobody was sure how Ruth would react, or the doctors and nurses. It had never occurred to Dudley that if Brian wasn't going for the moment of birth, he shouldn't either. Dudley stayed home with Brian, looking at his watch and waiting for the phone call with news. He was among the first to hold the new baby a couple of hours after her birth. Baby Dvorah, with whom he bonded immediately.

There were many other family events, and Dudley was always a part of them. When Karen completed her law degree and a courthouse ceremony was set for 'swearing in', Dudley responded to the invitation by saying he wouldn't miss it. He had watched her progress closely, and was proud of her achievement. Karen was surprised and thrilled to see an unusually large audience of judges and law clerks in the courthouse for her ceremony. Later, she was amused to discover that word had leaked out and everyone had wanted to meet Dudley!

Occasionally my close friend Jane Mason and I would spend a couple of days together somewhere in Pennsylvania. We had grown up in Philadelphia, and had been best friends since our early teens. We continued our close friendship into adulthood, having

marathon talking sessions a few times a year. The first time we wer
to Lancaster, Pennsylvania – Amish country – leaving Dudley
home with Brian, Dudley was soon on the phone.

'What are you doing?' he asked.

'Looking at cows in the field. Talking about husbands ar
children.'

'Oh. All right. I'll call you later. Bye.'

A few hours later my mobile phone rang again.

'What are you doing now?' Dudley asked.

'Talking about you,' I said. We hadn't been, but he liked th
answer, and laughed aloud.

'You mean about how many times I've called? I presume yo
don't mind.'

'I don't mind. Well, what are *you* doing?' I asked.

'Nothing. Watching TV. Cutting my toenails. Waiting to go
lunch with Brian.'

Finally, Jane, putting her psychology degree to good use, said, 'F
doesn't want to be left home. We'll have to take him along ne:
time.' I praised her insight. She said you wouldn't have to be a rock
scientist to know that Dudley felt abandoned.

We were sure Dudley would be bored to tears listening to us ta
for hours, stopping just long enough to breathe. We rarely discusse
music. But Dudley was patient and occasionally interjected wit
some very perceptive comments. To be fair, we had to invite Bria
and Jane's husband Bernie to be part of our 'girls' night out', as v
called it, even though it lasted forty-eight hours. We were relieve
when Brian and Bernie graciously declined; we could continue
talk about them. Dudley said he was fine being 'one of the girls, bu
do you want me to go in drag?' He liked women better than me:

enerally. At the same time, he felt that, 'being the token male', he
ould protect us from harm rather than sit at home worrying. He
nally used the word 'abandoned' to describe how he had felt stay-
ng at home during my previous Lancaster outing with Jane. We
ever left him at home after that first time. These trips continued
very few months until the month before his death.

We covered all the traditional sights of the Amish country. A ride
n the historic Strasburg Railroad was Dudley's first choice on the
st of possible activities. At the end of the ride, he bought a tiny
ewter railroad car in the gift shop. He called it his 'choo choo', and
old Jane it reminded him of his father, who had worked on the rail-
ays.

'Well, he certainly looks like Dudley Moore, doesn't he?' the
ashier said.

'Yes, he certainly does,' I replied.

It was as though no real person could be the same as the famous
ersion of himself.

We all piled into the back of a buggy for a traditional horse and
uggy ride given by a young Amish man. The Amish, who brought
heir Anabaptist traditions to the United States from Europe, have
ommunities in twenty-two American states and in Canada, with
he community of 18,000 Amish in Lancaster, Pennsylvania among
he oldest and best-known settlements in America. They live a sim-
le, eighteenth-century life, without telephones or electricity, and
heir community stresses humility, family and separation from the
nodern world. Never having seen a television or movies, our driver
ad no idea that Dudley was a celebrity. We all introduced ourselves
y name, and Dudley had an hour of anonymity, a rare sensation for
im.

In this instance there was only one version of Dudley; his famou
image was momentarily absent. He could handle it for an hour.

Dudley enjoyed the traditional Amish foods, in large quantitie
at a smorgasbord restaurant that became our own tradition. He wa
intrigued by the Pennsylvania Dutch shoo-fly pie, a sticky open pi
with a filling of molasses and brown sugar, so-named because i
attracts flies that must be shooed away. Dudley and Jane usuall
engaged in a competition to see who could eat the most chicken an
mashed potatoes.

By early 1999, life in our family was changing, and Dudley had bee
correct about Brian's concerns. Brian was worried about the future
about how we would cope with Dudley's worsening condition. H
had serious concerns for Dudley's safety, going up and down th
flight of stairs to his room many times a day. He was worried abou
all the little accidents – things that were dropped, broken or spilled
He never blamed Dudley for these problems; but wondering wha
would happen next made Brian tense.

He was also beginning to worry about how the closeness of m
friendship with Dudley would affect our marriage if Dudley were t
become a permanent member of the household. There were nev
minor tensions in the house. Brian and I were bickering over littl
things. We never had big fights, but the bickering was annoying t
anyone who was around. Dudley would try to resolve the issues
Whatever the cause of the argument, Dudley would say that Bria
and I were both to blame. An interesting, fair-minded approac
that worked well. These phases would come and go; then everythin
would be easier for a time.

One evening, Brian was asleep, and I was downstairs going

through the mail that had accumulated on the kitchen table. Dudley came downstairs to get a glass of apple juice.

'Why are you still up?' he said. 'It's I a.m.'

'I'm going through the mail. It's been piling up.'

'Shouldn't you be in bed at this hour?'

'Do I have a curfew?' I asked, a little amused.

'It's I a.m. right now.'

'I know.'

'Is anything . . . wrong? I know you and Brian were arguing about something.'

'Something really stupid,' I said. 'Trivial. I overheard him complaining to his friend Michael about my parking the car in the driveway and not leaving enough room for his. He was being ridiculous about it. They decided it had to be a passive-aggressive action on my part and they were psychoanalysing me.'

'Was it? Why didn't you leave room for his car?'

'It's a matter of interpretation. I left room, but he wanted *more* room.'

'That's *it*?' he asked.

'I told you it was a stupid argument.'

'Men need to *think* they are in charge, even when they aren't, really. I don't know any man who is in charge. Do you? You are supposed to let us *think* we're in charge. I thought all women knew that. Leave the extra five inches for his car if that's what he wants. Why would it make a difference to you?'

I knew Dudley was speaking from personal experience. Just a few weeks earlier, we had been in an elevator, on the way to see one of his doctors. When we got out of the elevator, he was annoyed. At the end of his visit with the doctor, the same thing happened. We went down six floors in the elevator, and when we got out, he was visibly annoyed. This time, all the way to the car and for the first ten minutes of the ride.

I could stand the mystery no longer. 'What's wrong?' I asked him.

'Nothing. Don't worry about it. It's *nothing*.'

'You seem annoyed about something,' I said. It was obvious.

'I'm *fine*,' he said.

'Don't you think by now I know you well enough to tell when you are annoyed?'

'The only thing I'm annoyed about is you asking me if I'm annoyed,' he barked.

'OK, I'm sorry, then. I won't ask again. You can file it away and just be annoyed for a few years.'

Steam was shooting out of both his ears.

'Oh, you are so *impossible*. That's what I do. I file things away and they fester. Why do I need to change my lifelong habits? I'm attached to them – that's why we call them *habits*.' — A long pause. — 'Well, if you *must* know, I'm annoyed about you always pushing the buttons.'

'What buttons?' I assumed it had been an analogy. I was wrong.

'In the elevator. You shouldn't be pushing the buttons. The man is supposed to do that. As well as turning the keys in the locks.'

I knew about the keys. I had learned that one the hard way on tour with Dudley. He had to unlock the doors to all the hotel suites. If they were computerised cards rather than keys, he invariably tried them backwards and upside down before getting them right, but it was worth the wait to see his ultimate satisfaction when the door opened.

But I did not know about the elevator buttons, and he had obviously waited a long time to tell me — until it came oozing out. He had probably been thinking about it for months, maybe years.

'You're right. I knew about the keys, and I can see that the buttons are just as important to you.' I could have said it was a ridiculous thing to get upset about, that little kids throw tantrums about elevator buttons. But this was so . . . Dudley. Letting somebody else control his finances but needing to be in charge of the buttons. He was an intellectual and had a deep understanding of the psychological causes for other people's problems. He was also a child, managing to encompass the full range more thoroughly than anyone I had ever met. He had voiced his annoyance, and that was a good thing. After that day, Dudley was forever in charge of the buttons. He would smile as I stepped aside, waiting for him to control the elevator.

From the male—female perspective, it had been a strange revelation, since Dudley was among the most liberal people I knew. He would gladly have marched for women's rights. He granted complete and total equality to any woman he respected. But there were some notable exceptions, blind spots in his vision, where male—female roles were simply not interchangeable. He wanted to be the one to drive, to turn the keys, to push the buttons and to select the restaurants. That covered all the categories, as far as I could tell. Once on the way into New York to go to the theatre, he apologised that I had to drive. 'This isn't right. I should be driving. I just want you to know that I'm really sorry I can't drive any more.'

He saw my 'parking space' argument with Brian in the same light. It was a 'male thing', he said.

We talked for a little while longer. 'You should go to bed. Brian is probably not asleep. Tell him you'll give him more space for his car.'

He wanted to be sure there would be peace in the household. I followed his instructions.

17

WHERE DID ALL THE MONEY GO?

DUDLEY HAD LITTLE IDEA of what went on in his bank accounts. His checking (current) account was a mystery. All of his finances were completely in the hands of his business manager, Hugh Duff Robertson, with whom he had a long relationship. Robertson's firm, A. Morgan Maree, had handled Dudley's money since the late 1970s, first under the supervision of Hugh's predecessor, who retired, and then under Hugh when he took over control of the company in 1987.

For a while, Hugh Robertson had been hinting that Dudley was in debt, and living on borrowed money. He had blamed some of it on Nicole, telling Dudley that Nicole had spent $600,000 of his money in less than one year. This made Nicole furious, as she had been blaming Dudley's financial problems on Hugh Robertson.

In his earlier years, Dudley had been meticulous about his money, keeping logbooks that showed how every penny had been spent. He kept some of the books for many years, and was proud of his talent for financial management.

But living in California, and having more income than he could easily negotiate, he needed someone to take care of things for him. Gradually, over a period of some years, Robertson had gained complete control of Dudley's finances. He was paid by Dudley for being his attorney, business manager and investment advisor. Dudley liked him – Hugh Robertson was jovial and outgoing, spending a lot of time on the phone with Dudley. Despite the fact that many of Dudley's close friends and relatives had advised him to change business management firms, Dudley said he was loyal to Hugh Robertson. Each of Dudley's wives and ex-wives had begged him to take control and move his money elsewhere. Brogan and Nicole had been very outspoken on the subject. Suzy had been concerned for years. Dudley's sister and brother-in-law were worried, and his close friend Else felt something was wrong. But Dudley refused to budge. Dudley told people close to him 'no, of course I don't trust him. But I like him'. The arguments with his friends would go on and on, but that only made Dudley dig in his heels. It wasn't until years later that he finally gave his reasons, which would have made sense to all his friends, if he had been willing to tell them. However, it wasn't until he had finally taken steps to pull his finances back from the brink of disaster that he was ready to offer an explanation.

Having solid finances was extremely important to Dudley, even though he didn't want to be bothered with it on a daily basis and didn't feel qualified to handle his own investments. Seeing his financial foundation begin to shake was frightening to him. Some of the court papers connected to Dudley's recent divorce from Nicole had indicated he had little money left, and these papers had leaked out to the press. Having reports in the press about his financial problems was a big blow to Dudley, and it made him feel like a failure.

By the late 1990s, Hugh Robertson had complete power of attorney over Dudley's finances, given to him willingly by Dudley. Dudley had stopped signing his own cheques. He didn't receive bills. And he had stopped receiving financial statements. Eventually, Robertson told Dudley he had to put himself on a budget, and he told me that Dudley was living totally on money borrowed against his house. 'It's a bad situation. He's a million and a half in debt.' This was devastating to Dudley; having money was important to his ego. He did not spend much on himself, but he liked knowing it was available for anything he wanted. He liked giving generous gifts to friends and family. He enjoyed good restaurants. Every year he gave a generous gift to his sister Barbara and brother-in-law Bernard, and he sent gifts to his friends, especially around Christmas time. He planned his holiday list weeks or months in advance, carefully considering what gifts people would like. With Dudley's health starting to decline, he began asking questions about how to finance his medical care. In 1998, he was still thinking about moving to England for part of the year, and Hugh Robertson told him it was out of the question. He wouldn't be able to afford private medical care and daily help, and he couldn't afford to purchase a flat.

With income down and medical expenses up, the debt kept increasing. With money borrowed against the equity in his home, as well as the mortgage on Nicole's house, he was nearly $2 million in debt, and he had loan payments of close to $8,000 a month. 'Hugh says I should sell the Marina house to get out of this debt,' Dudley reported after one long phone conversation with his business manager.

'What do you think?' I asked.

'I don't know. I love the house, but I may never live in it again. Maybe he's right. I should be able to get four or five million for the house. That may be the answer to this problem.' Hugh had valued the house at about three and a half million dollars in Dudley's statement of net worth. Dudley had spoken of the idea occasionally but never seriously considered selling it before. He had assumed he would have the house for the rest of his life, and that it could be his security in old age.

Dudley began going over the details in his head, over and over and over again. He was obsessing over it, trying to weigh his choices. I knew he couldn't really bear the thought of selling the house, his haven, but he also knew for sure that his days in the Marina house, and in Hollywood, were over. It was a difficult realisation for him, and he resigned himself to the fact that selling the house was his only option.

A few days later, Hugh Robertson called Dudley to report that he had a friend who was interested in buying the house, but that he thought it might have to be sold for about $2 million. Dudley was unhappy about Hugh's attempt to dispose of it so quickly. He did not say much to Hugh – only that he would think about it – but when he got off the phone, it was very clear that he was troubled. He was pacing the floors upstairs in his room. He was quiet. It was easy to see that he was angry and hurt.

It was a quiet moment, possibly years in the making, but when something was really over in Dudley's mind, there was no turning back. 'Something needs to be done about this. This disaster has gone too far. I'm going to be completely broke if this happens.' It was as though the final piece of a very confusing thousand-piece jigsaw puzzle had just been placed in its spot. It was all in focus for Dudley.

Not one to take action in a rash way with business dealings, Dudley asked if we could make an appointment to meet an attorney whom we knew and respected. He wanted to be sure it would be all right with me. 'If you don't mind, and if you have the time, would you go along with me to the meeting?' he asked, cautiously, quietly, as thought it might be the world's biggest imposition. In addition, he asked if another good friend, an attorney and judge on the west coast, could fly in on one day's notice for a meeting. Dudley feared that things were not as they should be.

Dudley knew he had earned more than 35 million dollars during his years living in the United States – this had been confirmed for him by Lou Pitt, with printed statements from ICM. Dudley didn't think he had spent enough to be in debt. However, he stopped short of accusing Robertson of doing anything wrong.

Dudley did not spend a lot on personal things. He drove a Lexus and owned several homes – his Marina del Rey home, Nicole's home, a house he owned jointly with Susan Anton and a small Las Vegas property occupied by Nicole's former mother-in-law. Periodically he bought a new supply of clothes – it was in spurts rather than steady purchasing, and they were of high quality but not extravagant. He occasionally liked to indulge in fine restaurants. While married to Brogan Lane, he had spent money on renovating and decorating the house, and bought custom-made furniture for it. In the high-earning Hollywood days, he had taken friends on vacations. He was always generous, and liked to pay the bill when he took his friends out. Still, none of it seemed to him enough to drain his finances to such an extreme level.

Dudley was very upset about his situation, but he wanted to

handle it in a low-key, private way. Finally he explained his reluc
tance, over the years, to make a change. He said that he did not wan
to be 'another one of those famous Hollywood stories, where peopl
would feel sorry for me, or else say, "How could you have let it hap
pen?" Maybe it *was* my fault. Now I've got to figure a way out of thi
situation, without it becoming a public spectacle.'

In February 1999, we set up a meeting with Gene Korf, a Nev
Jersey estate attorney who is a cautious, conservative solicitor. A
soon as Dudley began speaking, in the conference room of Gene
office, Gene was quick to see the situation. Both attorneys sav
Dudley's reluctance to offend Hugh, coupled with his firm resolv
to take control of his own finances.

'Here's what I think you could do today,' Gene Korf said. 'Jus
one thing. Sign a letter revoking Hugh Robertson's power of attor
ney. That's mild, and all it says is that you are taking control whil
we look at your situation.' Gene spoke slowly and distinctly. 'Thi
must be your decision alone. I can only advise you and explain wha
it means. You are in effect saying to Robertson that you want to sig
your own documents, you want to see what your financial situatio
is, and while you are examining things, he is still your busines
manager, but he can't sign anything for you.'

Dudley didn't need to hear any more. He liked Gene and what h
had explained. He felt it was a rational and conservative approacl
and would help him to take one small step forward while decidin
what to do. The pen was in his hand, and he paused for a long tim
before signing, reading the words over and over to make sure h
wasn't missing anything. It was only his signature. He had signe
his autograph thousands of times before. But with this one auto
graph, Dudley was about to take control and, despite Gene's mil

explanation, everyone in the room, especially Dudley, knew that an era was about to come to an end.

We left the meeting with the understanding that Gene would intercede in all communications with Hugh Robertson, and that there would be a period of several months during which every effort would be made to sort out Dudley's finances, and his control over them. A sense of relief came over Dudley. He had a big smile, and his step was buoyant. He had reclaimed a part of himself that had been drowning in confusion. Later that day he spent hours talking about the meeting and how he felt about everything that had just happened. He was ready to face the truth about his situation, whatever that might be.

It was a long, slow road and a very frustrating one for Dudley. He had endless discussions with Gene Korf about the direction to take. Dudley told his close friends, one after the other, the steps he had taken, and he received unanimous congratulations. Else Blangsted was particularly ecstatic, as she had watched Dudley's financial decline with considerable dismay.

Else told the story of an experience she had had with her own business manager several years earlier, and recommended her new manager. However, Gene Korf felt a business management firm in New York should replace Robertson, and set up a meeting with a colleague of his in Manhattan. Dudley liked the firm, and was set to make the change when Gene expressed some concern that it was too early in the process to make the transfer without having all the necessary information from Robertson's office. The information was coming in very slowly. Gene suggested continuing the process a little longer, with Gene interceding in all dealings with Hugh Robertson.

Dudley was concerned about the cost of the legal bills, and suddenly felt elated by having new-found control. He wanted to pick up the pace. He began signing his own cheques, looking at each one very carefully before signing, and holding it up to examine his signature. Finding out all the details of his own finances was not easy, as Dudley had given Hugh power of attorney over all his business dealings a long time ago and Hugh had stopped sending monthly financial reports several years earlier, when Nicole began reading them and arguing about them. Dudley had defended Hugh, and there was an ongoing feud between Nicole and Hugh, and between Dudley and Nicole on the subject of Hugh.

Not yet having full access to his own accounts, Dudley hired a private investigator to search for all his bank accounts. He was no stranger to private investigators. He had once learned that he was paying for a private investigator that Nicole had hired to follow him. He had appeared only mildly annoyed about it.

This time, he made the phone call without hesitation, arranging for a private investigator whom an attorney had recommended to him. Dudley and 'Jack' sat across from each other at a large table, papers spread out in front of them.

'I want to know about my bank accounts,' he said. 'In this country and anywhere else you can find them.' Dudley gave him the names and numbers of the accounts he knew about. They shook hands. Dudley gave him a deposit, $600 in cash, and that was the end of the meeting. It took only a few days for 'Jack' to discover that Dudley had more than a dozen bank accounts, most of them unknown to him – he thought there were only four – including several out of the country in the Cayman Islands, containing nearly half a million dollars. Next, he began the process of accessing the

ccounts. On Gene's advice, Dudley needed to clearly establish with
he banks that he was taking back control of his own accounts.

Now, with nobody else possessing his power of attorney, the
rocess of notification was something that only Dudley could do.
But because Dudley's voice was beginning to sound slurred, and he
vas slow on the phone under pressure, the process was gruelling and
ften made him feel frustrated or angry. He had to notify each bank
ivision that he had rescinded Hugh Robertson's power of attorney,
nd that he wanted to receive copies of his bank statements. In
ome cases, he was requesting back records for a couple of years, in
rder to get an accurate picture. He sent many faxes and sat on the
hone hour after hour, asking to speak with bank managers and then
xplaining what he needed. Sometimes it went smoothly.
Occasionally he asked me to be on the extension phone and to lis-
en. At times, he found himself blocked at every turn. Some bank
epresentatives refused to believe that it was really Dudley on the
hone and simply hung up on him. On more than one occasion,
eople took the information, but Dudley later learned that the
hanges had not been put into effect.

After a few weeks, large boxes of bank records began arriving,
nd Dudley started the process of poring over them. He felt over-
vhelmed and wondered if he would ever be able to sort it all out.

'There are hundreds of pages here. How will I ever figure this
ut?' he asked, surrounded by bank statements that were more
launting than he had expected. While going through one set of
ank statements, he was shocked to discover a cheque for $118,000
hat Hugh had signed in June of 1998 and deposited into another of
Dudley's accounts to pay for some of Dudley's expenses. The
heque effectively closed his son Patrick's trust fund, comprising

years of court-ordered payments specified in his divorce fro
Tuesday Weld. Gene Korf immediately wrote a strongly worded le
ter to Hugh Robertson demanding that the money be returned
Patrick's account and the trust fund properly re-established, but
was not done.

Dudley called Patrick to explain the situation. Patrick had h
own attorney and was enraged. There followed a feud betwee
Hugh and Patrick that ended badly. Despite Dudley's clear instru
tions to the contrary, Hugh Robertson cut off Patrick's access
medication he needed by closing his account with the Los Angel
pharmacy he used regularly. When Dudley heard about it, he imm
diately instructed the pharmacy to continue filling Patrick
prescriptions. In a juvenile act of rage, Patrick left a threatenir
message on Hugh Robertson's office voicemail. Although Hug
Robertson had known Patrick for many years, and should hav
realised that Patrick was angry, not dangerous, he used the tape
get a restraining order against Patrick. He also sent copies of th
tape to Gene Korf and Dudley. Dudley stood up for Patrick, laughe
when he heard the tape and said that Hugh Robertson should hav
known better than to try to stop his son from getting the medic:
tion he needed. It was an ugly few days that served to strengthe
Dudley's resolve to find a new business manager.

Gene Korf had a barrister colleague standing by, as he suspecte
there might be a lawsuit if Dudley chose to take an aggressive rout
It was not Dudley's style, but he knew Dudley might react strongly
pushed. Because of Dudley's PSP symptoms, Gene thought it poss
ble that questions might arise as to Dudley's competence. Wit
Dudley's neurological condition progressing, and his increasing di
ficulty in expressing his thoughts, particularly under stress, Ger

anted to be sure that Dudley's competency would not be in ques-
on. Wisely, Gene ordered a complete psychological evaluation and
ompetency testing.

Dudley found having to take such a test demoralising, although he
greed without hesitation. 'I'm as competent as I've ever been, and
at may not be saying much,' he quipped. But he was also anxious that
is inability to answer questions quickly might deem him incompe-
ent, even though the law seemed to be on his side and he could not be
enalised for having neurological problems. He was having trouble
nding the words when he needed them, and the slurring of his
eech was distressing. 'I seem doomed to become Arthur in real
fe,' he said, trying to enunciate every word as clearly as he could.

When it came time to undergo the long and detailed evaluation,
udley passed the test with flying colours. Gene filed away the
eport in case it might be needed, and continued working through
e transition.

It was an extremely difficult time for Dudley, who struggled with
e process every step of the way. He might well have taken a
ronger course of action had he known something important that
ever came to light in the three years that he lived after this transi-
on took place. Hugh Robertson had already been investigated by
e United States Securities and Exchange Commission, the federal
overnment's regulatory agency dealing with rules of conduct and
nancial infringements, and the primary American agency fighting
ecurities fraud.

In two separate instances, in 1997 and 1998, Hugh Robertson –
nd his companies including A. Morgan Maree and Armscott
ecurities – was brought up on charges, submitted to remedial sanc-
ons and fined for violations including charging customers

'undisclosed, excessive mark-ups', generating 'excess profits' an
employing 'devices, schemes and artifices to defraud', as well as 't
obtain money and property by means of untrue statements of mate
rial fact'.

A. Morgan Maree was also charged with recommending securi
ties to advisory clients in which Robertson's company had a
ownership interest. The SEC issued a 'Cease and Desist Proceeding
against A. Morgan Maree, Jr and Hugh Duff Robertson, as AMM'
president and sole owner, stopping his activities as a broker.

In addition, the company Armscott, owned by Armscott Capita
Group (of which Robertson was the sole owner), engaged 'in trans
actions, practices and a course of business which operated as a frau
or deceit upon purchasers of securities'.

However, Dudley knew nothing at all of this matter. Neither di
anyone working for him at that time. He only knew that he ha
earned more than $35 million over a twenty-year period, but wa
now living on loans. He was disillusioned and desperately con
cerned about his precarious financial situation. After a fev
transitional months had passed, Dudley felt things were moving too
slowly and it was time to hire a new business manager.

'Maybe I don't need a business manager at all,' he said. 'I haven'
got much money left to manage.' Briefly, he thought about handlin
his own finances. 'I used to watch every penny years ago. When
was younger, I wrote everything down – everything I purchased –
even pens and notebooks, paper clips, pencils. Maybe it could reall
work out now, too.'

This was both powerful and touching, but the prospect was daunt
ing. I knew he would realise that, but the fact he even considere

taking on his own financial management was major progress in reclaiming control.

'I would be really concerned about this,' I said, with incredible mixed feelings. It was what we had hoped to see – Dudley feeling like his life was in his own hands. He was taking charge of the big things. I was scared to burst this bubble, but if he attempted to take on too much it could backfire.

'It would be hard to trust another business manager after what has happened,' Dudley said.

'But maybe you can find someone who believes you should be *involved* in the process – not someone who will take over and sign everything for you,' I said.

He accepted my answer. I believed there had to be someone who could do the job well and keep Dudley actively involved, despite what we knew would be his declining physical condition and his decreasing ability to communicate easily.

Dudley always seemed to have some surprising contacts up his sleeve – people whom he had met and who had offered help if he ever needed it. It only took a few of days for him to make contact with a CIA agent he knew on a casual basis socially. We were planning a trip to Los Angeles in May to sort through his possessions. Dudley explained the situation and asked his contact for the five best attorneys in the Los Angeles area. Three days later, he had the list.

Dudley said we would have to meet with all of them, one after the other, and see what they recommended.

'You want to see five lawyers?' I asked.

'All five. And we can pick the best one.'

Dudley planned carefully what he would say, and reviewed his notes as though he were learning a script.

'They need to know the background. And the problem. And I want you to jump right in if I leave anything out. Or if I get stuck.'

In one very busy week in California, Dudley made decisions about his furniture, met with friends, went to Disneyland (he said it was his first time there) and saw four of the five lawyers on his list. He liked Patricia Glaser and her colleague Joan Vento best, and felt they completely understood his needs and his situation. The prominent firm had a reputation for being very tough and Dudley was at first a little intimidated by Glaser's highly publicised reputation. But the meeting with Glaser and Vento was direct, real and quiet. Despite their tough reputation, they were gentle and considerate of Dudley's needs. They spoke directly to him, and did not expect me to fill in the answers. They waited patiently while he formed his words, which were sometimes slow in coming. Glaser advised him to contact her colleague Joel Mandel, with the Management Group. 'He's the best business manager I know. He will help you pull things together.' The question of whether there were grounds to file a lawsuit was left on the back burner. Top priority was rescuing Dudley's financial situation and establishing security for him.

When we left their office, it was 5 p.m. on the last afternoon before we were due to fly back to New Jersey. Dudley thanked them, and said he would keep in touch as things progressed. They said they would stand behind him and help with his decision. Seeing his situation, they refused to charge him for the meeting, or for their subsequent advice. He said that meeting with them gave him the strength to move forward.

'I'll never tell another lawyer joke, after meeting them,' Dudley said. 'Not even the one about two hundred lawyers at the bottom of the ocean. This will be one of the supreme sacrifices of my life. But viola jokes? I can easily substitute those. What's the difference between a violin and a viola?'

'I don't know,' I said. 'What?'

'A viola burns longer.'

When we got home, one of Dudley's first calls was to Joel Mandel. He was glad to speak with Dudley and said he would need a few days to review and assess the information Dudley said he would send him. There were several more phone calls. Joel said he would be pleased to help Dudley, but advised Dudley to take time and think it over. He wanted Dudley to be sure of his decision. Dudley waited a few days and made one decisive phone call to Joel Mandel.

'I would like you to take over my financial management,' Dudley said. 'I have no doubts about this.'

The next phone call was to Suzy, who was ecstatic.

The following day, Dudley composed a letter, with the wording advised by Joel Mandel. He notified Hugh Robertson that he would no longer represent him, and asked for his records to be transferred to the Management Group. He sent certified copies of the simple one-page letter to his new legal group. It was another big step in taking back control of his life, and Dudley once again felt very proud and hopeful. He had made a big decision and acted on it.

It took a while for the Management Group to pull Dudley's finances out of the danger zone. But as his condition declined he made the decision not to engage in what he knew would be a long and protracted investigation into what had gone wrong.

18

THE ANNEX

THE NEXT FEW MONTHS, early in 1999, were a whirlwind of activity and change for Dudley. He resumed his therapy programme, this time going to the Kessler Institute in New Jersey for several hours a day, three times a week. A large team at Kessler was working with him. Although he hadn't yet fully accepted his diagnosis of PSP, the Kessler Institute was well equipped to deal with neurological problems. They set up a comprehensive programme that included psychological help in dealing with some of the effects of his condition. Dudley would participate in the programme for a while, then quit, then return to it after a break lasting weeks.

The staff would set up periodic evaluation meetings that included Dudley and our family; Dudley always expressed concern that he wasn't improving. He found it hard to accept the fact that there was value in therapy that would merely slow the progression of his condition, but not improve it dramatically.

Even with exercises designed to help, his balance was getting worse, and we knew there would be a time, fairly soon, when he would not be able to negotiate the stairs by himself or would progress to the use of a walker or wheelchair. His legs were developing stiffness, and he could no longer compensate for his club foot, as he had been able to do for many years. These combined factors would cause him to fall. Dudley wanted to build an addition to our house, with an elevator, and we consulted an architect, but the project had many complications and was not moving forward very quickly.

One spring afternoon, I was in the office, Dudley was at home and Brian went home to pick him up for lunch. We were in Dudley's 'chicken quesadilla' phase, which lasted for more than a year. It was the house speciality of one of the restaurants we frequented. Quesadillas made with grilled chicken, sour cream, bacon and cheese. He would order: 'Chicken quesadillas – hold the bacon, hold the sour cream, hold the cheese.'

We were going to meet at the restaurant. On the way, I got a call from Brian on my mobile phone. His panic was coming right through the earpiece.

'What's wrong?' I asked.

'It's Dudley,' Brian said. 'I'm really shaken. I was at the bottom of the stairs, and Dudley was coming downstairs. Halfway down, he remembered something and turned to go back up. But he lost his balance.'

'He fell down the stairs?'

'No, worse,' Brian said, the fear still in his voice. 'I tried to catch him, but I missed and he went over upside down. Over the side of the banister. I watched him just flip over – he couldn't grab the banister, and I couldn't break his fall.'

The scene Brian described was horrifying. It was impossible to believe he had not been seriously injured. Dudley had toppled completely over the banister and had fallen a distance of about six feet, head first, onto a table underneath. He had managed to crack not only the table but also a thick wooden chair. Yet his head was fine — not a mark on it or anywhere on his body — and he said he was '*fine*'. He refused to be checked by a doctor and insisted on going to lunch. He showed no signs of damage — not that day or any time after.

'I told you I'm tough,' he said. 'And my head is hard as a rock.'

That did not help much to allay our fears of future incidents. He might not be so lucky the next time. Dudley really was fine this time, and never showed any ill effects from a fall that no professional stunt artist would dare to attempt. But Brian and I were both scared, and thought it had to be a warning sign that we should not ignore.

In one of the most bizarre pieces of timing we had ever experienced, later that afternoon a real estate company placed a 'For Sale' sign on the lawn of the house directly next to ours. The house had previously been on the market, but was sold a month earlier. However, we were not aware that the sale had fallen through, and the house had gone back on the market that fateful afternoon. It was a ranch house with a finished basement. Nevertheless, Dudley could have everything he needed on the main floor. We were amazed to see the real estate sign — it was, truly, a *sign*!

Dudley was not happy about the idea of moving out, even if only next door, but he too wondered if he might break his neck in another similar fall. Time was closing in and his balance was getting worse by the day. There was not enough time to build an addition, which could take many months to complete. We called the real estate agent and toured the house the next day, telling the agent that Dudley was our Uncle Dave. He played along but knew perfectly well that Uncle Dave was Dudley. There was an unspoken understanding that he would keep the matter confidential, and he did.

We knew that even though Dudley was well aware of all the good and logical reasons for moving out, he might also feel rejected and depressed. Before considering the move, we determined that Elise would be willing to live in the house with Dudley. They were good friends and Dudley appreciated her easy laughter and earthy sense of humour. She was between apartments and had moved back home for a few months, so the arrangement worked well for her. She would help Dudley in exchange for a place to live. While she was out at work every day, someone would be hired to help Dudley with his daily routine.

There were also good legal reasons in support of this move. Even though Dudley's financial situation was still unresolved, both Gene Korf and attorneys who handled matters for Brian and me suggested that the move would avoid future problems with Dudley's estate. It was better for Dudley financially to clearly establish his New Jersey residency by owning property. And it would be easier for Dudley, when his condition declined further, to have full-time care in his own home. Gene Korf was just beginning to work with Dudley on updating his will and trusts, and had already spoken to him about the advantages of owning a New Jersey house. Had it not been for his dramatic fall, Dudley might not have acted upon Gene's suggestion.

When we toured the house, Dudley said he thought it was functional and would suit his needs, but he did not love it. He said he would have to think of it as the 'annex', and quickly agreed to the purchase, with only one month until the closing date. We planned to build a connecting bridge between the two houses, but found it was easy enough to go back and forth. There were two steps up to our front door and four to Dudley's. With a little help, Dudley negotiated the steps well.

Dudley was trying to focus on all the positive elements. He felt happy about having the space to bring many of his possessions from the California house, and participated eagerly in plans for decorating the main floor of the new house as well as the large lower level, where he decided to put two of his three concert grand pianos when they arrived from California.

It was a three-bedroom house. Dudley would occupy the master bedroom, with Elise across the hall within easy earshot in case Dudley needed help during the night. The third bedroom was set up as a guest room.

The transitional period between purchasing the house and moving in provided a good opportunity for Dudley to get used to the idea. There were many decisions to be made. Having begun to take control of many aspects of his life, including his finances, Dudley learned that he could also enjoy making decorating decisions. We found a talented carpenter, Armando Valles, to do the renovations needed to transform the basement level into an office and piano studio. The work had to be completed on a very tight schedule, and the team put the last few tacks in the carpeting Dudley had carefully selected just as the truck arrived from California with his furniture.

In May, a few weeks before the move, I had to be in Los Angeles for a series of Music For All Seasons programmes. Dudley was coming along, and could make decisions about the furniture in his Marina del Rey house. Stacey Herman, his former assistant, had

continued to watch the house and supervise any maintenance tha
was needed. She offered to help with the move and paved the way b
selecting two moving companies to estimate the cost of the cross
country truck drive.

Dudley was most emphatic that he wanted all three grand
pianos, and his childhood upright piano, brought to New Jersey. The
new house was much smaller than his LA residence, but the living
room could accommodate his beloved Bösendorfer piano without
problem, leaving room for the upright, a sofa, chairs, television and
couple of tables. The studio in Dudley's California house had been
built around the Bösendorfer, a magnificent nine-foot Imperia
Grand with a luscious sound. Now the moving-company represen
tative stood inside the studio, assessing the piano, the organ, the
speakers, the recording equipment. He determined that the piano
would not fit through the door, even without its legs and lid.

'Unless . . .' he said. He was staring at the wall in the studio
knocking on the soundproofed walls. We could see the wheels turn
ing. We waited patiently. Finally he spoke again.

'Unless we go right *through* the wall,' he said.

'How can you do that?' I asked. It was a solid, thick wall, curved
over the staircase.

'Easy. We can just cut through the wall, take the piano down the
stairs and we're done. The wall can be patched later.' Dudley agreed
He wasn't going to leave his Bösendorfer behind.

A few months later when we visited the house for the last time, i
was impossible to tell there had ever been a huge piano-sized hole
cut in the wall.

Whether or not Dudley could play them as well as he had in the
past, he was attached to his pianos. His life and emotions – hi

history – were wrapped up in them, and he wanted the security of having them with him. Finally knowing he could take all his pianos along, Dudley sighed with relief and sat down at the Bösendorfer, opening the lid and beginning to play the theme from *Six Weeks* slowly, sweetly, bringing out the sad melodic line. He was having trouble playing, but that didn't surprise him. *Six Weeks*, made in 1982 and directed by Tony Bill, was about a politician who befriended a thirteen-year-old ballet student, played by Katherine Healy, and her mother, played by Mary Tyler Moore. In the film, Dudley's only serious role in a movie, the young dancer is dying of leukaemia and Dudley's character helps her to fulfil her dream of dancing Clara in *The Nutcracker*. It was a film he adored and the music he composed for it was without a doubt the work he loved best. As he sat at the piano, he was still able to express his emotions through the music.

When the New Jersey house was ready, with the walls painted, carpeting laid, phones and security system installed and television cables placed in all the strategic points, Dudley wanted to watch the all-day move. He couldn't imagine missing any of it, and wanted to be sure that his furniture was placed exactly where he thought it should go. He took a folding chair from the kitchen and sat inside the still empty house, a few feet from the door and just out of the way of the five movers. Armando, who had just finished working, stayed to be certain everything would go in properly.

Two huge moving vans drove up, looking like they contained more than anyone could fit into the modest house. Dudley talked to everyone and offered to provide lunch for the group, ordering a large Italian meal to be delivered from a local pizza parlour.

Dudley was ecstatic to see his pianos, and went over to the

Bösendorfer to play it as soon as he could get to the keyboard. It had been a few weeks, and it felt good to be playing his own piano in his new home. After the Bösendorfer's complicated exit from its California location, its grand entrance into the New Jersey residence was smooth and flawless.

It looked like it was going to be a tight squeeze to get the Steinway and Yamaha pianos downstairs, however. The measurements had been taken very carefully, from all angles at which a piano might be carried. It appeared that there would be one inch to spare. The movers tested their beliefs with the lid of each piano. The Steinway lid slipped right through the available space with more than an inch to spare, and was now perched against the wall waiting for the rest of its body. The lid of the Yamaha, however, became stuck at its widest point. There was no way it could be turned to make it go through.

Armando, who had recently painted the ceiling over the stairs, was crestfallen. He pulled out his saw and cut out a piece of the ceiling just large enough to allow the piano to come through. Then he patched the ceiling while the movers were setting up the pianos. There were two railings installed on the staircase going down and, with carpeting and thick padding, no way for Dudley to get hurt even if he were to fall. But since everything he needed, including his favourite piano, was on the main floor of the house, his chances of getting hurt were minimal.

Finally, it was time for Dudley to move in. We had it arranged so that he would rarely be alone in the house. Pat Bruno was appointed to cook and keep the house in order, with substitutes lined up for days when she was unavailable. As always there was a concern about confidentiality, and extreme care was taken, starting with signed legal documents, to ensure that no details of Dudley's life would ever become public unless that was his decision. We trusted Pat completely, but each time a new person came into the picture, it was hard to be sure.

When Dudley was ready to sleep in his new house for the first time, he carried his dressing gown from my house to his. He said he would get the rest later. I helped him move some of his clothes, but he never wanted to empty his room. 'That way, this can continue to be my room and that can be the annex,' he said. I wondered if he would really be OK with the move.

This was new for Dudley – having his own home but knowing he would probably never marry again. He had our family network, bolstered by our close friendship, but I wondered if he might still feel lonely. I was very touched when he said we were his family, 'the family I always wanted', and his support system, and that nothing could sever this tie.

Dudley had arranged with Armando to renovate the kitchen after moving in. The old kitchen was ugly and in poor condition. Dudley wanted to select the new cabinets, floor tiles, fixtures, countertop and even the knobs for the cabinets.

Since I was a good bargain appliance shopper, Dudley assigned me the task of finding a new stove, dishwasher and refrigerator, and we had a ritual to go through as each appliance arrived.

'What do you think of this stove?' I would ask.

'I know you want me to say it's the most beautiful stove I've ever seen. This is, without a doubt, the most beautiful stove I have ever seen.'

The stove was white and it looked like any other stove. But I was proud of its quality and price.

'And these buttons. They are amazing. How do they work?' would ask.

He would examine the controls very carefully. We both knew was humouring me. He knew I needed the praise, even if it was su plied in jest.

'This one. It says "On". I imagine that's how you turn the ove on. And there's probably an "off" somewhere.' There wasn't. It w a fancy computerised thing that had a spot to touch for 'cancel'.

More amazing was the refrigerator – a beautiful modern frid with an ice and water dispenser in the door. Dudley liked gadge and was glad to have this one. Although all of Dudley's meals we cooked for him when he was at home, and our daily lunch outin continued, he still spent a lot of time in the refrigerator – looking what was in it, finding snacks, rearranging things, pouring juice, tal ing his daily dose of blended malt and cod liver oil (which mac most Americans cringe, but he loved it and had it specially importe from England).

Elise slept lightly and was usually able to prevent disasters in the making. But there was the odd occasion she was awakened by a b crash and a loud 'OH FUCK' coming from the kitchen. She woul dash in to find the floor covered with all the bottles that had some how fallen out of the shelves on the refrigerator door – glass on the floor, barbecue sauce or ketchup on Dudley's white socks, a hug mess. She would invariably clean it up while Dudley apologise They would both end up laughing about it. He would never ask for help. Later, even weeks before his death, when medical aides wer providing 24-hour care, Dudley would slip out of the room as qu etly as possible so that the room-to-room monitor wouldn't pick up. We had a buzzer hooked up to the side of his bed so all he had t

was press it. We counted on one hand the times he voluntarily
ed the buzzer. More than one assistant tried spending the night
a chair in the room, but Dudley hated trying to sleep with some-
e watching him.

'I didn't want to bother anybody,' he would say, after another
cape. In reality, we all knew that it was his last remaining bit of
dependence.

'Dudley, they are paid to be here and help you. This is for your
wn safety,' I would tell him.

'Oh, fucking hell,' he would say, the words coming out so slurred
at even he would laugh. 'Fine. I'll call next time.' He wouldn't.

He perfected his technique, slowly getting off the bed without
aking a sound. But there was a tiny squeak in his door that
mained un-oiled so that it could be heard on the monitor when he
ened it. After one escape, when he fell, I told him that he
minded me of my teenagers, who, I had learned years later, used to
eak out in the middle of the night. Karen, by day the least rebel-
us of the bunch, had once taken a midnight bicycle ride on the
ew Jersey Turnpike (similar to the M4 on a bad day). Dudley
ughed heartily and said he was 'proud to be in such skilled com-
any. I'm aiming for the Houdini Award,' he added.

Dudley was doing well in the new house. He was alone less, safer
ith no stairs to climb and satisfied that he was still as much a part
f the family as he had been before the move. He felt neither aban-
oned nor rejected. We spent a lot of time together, in the morning
efore I went to the office, during the day over lunch and in the
vening. He would come back from the 'annex' to the 'main house'
d we would watch rented movies, or go out to the movies, or con-
rts and plays, several times a week.

He was also pleased that his new business managers were beginning to pull his finances back together. There had previously been some nasty press suggesting that Dudley was bankrupt. He h heard about it and was very upset. The Management Group took aggressive approach to Dudley's financial situation. Dudley own several properties and was paying high costs for maintaining all them. One by one, the Management Group took steps to reduce debt by selling each of them. There was his primary Californ house, Marina del Rey, the sale of which would enable him to wi out the large debt he had accumulated, and provide a cushio Another was Nicole's house, about a mile from his. There was not ing he could do about this one. It was part of the divorce settleme and was his responsibility. Another was a house he owned joint with Susan Anton, with whom he had been involved for seve years during the 1980s. There was no reason for him to contin owning the house and paying expenses on it. Susan was not living it and was also looking to sell it. Another burden was the Las Veg condominium he had bought, several years earlier, at Nicole's ur ing, to provide a rent-free space for the mother of Nicol ex-husband Charles. Dudley was paying all the expenses on th house, including insurance. When the Management Grou informed her that Dudley was planning to sell the condo, she hire an attorney affiliated with the NAACP, accused him of racial preju dice — she was black — and tried to stop the sale. Dudley was n only shocked, but hurt. There was no person on earth less preju diced than Dudley. His attorneys informed him that fighting h action in court would cost him more than the value of the cond They recommended paying her $25,000, which he did.

Joel Mandel and his entire staff understood the background

Dudley's situation. They understood that he would not give them power of attorney, and they didn't request it. They sent him a package every month containing all his bills, prepared to be paid, with every cheque ready to be signed – only by Dudley. Whenever there were financial decisions to be made, they spoke personally with Dudley, explaining all his options and waiting patiently until he had asked all his questions – however long it took, and until he heard, and understood, the answers. Every month Dudley received a detailed business report from them, showing how every penny had been spent. He would study the reports carefully, and phone with questions. And they did not take a fee until Dudley's finances were once again solidly in the black. It had been a close call for Dudley.

Not long after Dudley's move into the new house, it was time for another summer trip to Nova Scotia. Brian's father and stepmother had arranged to join us. They flew first from Gatwick to Newark, and the following day I travelled with Dudley, Fred and Wynne up to Halifax. Brian had gone ahead a week earlier to open up the house and prepare it for the visiting group. Since I tended to be calmer under the pressures of travelling, I had volunteered to bring all three. Brian and I thought it was a fair division of labour.

While, under normal circumstances, Fred, Wynne and Dudley were able to walk, they would have trouble with the long distances in an airport. We ordered wheelchairs for all of them. Airport staff were cooperative and helped to wheel them. The flight was under two hours, and they were still in good moods when we arrived. At Halifax International Airport the route from plane to Customs desk is very long. Two airline representatives wheeled Fred and

Wynne. I wheeled Dudley. Finally arriving at the desk of a Customs agent, we lined up in front of her. Three wheelchairs in a straight line. Fred and Wynne were displaying their best full-toothed grins. Dudley looked serious. The agent recognised him immediately.

'Who's in charge of this group?' she asked sternly.

'I am,' I replied, handing her all four of our passports and Customs declarations. 'The top one is mine.'

She looked at them all, opening the passports and studying each person closely.

'So . . . you are going to a farm?' she asked. I assumed she was joking.

'Not exactly a farm. I've got a cabin in the woods, on the beach, and they are coming to visit for three weeks.' I knew it was really a 'cottage' now, in its improved state, but 'cabin' slipped out and it was too late to correct it.

'Well, it says here you are going to a farm.'

Because of stringent controls relating to the spread of agricultural diseases, one of a long list of 'yes' or 'no' questions was 'Will you be visiting a farm?' I had not been paying attention and had ticked off 'yes' instead of 'no'.

'Well, which part of this question did you not understand?' she asked.

'I guess it was the yes or no part,' I said. I was only slightly flippant. I knew it was considered inappropriate to make jokes to officials in an airport. Dudley, who had just closed his eyes and appeared to be napping, began laughing. Fred and Wynne had not yet turned on their hearing aids after the plane trip. They were still grinning.

'Do you have any liquor with you?'

'No,' I replied.

'Are you absolutely sure?' she asked.

'Yes, absolutely sure,' I said.

'Let me get this straight,' she went on. 'Three weeks in a cabin, and no liquor?'

'They all drink a lot of tea,' I said. 'They're English.'

'Well, if I were you,' she whispered, finally cracking a smile, 'I'd pick up a bottle on the way there.'

PART III

PART III

19

LETTING THE WORLD KNOW

IT TOOK SEVERAL MORE neurological evaluations before Dudley was finally willing to accept the grim diagnosis of Progressive Supranuclear Palsy. By that point he was under the treatment of several physicians. He was participating in trials at major medical institutions testing new drugs to see if they had any effect on PSP.

Progressive Supranuclear Palsy (PSP) was first clearly defined in 1963 and often mimics Parkinson's disease. It is a fatal degenerative condition that affects one in 100,000 people. It is caused by clumping of abnormal (tao) proteins in brain cells and leads to a wide range of symptoms, including poor balance (particularly falling backwards), slurred speech, slowed eye movements and general difficulties with coordination. Swallowing becomes increasingly difficult, with most patients turning to a diet of thickened liquids or using a feeding tube. Most victims of PSP survive from three to eight years after diagnosis, and most end up in a wheelchair or bedridden.

PSP is not the actual cause of death. People die from complications of the condition, not from the condition itself. The most frequent cause of death is aspiration pneumonia. Because of the decline in the swallowing mechanism, small particles of food or liquids can accumulate in the lungs, eventually causing pneumonia.

When Dudley was sure that the diagnosis was correct, he wanted to set the record straight and let the public know what was happening to him. In the autumn of 1999 Dudley returned to the Kessler Institute to resume therapy, still depressed that he was continuing to decline, but nevertheless putting aside his reluctance to engage in the challenge of physical therapy and trying it one more time.

For several weeks there were discussions about how to release the news. Kessler's public relations department was ready to assist, and with Dudley's permission they called in a press consultant the institute used for high-profile announcements. Brian and I joined Dudley, Kessler's administration, and Dudley's treatment team, headed by Dr Thomas Galski. They talked through all the options. Dudley wanted to be on camera and to have a press conference. Another idea was to have Dudley speak with one major reporter, on or off camera, instead of a barrage of press, which the doctors felt might be too risky. If he were to have a bad day, his condition might appear even worse than it was. Since Dudley wanted to speak, another option was to first have a printed press release sent out over the news wire services, and later to do one television interview that could be taped. When we left the meeting, it seemed likely that there would be a press conference sometime within the next few weeks.

However, when Lou Pitt and Michelle Bega (his press representative from Rogers and Cowan in LA) were consulted, they both felt that a press conference was a very bad idea. Michelle felt Dudley would be put on the spot, with negative results. People would be shocked to see his condition without first having a chance to hear all about it. Michelle proposed having a carefully worded press release, with contact numbers for medical personnel who would be available to answer questions.

Over the next few weeks, the press release was written, re-written and passed along for feedback to every person quoted in it or closely connected to Dudley. It was to include a fact sheet on the condition, with a bullet-point description of the symptoms and prognosis. Finally, Dudley said, he wanted to put a statement of his own into the press release.

> I understand that one person in 100,000 suffers from this disease, and I am also aware that there are 100,000 members of my union, the Screen Actors Guild (SAG), who are working every day. I think, therefore, it is in some way considerate of me that I have taken on this disease for myself, thus protecting the remaining 99,999 SAG members from this fate.

Dudley had wanted to say 'from this fate worse than death', but much to his annoyance it was vetoed by several others, who felt it was too true and too depressing to be in a press release.

A few weeks went by. The public relations team prepared everyone for every possible reaction that might occur. The four physicians named and quoted in the press release were briefed, and all were ready to greet the press with the most salient points and concise information about Dudley's condition.

On the day the news was to be released, everyone was ready. We knew exactly what time the release would hit the news wire services, and we waited. The news spread like wildfire. People were shocked, depressed, amazed, sympathetic. There was an incredible outpouring of support for Dudley. The media went into a frenzy and within hours there were phone calls to the Kessler Institute, all the doctors, Lou Pitt, Michelle Bega, our house, the MFAS office, my mobile phone. The press were on the doorstep. The tabloids – American and British – were on the case immediately. We could barely leave the house without being followed, and the possibility of any privacy had completely vanished. We were expecting this, and already used to dodging the press from their previous attempts to follow us.

Dudley's own statement was quoted everywhere, eliciting great respect from the news commentators who were amazed that he could announce such a serious condition and yet manage to retain a sense of humour, as though he were trying to soften the blow for his millions of fans.

As soon as word was out, the PSP Society was eager to form an alliance with Dudley. He wanted to help, but was hesitant to become involved with the Society and kept postponing meetings that both the American and British organisations wanted to set up with him. Eventually, he lent his name to establish the Dudley Moore Research Fund for PSP, an international research fund set up by MFAS with a grant from the Virgin Healthcare Foundation, and administered through the Baltimore branch of the Society. He regularly asked about the progress of the fund and the various research projects, but kept his personal involvement to a minimum. 'This disease is dreadful. I don't want anyone to go through what I am going through. But I want people to remember my music, my piano, my films, my humour – not primarily my illness.'

It was a difficult situation. The world now knew of Dudley's affliction and his struggle, and Dudley was relieved to have the public know what was wrong with him. He was also sad that he didn't hear from many of his old friends – people he thought might have called to say they now understood why he had dropped out of sight for so long.

Almost immediately, the major television personalities began asking if Dudley would appear on air for an interview. He was willing, in fact eager, to do it. Lou and Michelle felt it would be a good idea only if it was the right programme. Over the years, Dudley had been interviewed by all of the best-known talk show hosts in Britain and America. He had always enjoyed being interviewed, but this was different. Now he had a mission. Of the many requests that poured in, only ABC-TV's Barbara Walters (20/20) seemed to be under consideration. Dudley knew her, liked her and trusted her. She asked him only to visit her once, and promised Lou that she would not push him to do an interview on air. She arranged a limousine, and Dudley and I went together to meet for breakfast at her New York City home.

She was warm and charming to both of us, but this was no simple social visit. There was no question of her agenda. She intended to have Dudley on air. Barbara was very sympathetic about his condition and spoke with Dudley at length about what he was going through. It was a while before she broached the subject of an interview, and Dudley said yes before she even finished her question. He wanted to tell the world about his condition, his struggle, his unhappiness and his despair about not being able to play the piano. After a short while, Barbara turned to me and said, 'And of course we'll have you join him on air,' I gasped, audibly. I thought I would feel too exposed on national television talking about Dudley and his condition. I had gained weight from too many lunches out and not enough attention to the menu. I wasn't happy about the idea at all.

Barbara was reassuring. She patted my arm; she knew exactly what I was thinking before I said a word. 'We have make-up,' she said, smiling. She told Dudley the interview would be videotaped. Anything he was not happy about, he could say over again. It had never occurred to me that I would be invited to appear on air with him, and this gave me a lot to think about. On the one hand, I felt I could help to explain things. On the other hand, this wasn't about me. Barbara Walters felt otherwise. It was my story too, and she planned to say that on air. On the way home, I asked Dudley how he felt about my joining him on the programme. 'It's great,' he said. 'It will be comforting and reassuring. I shall do better if you are there.' That was all I needed to know. I stopped worrying about it.

For the intervening days, I was nervous about the whole broadcast. Early on the morning of taping, they sent someone to Dudley's home to do our hair and make-up. Dudley seemed confident that all would be well, but it was a big step. He wanted to set the record straight. There had been so many rumours about his drinking and he was very angry about that.

'I just want people to know the truth and to know what I'm going through, why I've dropped out of sight and what this disease is doing to me. I want them to know I'm going to die from this.' He was sombre, serious. His thoughts were clear. We were both quiet on the way to New York that morning. Dudley stared out of the window for a long time.

When we got into the studio, we spent some time waiting. We

knew that Lou Pitt was also on his way there and that Barbara was going to interview him afterwards. It was good to see him; Dudley was always happy to see Lou. It never mattered how much time had passed between their visits – they both picked up exactly where they had left off. They had a comfort and a closeness that brothers often have.

The studio was set up to appear as though we were in a living room. We had two chairs side by side, and as the camera focused on both of us, I realised I was going to be on camera with Dudley the entire time. I was not really happy about this, since it was Dudley's chance to be seen and heard for the first time talking about his condition. But I quickly asked him about it and he was comfortable with it.

Dudley was having an increasingly difficult time expressing himself, and everyone who knew about the broadcast wondered if he would be all right, and hoped that he would rise to the occasion. He did. When Walters began the interview, Dudley was clear and articulate. The slur in his voice was a minor problem, and he was able to express exactly what was on his mind. Clearly, he had been thinking about what he would say.

Walters was direct, knowing his biggest concerns. 'People thought you were Arthur. They took the character from the movie who was drunk, and said, "That's Dudley."

'It's amazing that Arthur has affected my body to the point that I have become him,' Dudley replied.

'Your mind is intact, so you know very well what is happening to you?' Walters asked.

'Yes, I know very well what is happening to me – particularly what people say and what they think,' Dudley said.

'What do you most want people to know?'

'I want people to know that I'm not intoxicated and I'm going through this disease as well as I can,' he said.

Dudley went on to say: 'I'm trapped in this body and there's nothing I can do about it.'

From her initial meeting with us, Barbara had clearly understood our close friendship. On camera, doing what she does best, she asked questions that were direct, poignant, heartfelt. She got Dudley to open up completely. He had yearned for this opportunity since first beginning to accept the fact that he had a degenerative disease from which he would never recover.

The interview was strange for me. I had thought I would be with Dudley for moral support. I had not considered that the focus would ever turn towards me, towards my relationship with Dudley. Barbara asked Dudley about me, and about who would care for him if it weren't for me. Dudley described me as a 'saint', and said nobody else would take care of him. It was the first time he had been so clear in his appreciation.

The interview was over in an hour, and we thought it had gone well. We stayed in the studio for a while, had lunch, talked to people on the staff and waited for Lou's interview. Dudley was calm and satisfied that it had all gone so well. We knew the programme would not air for another few weeks.

When we got home, I couldn't stop thinking about what Dudley had said. 'Did you mean that? What you said about me?' I asked him that evening.

'Every word,' he replied.

'You've never said that before. Why on national TV?'

'It's easier for me. Easier to tell the whole world,' he said. Strange, but true for Dudley.

'Well, thank you,' I said, with some understatement.

'And, incidentally, I have said it before. But perhaps this time you ill hear it. At least you can rewind the tape and play it again – that ill save me having to repeat it,' he said, momentarily amusing imself.

I was silenced. He had said it with a kindness that was softer than sual. He was probably right. I hadn't been listening.

'I couldn't get through this without you,' he said. 'You are why 'm here, why I'm still alive.'

I hugged him, stunned that he had been so outspoken, that he ad been able to express so much to me. It was always a big thing for)udley to say how he felt, once he finally, really, *knew* how he felt. At hat moment I was struck by my own many conflicting emotions. I vas glad he could communicate how he felt. I also thought that ometimes it is easier to be taken for granted. I didn't know how to eact. Things were changing. Dudley was learning to say what was in is heart; it was taking him less time to figure out how he really felt. t seemed so cruelly ironic that the more he learned to identify and xpress his feelings, the more of a challenge it would become for im to speak at all. Less than two years later, his voice would be educed to a whisper and his words barely understood.

At this point Dudley was still functioning reasonably well, lthough walking with a cane – it had the carved wooden head of a are and had been named 'Maurice' by Dudley. He was dwelling on he steady deterioration in his condition, even when it wasn't obvi-us to anyone else. The tiniest points about his balance or speech, or he problems in his hands – these would occupy his thoughts fre-uently. Besides his physical therapy sessions at the Kessler nstitute, he was having speech therapy and psychological counselling, but he didn't feel they were helping and he didn't see the point. Everyone in the family encouraged him to keep going, to keep trying. We thought he continued going simply because he knew we wanted him to do so.

His therapies and his daily life were part of the 20/20 broadcast. The crew spent several days filming Dudley at the Kessler Institute as well as at home, at the piano and attending Music For All Seasons programmes. The 20/20 broadcast would provide a comprehensive and accurate picture of what his life was like, how he was struggling and what he was doing to keep going against all odds.

Nearly a year earlier, Dudley had agreed to do a performance in Philadelphia for Music For All Seasons and Concerto Soloists of Philadelphia. His original plan was to narrate Prokofiev's *Peter and the Wolf*, which he was eager to perform once more. Larry Gelbart's clever narration had caught his attention and imagination, and he had enjoyed doing the Carnegie Hall performance a couple of years before.

However, as the months went by and we came closer to the Philadelphia performance date, Dudley's speech became more and more slurred. It was obvious that the demanding narration of *Peter and the Wolf* would be impossible for him. Through a combination of circumstances, and with help from Dudley's old friend Tony Adams, we contacted Julie Andrews, who agreed to share the stage with Dudley. Dudley and Julie had a friendship that went back many years. They had loved working together on the film *10*, and Dudley had kept in touch with both Julie and her husband Blake Edwards. They all liked and respected each other. Julie and Blake were aware of Dudley's condition, but not familiar with all the symptoms. As soon as Julie heard that Dudley wanted her to join him in a performance, she said yes. Dudley thought *Carnival of the Animals* would be a good idea, with Brian and me playing the two pianos and Dudley and Julie sharing the narration. Although we were concerned it might serve as an uncomfortable reminder that Dudley could no longer play the piano, he was happy with the plan, and excited that he could be onstage once again.

At Kessler, Dudley spent several months in his speech therapy sessions working on the narration, which had come so easily to him in the past. It was difficult watching him struggle to say the lines that had flowed so brilliantly just two years earlier. When had all these changes taken place? It had been so gradual that we barely noticed a difference from day to day, from week to week. But looking back over six months or a year, the deterioration was marked.

Monique Kaye was Dudley's speech therapist at Kessler. She was always charming and quietly elegant. Like most of the staff there, Monique did not alter her approach because of Dudley's status as a celebrity. While he was there, he was treated like any other patient. Monique didn't push Dudley; she inspired him to improve his speech. She was endlessly patient despite his enormous frustration with the process. He had resigned himself to the fact that he would never play the piano in public again. Now he had to face the fact that his speech was deteriorating – there wouldn't be many more opportunities for him to perform narrative works.

Although Monique gave him exercises to practise at home, Dudley rarely did his 'homework', even with encouragement from those around him. However, he still wanted to perform, and it kept him going to know he had one performance date on the horizon. Occasionally, he would share his concern that he wouldn't be able to narrate well enough. Sometimes he was angry about his condition, but he longed to be in front of his audience, to feel the warmth, to hear the applause.

It was Wednesday, 17 November 1999, and we were in Philadelphia to prepare for the performance the next day. Tickets to the concert had sold quickly and there were none left. All of Philadelphia was buzzing about the fact that both Dudley Moore and Julie Andrews were going to be onstage together. The orchestra's management had titled the programme *A Perfect 10*, in honour of Dudley and Julie's reunion.

It had been only two months since Dudley had announced his condition to the world, but a lot had happened during that time. People understood that there was an explanation for his symptoms; no longer did they assume he was imbalanced from drinking. This change in the public's perception was very comforting to Dudley. People were offering words of support, sending letters and gifts; but it was little compared to the flood of support he was about to receive. The *20/20* broadcast would be shown the night after the Philadelphia concert, but word about Dudley and his struggle had already spread internationally.

The dress rehearsal was hard work for Dudley. By mid-November, he had abandoned his single walking stick, Maurice, and was now using two specially designed canes that had flexible flat bottoms and looked like crutches. For long walks he had recently begun to use a wheelchair. Dudley took his preparation for the performance seriously, but was still able to appreciate the humour of the Ogden Nash verses, which he shared with Julie. She was wonderful in the rehearsal and subsequent performance, drawing him out and helping, without being obvious, anywhere that he was having a problem.

Dudley's speech therapist, Monique, attended the rehearsal, helping him to project and reminding him to speak slowly and distinctly. He did everything in his power to compensate for the unpredictable moments when words would slur or come out incorrectly, and Julie was ready to rescue with a gentle touch.

There was a standing ovation at the end of the performance. It had been a monumental achievement for Dudley – his first time onstage in more than two years. Everyone in the room knew it would probably be his last concert performance.

We all attended the celebratory fundraising dinner after the concert. That evening, the Dudley Moore Research Fund for PSP was launched in a small ceremony during the dinner, with several members of the Baltimore-based Society for PSP in attendance.

When the formal part of the evening was over, we all went back to the hotel. Julie had been very touched by his struggle, by the performance they had just given and by the way Dudley had risen to the occasion. He was thankful that she had done so much to help him, to make him feel that he could still perform.

Their friendship over the years 'grew sweeter whenever we met', Julie said. But they hadn't seen each other in a few years prior to the Philadelphia event, 'and I had no idea his condition was so bad – or how brave he was. The performance was hard for him; I helped to give him as much dignity as I could.'

As Dudley and Julie sat together on a couch in the suite, reminiscing, she said, 'There was enormous ease and friendship coming from him.' They had always communicated easily, warmly. 'We sat very close, and talked.' Julie expressed to him her sadness about his condition. 'He said to me, "I hear what you say and I comprehend what you say, and by the time I've formulated my response moments later, I can't get it out. It's like a wall is being built around me, and I can't get out. I'm sealed inside myself." I was so terribly grateful to have shared that time with him,' she said.

The next day we went home, and that evening the family gathered at my house to watch the airing of the Barbara Walters interview on 20/20. Dudley could not have been more pleased as he watched the final edited version of many days of filming come together in a programme that admirably told the story of his struggle.

Long before we knew the date of the broadcast, Brian and I had arranged to visit Joel and Mary Ellen and our three grandchildren in Atlanta. Dudley, as always, said he would come along. He liked them all, but felt particularly close to Joel, a cellist who, he said, 'plays Bach exactly the way it should be played', a high compliment from Dudley. Dudley had watched Joel's growth through his teens and into adulthood and rooted for him as he auditioned for a position in a major orchestra. Dudley had joined us for every one of Joel's orchestral concerts as principal cellist of the Delaware and Reading symphonies, attended his solo concerts and stated that 'I take my avuncular duties very seriously. I've always wanted to be an avuncle to a cellist.'

'I've always wanted to be a titular head as well,' he added once. 'That has a nice evocative sound to it.'

Joel's partners in the cello section were accustomed to Dudley's supportive visits backstage. We never had to wait long at the stage door. And no matter who the guest soloist was for the evening,

Dudley garnered all the backstage attention, greeting his fans and signing autographs.

Joel had recently joined the Atlanta Symphony, and Dudley was very proud of him.

On the way through the airports in Newark and Atlanta, Dudley was in a wheelchair, and the support from his fans was palpable. Many called out to him, 'Keep fighting, Dud,' or 'We're rooting for you.' There was a warmth and support in their good wishes. Dudley had never doubted it was a good idea to come forward with his story, but this response confirmed his decision. He needed the support of his fans more than ever, and people came through for him, held him in their hearts, carried him forward.

20

COMING TO TERMS
WITH THE LOSS

AFTER ALL THE DUST settled, and the world knew about Dudley's medical condition, Dudley expected to feel better. His secret was out. He was doing his best to cope. He was getting a lot of support and sympathy. People understood that he wasn't drinking, that his problems were not self-induced.

For months we had all been incredibly busy dealing with decisions relating to the big announcement, discussions about the press, the broadcast and the wide-ranging ripple effect of everything surrounding Dudley's decision to tell the world about his condition.

'This is like climbing a huge mountain,' Dudley said. 'Now I'm at the top of this mountain. I'm out of breath and exhausted,' he added, having difficulty saying the word 'exhausted'. He could never predict which words would cause him trouble. He considered the word 'exhausted' complex enough to justify at least a minor problem squeezing it out.

'My tongue must be exhausted, too,' he said with the hint of a smile, the word coming out perfectly this time.

More often than not, it would be an absurdly simple word that would slur or get stuck in his mouth. He remained able to laugh at himself and his troubles, the major exception being his inability to play the piano. I knew that he would sometimes try to play one of his three grand pianos when he was sure nobody else was in the house. It was possible to hear faint sounds of the piano just outside the house, but the music would stop the minute the front door opened. Dudley always knew when somebody was coming in. He had the alarm system set to beep loudly whenever an exterior door was opened.

In my car, Dudley's *Songs Without Words* was one of the six CDs in the CD player – one of only two that had permanent spots; the other was a CD of cello concertos played by Steven Isserlis, one of the few people with whom Dudley kept in touch. Steven was also among the chosen few whom Dudley would visit on his infrequent trips to London, and Dudley would travel to New York or Philadelphia to hear Steven play on his United States tours. Dudley loved Steven's playing, and he liked Steven's liberal and unconventional personal style.

It was acceptable for the other four CDs to rotate in the remaining available slots. Those two had to stay in their assigned spots (numbers 1 and 2) so Dudley could press a button on the car stereo and find them easily. Usually he would shed a few tears as he listened to his own piano playing, so warm and expressive. Most of Dudley's compositions, particularly those for the piano, were sad in nature, more often than not in a minor key. After the first few moments of listening to his own playing, he would be OK. He could make the transition from sadness to acceptance, and finally to pride that he had created so many beautiful pieces. But there were times he couldn't make that transition, and the emotions would go in the opposite direction. 'Are you sure you want to listen now?' I would ask him at those times. 'Yes, I need to – even if it upsets me, I need to hear it. It's almost as though I can play again when I hear this – as though I *am* playing.'

One day in the car, we were listening to his music and he wasn't going through the transition to acceptance. He was stuck in sadness, and already on the third track of the CD.

'Why did this happen to me?' he said. 'I have to ask that. Why me? Why my music?' I knew we would not get to 'acceptance' this time.

'I know there's no answer, but I keep wondering why me? Why me?' His right hand was in a tight fist; he was staring at it. Then he opened his fist and looked at his fingers. 'I've tried to be humorous about it. To think of it as some tragic irony. I've tried to *understand* it. Maybe I've done something to deserve this. Perhaps I'm supposed to learn humility, or some other lesson, although I'm hardly conceited – I don't think of myself as any better than the next guy. So I keep coming back to the same question. Why me?' He turned the volume up. He was having trouble getting some of the words out, but he kept going.

'I hear myself play and wonder why this would be taken away from me.' There were tears streaming down his face. His grief was deep and I had never seen him so profoundly upset – about anything. He had turned up the volume during a passage that was sad enough to arouse deep emotions even in a listener who had started out convinced it was the finest day of his life. But Dudley had begun

this journey at the bottom of sadness, already on the brink of tear
I pulled the car over. There was no point in driving. There wer
tears flooding my eyes too and I couldn't see the road. We ha
bought coffee half an hour earlier and the cups were in their holde
between the two front seats. The lids were unopened, a bad sign, a
the coffee would normally have been half gone by now. Not muc
could interfere with our coffee drinking. I took a paper napkin tha
was wrapped around one of the cups and dried some of his tears. H
put his hand around mine and continued wiping his tears.

'I don't know how I can go on without the piano. You can put a
the rest into a thimble. I would give up what's left of my legs, m
balance, if I could play the piano again.'

He stopped speaking. His crying had descended into sobs. H
had turned the music up so loud that it was almost deafening.
leaned over and held him. We embraced and cried – he wept unt
he was exhausted and there were no tears left in his body. Then w
were both quiet, and sat in the car, holding hands, for a long time
until the music ended.

'I can't change this, can I?' he said very softly, knowing th
answer.

'You can remember what you have created, and try to let that b
some comfort to you.'

'I know,' he said. 'Sometimes I can barely breathe. I feel like I'
drowning without the piano. It's as though the piano were the sh
that sails me through life. I think that's a pretty good analogy.' H
smiled for the first time since he had turned on the music in the ca
'Without it, I can't sail through life. I stumble, and I'm lost. Th
music is still inside of me, but it's trapped, fighting to get out.
hurts so much.' He was finished talking. He looked at his watch.

An hour had evaporated, sitting on the side of the road, and we were nowhere near home yet. 'I think we'd better get you home before Brian thinks we've left the country.'

'Fiji,' I said. 'Nothing less will do.'

'Bora Bora would be my choice. It's the most beautiful spot on earth, and I drank my espresso on the balcony there every morning,' he said.

'Note the island theme,' I said.

'It must be this godawful weather.' It was the beginning of December, and chilly. It was 5 p.m. and already dark.

'Wait a minute,' I said. 'Isn't Great Britain an island?'

'Hardly tropical,' he said. 'Why do you ask?'

'Because we'll be there in a few weeks,' I said, remembering our upcoming Christmas trip to England.

'Oh, good,' he said. I knew that as long as there was something coming up, something on the calendar, Dudley would pull through. He would get out of the depression and return to feeling some sense of hope.

Dudley never reached such a low point again over his loss of the ability to play the piano. His outpouring of grief was so complete that day it was as if he had literally emptied it all out. He had reached his emotional bottom, and there was nowhere else to go. He had to rebuild, to find hope, to see the good in his life, to appreciate what he had achieved and created. Without saying it in words, he slowly began to show his determination to accept the way things were.

Dudley's physical condition would decline almost imperceptibly day after day, but periodically would move down a definable level.

g would get just a little worse, and never return to the pre-
igher level. There were several drug trials, including one
long study by Yale University, which involved travelling to New
Haven, Connecticut for a complete evaluation before and after six
months of testing a drug. Dudley was eager to participate in any
study if there was a chance a cure would be found. So far, Sinemet, a
drug used for Parkinson patients, was the only medication that had
any positive effect. It appeared to help with balance and coordination, but would not cure the condition.

One afternoon we were driving home after a day of therapy at
Kessler Institute. Dudley was tired from speech therapy that had
not gone particularly well, despite Monique's encouragement.
Physical therapy had also been a struggle; his balance was worse –
his condition had recently done one of its little downward leaps.
Dudley had many eye complaints. Dr Gizzi had tried a variety of
prism glasses (lenses that shift an image to where the eye is looking,
rather than magnifying it), and an optometric consultant at Kessler
had been experimenting with prisms ground into Dudley's regular
prescription, none of which helped him markedly. He was talking
about having his prescription tested again.

Dudley's glasses collection had always provided some levity, no
matter what else was going on in his life. Long before his eyes had
been affected by PSP, he was in the habit of having many pairs of
glasses for a variety of situations. His jacket pockets would be filled
with them – at least three, sometimes four or five (some in cases,
some loose with their earpieces bent in strange directions). He used
bifocals, but one pair was never enough. He had a pair he loved best
for reading. Sometimes it was an older prescription that he couldn't
bear to give up. Plus a pair of bifocals whose old distance segment

as slightly more soothing than the newer prescription. He was
onstantly losing and reordering his glasses. No sooner would the
ew pair arrive than Dudley would invariably find the original pair.

One drawer in his bedroom was overflowing with glasses in a
ariety of soft and hard cases, or just thrown in with no case at all.
His old leather briefcase was the setting for another collection of
lasses. And most of his jackets had a pair or two in the pockets.
Nevertheless, there were two or three special favourites − either
ames or prescriptions he liked best − and if those were lost, he
ould have them reproduced exactly rather than dig through the
rawer for a different pair.

During the last few years of his life, my nephew, Ronald Platt,
upervised Dudley's eye care. Ron is an optometrist with an office in
hiladelphia. Roughly once a year, Dudley would arrange to have an
xamination, a glaucoma test and to have his prescription checked,
ven though it was duplicating some of the testing frequently done
t Kessler. In Dudley's opinion, Ron had the definitive answer to
ny eye questions. Dudley would carefully place many of his glasses
a bag, or in various pockets, and we would turn up for an exam
at was reminiscent of his medical doctor visits.

'Well, I don't know,' he would say, seated in the examination
hair. 'That letter is definitely an "a", although if I were to squint
ver so slightly I would have to admit that it might possibly be an
:". Oh . . . you probably meant the line above, the line I can actu-
lly *read*, although that one is fuzzy as well.'

'The first line that's completely clear for you − that's the one I'd
ke you to read,' Ron said good-naturedly.

'Well, how are Sue and the children?' Dudley asked. 'Oh, sorry,
ou were probably waiting for this line of text that's in front of my

nose. The children must be getting big by now.' The card would b
inside a machine in front of Dudley's face, and he would be makin
funny faces for the benefit of anyone who was in the room with hin

Ron always had to schedule extra time for Dudley's visits, as th
exams would be interrupted by long discussions about whatever w
going on in Dudley's life, and whether or not Ron thought th
Dudley's glaucoma was getting worse. Fortunately it remaine
under control; they would, nevertheless, have long discussions abo
the condition. They also discussed eye drops at great length, an
Dudley liked getting a large collection of sample packages.

PSP affects not only eye movement (and as a consequenc
focusing), but also the blinking mechanism. One of the characteri
tic symptoms is what some doctors refer to as the 'Mona Lisa star
It is a wide-eyed look that comes about when the blinking mech
nism stops working properly. It is important to keep the ey
artificially lubricated. Dudley was interested in the variety of ey
lubricants available to him, and would discuss the pros and cons
each type with Ron, or anyone else willing to listen.

If anyone else had been discussing their own eye drops, Dudle
would have said a wry *fascinating*.

Taking small steps to live in the present and not dwell on his losse
Dudley wanted to work on a new project, and we were discussir
what our production company could do next. We still hadn't dor
our intended documentary on circumcision, but at the moment a
musical project, I thought, would be more likely to cheer Dudley u

We had recently closed our California-based production con
pany. Dudley had never received the bank records he had bee
requesting literally for years. We finally gained access to the info

ation and closed the bank account and the company. With legal
elp and advice from both Gene Korf and Stephen Rodner, an
ntertainment attorney in New York and a Music For All Seasons
ustee, Dudley and I had established a new company called Martine
venue Productions, Inc.

Finding a new name for the company was not easy, as we couldn't
gree on any name for weeks. We would drive around looking at
gns or symbols. Once we were driving past a place called the
ismal Swamp, somebody's idea of a good name for a tiny local
ond. Dudley thought Dismal Swamp Productions had an intrigu-
g ring to it. Not that our driving routes were habitually filled with
wamps, but less than a week later, we happened to be driving
rough the Great Swamp, a well-known wildlife refuge. 'Great
wamp Productions sounds more impressive than Dismal Swamp,'
e said. We were grasping at straws. Passing a picture of a fox on a
llboard, I suggested Swamp Fox Productions as a possible alterna-
ve. We liked that one best.

'Maybe we would get tired of anything swampy after a few weeks;
then we could be stuck with it. This needs some serious thought,'
said.

'Try saying it several times in a row, fast,' he said. 'Then we'll
now if it goes funny. Does that happen to you? You know, when you
y a familiar word over and over and then it goes all funny on you,
d it no longer sounds like a word you know at all.'

Sadly, I knew exactly what he meant. We both tried it. I went first.

'Swamp swamp swamp swamp swamp swamp,' I said.

Then he tried it. 'Swamp fox swamp fox swamp fucks swamp
cks fuck swamps fuck swamps.'

I was reminded of creating our original company, and noted the

fact that now, only a few years later, this discussion didn't seem at a
strange to me. We needed to put the name of our new compan
through rigorous testing to make sure it wouldn't go funny on us.
knew that other people put their proposed company names throug
a corporate name search and other legal processes. We would d
those legal things too, but in Dudley's opinion they were all missin
the critically important first step.

We looked at each other. Dudley started laughing. 'Nope,' h
said, a word I only heard him use a few times, and never outside c
the United States. 'They are *both* going funny on me. We'll need
different name for this company.'

'What about Martine Avenue Productions?' I said, tossing it ou
but not believing it could work. It was the street on which we lived

'It has a nice ring to it. A classy, successful sound. Yes, I like that

'Then everyone will know where we live,' I said.

'Don't be silly. Nobody will think we're stupid enough to nam
the company after our street. All the press already know where w
live, anyway,' he added. That was only partially true. We had success
fully managed to keep quiet the fact that he had moved next doo
into the 'annex'. For many reasons, we were glad it was still a secret.

'We could think about it,' I said.

'We'll have to put it through some rigorous testing,' he said. 'Yo
go first.'

'Martine Avenue Productions Martine Avenue–' I stopped
'Wait a minute. With or without Inc?'

'With Inc, I should think.'

'Nice rhyme,' I said. 'And *don't* suggest Nice Rhyme Production
Inc.'

'Martine Avenue Productions Inc. Martine Avenue . . .'

It didn't go funny on either of us. We both said it five times as fast as we could. There was a limit to the speed at which it could be said. That, I thought, had protected the name somewhat. The name had passed the first, and most critical, test. A week later it was still top of the list.

Dudley often spoke of his 1992 concert at the Royal Albert Hall. It had been a monumental programme and Dudley had enjoyed his many roles – as classical soloist with the BBC Concert Orchestra (conducted by Kenneth Alwyn); as jazz pianist with the Dudley Moore Trio, with his good friends and long-time trio partners Chris Karan and Pete Morgan, and as soloist in his own wonderfully funny parodies. It was a programme that had made a wildly successful UK tour, and it was easy to see that it had been Dudley's best concert and one he remembered with great fondness.

While in England for the December holiday in 1999, and with cooperation from the BBC, we managed to set things in motion for the production of the new CD, obtaining the original recordings which we could edit.

Most of the holiday time was spent with family and friends. Dudley was always glad to be back in England. In long periods of absence, he would become nostalgic for the English countryside and the traditions and history of his homeland. He felt connected to England, although he said he felt more comfortable, and less restricted, in America. Perhaps thinking about his own youth in England, Dudley reached out in an extraordinary way to a young composer and arranger.

He had been surprised to receive in the mail an unsolicited piano transcription of his score to *Bedazzled* – particularly remarkable since the score had been misdirected and spent months travelling the United States before finally landing in Lou Pitt's office, when it was promptly mailed to New Jersey. Dudley knew nothing of the young composer/arranger who had sent the score as a gift for Dudley, whom he had always admired. Dudley was impressed and thought he had talent. He read through it a few times, then dialled the UK phone number that Steve Law had included in the package. Law, a shy young man in his mid-twenties, was astounded to receive a personal phone call from Dudley a year after mailing his package. Not only did Dudley thank him, but he invited Law to meet him in London, where they discussed music they had both written. It was clear that, even in his condition, Dudley was ready to act as a mentor to a talented musician.

Halfway through our first week in London, spent visiting Suzy and Elodie, I rented a car and braved driving to Oxfordshire to visit Dudley's sister Barbara and her husband Bernard Stevens. As always, the visit began with a long embrace between brother and sister. Barbara had been the victim of a stroke several years earlier, and was partially disabled. Bernard gave me a tour all around the community that encompassed their new residence, leaving Dudley and Barbara to catch up on events in their lives since their last visit a year earlier.

We had arranged rooms in a hotel that was half an hour away from their home. It would have been too tiring for Dudley to go back to London that evening, and I assumed that he would want to visit his sister again the following day. But they had spent one long afternoon together. They had caught up on the family news and Dudley's condition. They had reconnected. The visit was warm and friendly, but it would not continue the next day. Dudley and Barbara embraced again, Barbara struggling to hold back the tears this time. Dudley said he would see her again soon.

That was a difficult year for Brian. His stepmother, Wynne, was eighty-seven and recovering from a stroke, and we discovered not long after our Christmas visit that Brian's father, Frederick, had lung cancer. At eighty-three, his prognosis did not look good, but in February Brian went back to England to bring them both to live with us in New Jersey. If Dudley as a full-time resident in our house had caused some stress, we had no idea how we would survive two ailing octogenarians in the house. But we and all our children adored them both, and knew that, used to living independently, they would soon insist on finding a place of their own. We wanted to get Fred into treatment and find a place where Wynne, who was recovering well from the stroke, could continue her outpatient therapy sessions.

Dudley was pleased they would be joining us. He was attached to Fred, and felt secure in his presence. Like the rest of us, Dudley called him 'Pop', and he thought Wynne was unusual and delightful. Both were hard of hearing and Wynne would forget to turn on her hearing aid.

'What's the name of this tune?' Fred would ask.

'No, I do *not* need a spoon,' Wynne would reply, annoyed. She never gave him the benefit of the doubt. She would get annoyed first and clarify what he had really said afterwards. Dudley said they were 'as good as any vaudeville act I've seen'. He was constantly laughing when he was around them. Eventually Fred and Wynne caught on, and they would laugh as well.

'Oh, I suppose I should turn on these damn hearing aids – I'm always forgetting,' Wynne would say.

She was as bawdy as Dudley, with a great sense of humour. She never walked out of the door without being well dressed, without make-up on. 'I have to be ready for my public,' she explained. She was sharp as a tack and not kidding about her public. She truly believed she might encounter someone who would remember her from her earlier years onstage as a dancer.

Even Dudley nearly gagged on one of her stories. A couple of years earlier, she had gone into a British department store looking for a perfume she had liked. It was called Organza, but once inside the store, she couldn't recall the name. 'I told the sales clerk I couldn't remember it exactly, but I thought it was called Orgasm. The clerk started laughing, and I realised what I had said. I told her it was funny that had popped into my head. I had the perfume only a month ago, but I hadn't had one of *those* in years.'

Arriving in New Jersey, Fred began chemotherapy. But his condition was advanced; he was discouraged. Less than a month after his diagnosis, he was in hospital. He waited until all his grandchildren were gathered round him and said, 'I'm glad you are all here. I wanted to tell you that I love you all.' He said goodbye and died that night in his sleep. Wynne stayed with us for three months, and she died from a tumour on her heart.

It was a difficult time for all of us. For many years, we had wanted Fred and Wynne to live near us, but they had been hesitant to make such a big move. When they did, their time around the family was too short. Although Dudley hadn't known either of them very well, he had become attached to them both, and it was a big loss for him too. He cried softly at Wynne's memorial service, as we listened to 'Vissi d'Arte' from *Tosca*, the operatic aria she had loved best.

21

LIVE FROM AN AIRCRAFT HANGAR

WE BEGAN WORK ON the CD that would showcase Dudley's cherished 1992 concert at the Royal Albert Hall. We knew it would take a long time, but it was the one project Dudley was not only able to handle but enthusiastic about tackling. There was no point in rushing through it. He was a perfectionist and was deriving great satisfaction from the entire process. Dudley wanted to write a large part of the CD booklet, and insisted on editing anything he hadn't written himself. Proceeds from the CD were to be distributed to both Music For All Seasons and the Dudley Moore Research Fund for PSP.

The original concert had been performed several times and taped more than once for broadcast by the BBC. When we began work, there were at least two good versions of each work. Sometimes the distinctions were subtle, and we would listen over and over in order to find the best possible performances. If there was a wrong note or a passage Dudley didn't consider effective enough, he would discard that version of the work.

Dudley was adamant about not patching together parts of each piece from different performances. He wanted the final CD to sound as live and spontaneous as the performances themselves had been.

Working on the production of a CD was having a positive effect on Dudley. The process lasted nine months, start to finish, and Dudley did some work on it nearly every day. There were the inevitable jokes that a baby could be produced in the same length of time, and possibly with less agony. The title was one of the first decisions we made, a surprisingly easy one. Dudley thought of using the term 'Live From' but not in a serious way – 'spoof-ish', he said. He liked adding 'ish' to words; he said it reflected his 'indecisive-ish-ness'. I remembered that during the concert he had referred to the Albert Hall as 'this . . . this aircraft hangar', and it only took about a minute for us to put it together with 'Live From' and agree that *Live From an Aircraft Hangar* was 'the perfect title', as Dudley said.

He was emphatic that he didn't want anyone else editing the CD – just the two of us. I knew there were two reasons. He was empowered by the act of producing a CD as president of his own production company; and he didn't trust anyone else to take over the large role he had assigned himself. He wanted to select and time all the pieces, decide on the order, assemble it, write the notes, supervise the design. But if he thought he was being 'presidentially dictatorial', he said, laughing at the subtleties of the image, he asked for my opinion and thoughts about every aspect of the production, except the amount of air between the words or sentences. This was a question of comic timing, and it was his territory alone.

Because of his condition, the 'studio' was Dudley's bedroom, and we set out all the necessary equipment on his king-size bed. Stopwatch, pens, pencils, notepads, extra pillows. Elise and Karen had given him a stereo set for Christmas – a compact CD changer and tape player that sat on top of his dresser. Dudley had protested the gift, saying he couldn't possibly accept it. It had been a sore point. Elise thought he hadn't appreciated it. Dudley had everything he needed in the house, but they had found the one thing that was missing – a good system for playing music in his bedroom. He had been using a small CD player and radio, but this new system was much better, with excellent sound and space for three CDs. Spending more time now in his room, it was the only thing that made sense.

Dudley had objected because he felt he didn't deserve such an extravagant ($300) gift. He said he wanted to be the only one in the family giving extravagant gifts. He thought of my daughters as his nieces. He worried about them, gave them advice, cautioned them about their choice of boyfriends. Elise and Karen understood his feeling and said they wouldn't be 'extravagant' too often; Dudley overcame his objection and used that gift every day for the rest of his life.

In editing the CD, I took my spot on a chair in front of the stereo system. Dudley took his place, seated in bed, propping himself up against many pillows. He had a stopwatch in one hand and pen in the other, with a large yellow legal pad on his lap. He had agreed to wear clothes, not just a dressing gown, for these editing sessions. We compromised on a long T-shirt that had the large head of a well-known wrestling figure, 'The Rock', on the front. Dudley had no interest in wrestling – tennis was the only sport he liked – but he thought that wearing the shirt, a gift I had once given him as a joke, was incongruous enough for the President of Martine Avenue Productions, Inc. to wear for important editing sessions. He would occasionally look down at the gruff face on his chest and giggle.

As unorthodox as the trappings of professionalism tended to be, Dudley's work on the CD itself was the portrait of the ultimate professional. He was a perfectionist in every aspect of the project. His style onstage had been informal, rambling, vulnerable. He came off as completely spontaneous. In performance, he appeared to be thinking of the material for the first time, although in reality the same pauses and spontaneous touches were there, in the same places, every time. All of this worked brilliantly onstage, with the added visual element, and Dudley could bring down the house with just a glance over his shoulder from the piano. But listening to it, he quickly came to the conclusion that he didn't need those visually effective pauses on a CD. He wanted to pick up the pace, and was diligent in identifying every spot, every second, where things that had worked onstage had to be adapted for a CD. Undertaking such a project start to finish was new for Dudley. He had hated feeling as though he was 'retired', simply because of his condition. It made him feel better to know he was working on a large project with something to show at the end of it.

For the process of editing, Dudley's two-hour rule was abandoned. We would work three or four hours in a row, until he was either hungry or tired, sometimes both problems occurring at the same moment without warning. It was never simply time for a break. 'I'm *starving* and *exhausted*,' he would announce with a hint of annoyance, as though this emergency could certainly have been avoided if anybody had been paying attention.

Selecting the music to include on the CD was only the first step. Dudley wanted to include portions of his original commentary before each composition. In the live performances his commentary had sometimes continued for a few minutes before the music would begin. Only a short extract was needed for the CD introductions. He was surprised to discover how much he enjoyed listening. He laughed as though he was hearing the material for the first time; sometimes it was as though he was listening to somebody else performing.

He was nostalgic about his old works – his movies and his tapes or CDs of musical performances. Periodically we would hold Dudley Moore film festivals, gathering his films and watching every night for a week or so. Dudley would laugh as though he had never seen them before. If anyone visiting had not seen one of his films, he would pull it out and watch along with them. It was double the show – the movie, and Dudley's reaction to the film, and to himself on screen.

Although this was at a time when Dudley knew his film career was over, there seemed no bitterness or sadness, only the joy as he watched, always with commentary that only he could provide. Lines changed spontaneously on the set; Bo Derek giggling in *10* when she was supposed to be serious; his favourite line in *Arthur* ('You must have hated this moose') and other choice moments.

He would light up when asked about his career, and would engage in long discussions with anyone about his musical or film careers. But Dudley was also able to listen objectively and critically to his own performances while editing, and he was a tough critic – not just musically, but in every detail.

'That sentence – too many "ums" – we'll have to remove at least

three of them,' he said. The handwritten notes for Skipp Tullen
who was mastering the CD, were many pages long, and hard to read
as his handwriting was by then seriously affected by his condition.
As was often the case with Parkinson patients (another similarity to
PSP), Dudley's PSP-affected handwriting was becoming smaller
but not consistently so – sometimes it was very large and other
times very tiny. He had been appalled to find that a newspaper had
published his signature on two documents – one current and one
from several years earlier – as though it was everyone's right to
know that his hand coordination was so affected.

We had learned that Dudley did not want to be protected from
reading what appeared about him in the press. I had only once sheltered him from an article – the one in Australia when the headline
of one review wondered if he had been drunk onstage. He had
learned about it later. He said in that instance it had been OK
because of his vulnerable state, and half a tour left to play, but in
general he wanted to be the one to decide whether to read a story or
toss it in the trash. He wanted to know everything that was being
said about him, even if it upset him. Sometimes it upset him a lot. At
one point, he became so disgusted with the press repeatedly reporting that he was at death's door, years before he was, that he sent an
'open letter to the international press' asking them not to jump to
such conclusions. He challenged the press to set the record straight
by printing his statement, and they did. 'I should like to emphasise
that "rumours of my death have been greatly exaggerated",' he
began. 'You have been writing about my being "near death" for two
years, and imagine my surprise to be informed this morning . . .
that I have only weeks to live. I should, I imagine, let my doctor
know this. I suppose my imminent death will sell papers, while my

positive and life-affirming work is of no interest to anyone. I am hurt and discouraged by your cruelty.'

The letter was taken seriously and published widely in December 2000; he felt it had been a strong and positive action on his part.

Dudley had been proud of his good handwriting in the past, and was disturbed that he could now barely read his own notes. I would type them up at the end of every session, often having to call for help deciphering the words scribbled on the page in differently sized letters.

He had arranged for the installation of a computer, printer and scanner downstairs, creating a small office space with equipment purchased by phone during late-night-television shopping sessions. He was fascinated by the internet, although he required a fair amount of help using the computer. He spent one entire evening reading what was written about him on the internet. When we were ready to launch the CD, we realised we had no company website, and spent an intensive week working together to create one, with help from a small design company in Boston that was happy to treat it as a website emergency.

There were several different phone lines in the house, and to save Dudley the trip downstairs, I would either phone him or run up and down the stairs with questions.

'This looks like "Tleven fawn fix Welts",' I said. 'Any clue?'

'Ha! That's a good one,' he said, laughing one of his loud cackles. 'I like that a lot. We could list that as one of the titles – "Tleven fawn fix Welts".' It sounded even funnier, as the whole thing had come out slurred when he said it. 'Let me see that.' He grabbed the legal pad out of my hand and stared at it for a few moments. Well, it's between this one and that one. The timing is eleven minutes. This has to be the "Theme From Six Weeks". I should say it's a good thing I'm here to decipher this. God knows what titles you would put on the CD if I let you loose with my notepad – and my disastrous handwriting. In fact, perhaps that's not such a bad idea. Hmm . . . would it sell with a title such as . . .' – he turned back to the first page of the legal pad, about forty pages earlier, the pages all puffed out and swollen from an encounter with apricot nectar and other forms of legal pad abuse; he was studying the heading at the top of the first page – '"Line Fawn an Assrapt Banger"? Yes, that works every bit as well as "Live From an Aircraft Hangar". I'm just not convinced it has the *ring* of a best-selling CD. What is an Assrapt Banger? Find me my dictionary . . . please.'

'How many volumes do you want me to bring up?' I asked. Dudley had the complete, unabridged Oxford English Dictionary on the shelves downstairs. Twenty volumes, each weighing about ten pounds. I didn't know any other civilian who owned the complete set. 'I'm sure line, fawn and banger will all be in it. Is it "assrapt" you need to look up?'

I had said it with a straight face and as much seriousness as I could muster. He looked at me, a momentary delay before reacting, then burst out laughing. It wouldn't have been the first time he insisted on looking up a word that couldn't possibly exist. Occasionally the non-words – such as zobo and ycch – would make a guest appearance in the dictionary. He was, nevertheless, convinced they didn't *really* exist.

'You would probably make up words too if you were the editor of a million-page dictionary,' he said. 'What else could you possibly do for amusement?' I had to admit to him that while writing for the

New York Times, I had occasionally slipped in some outrageous non-word to see if my editor, who had a wonderful sense of humour, could catch it before the story went to press. Dudley said I had just proved his theory about the dictionary.

Dudley's departure from the task at hand could last half an hour, while he examined randomly chosen pages in the dictionary, occasionally calling out an unusual word and saying, 'I'm ashamed to admit, I've never come across this one before.'

Strange things would elicit an outburst of laughter from Dudley. His daytime medical aide, Peter Clarke, was able to get Dudley laughing every morning, with a series of fast exercises and jokes. Peter was always trying to increase Dudley's level of activity and was extremely pleased to see him working so energetically on the CD.

If things were ever getting too serious in the household, Elise only needed to pull out the battery-powered, remote-controlled 'fart machine' that was kept in a drawer and call it into action. Dudley found farting sounds the funniest thing ever, ranking far above any dirty joke he had ever heard. This particular device was a far cry from your average 'whoopee cushion' – it was a high-class contraption, with six varied fart tones, from a small 'plllbt' to a loud and long melodious one. Dudley once laughed for the entire duration of a 45-minute car trip during which Elise used the machine, repeating one of the six sounds as soon as he was quiet and had caught his breath.

When the editing was nearly completed, we realised we needed a photo for the CD cover. Dudley had a collection of model airplanes that had previously hung at strategic points in his California house. In New Jersey, he had placed them on top of the bookshelves downstairs. Perfect for the photo, he thought. We moved them all

upstairs, and tried taking photos of Dudley with his model plan
He looked bored, disinterested. His smile was fake. It was obvio
that he couldn't look enthusiastic enough no matter what he d
with his model airplanes.

'Oh fuck. This is a stupid idea. We need to be in a real aircra
hangar,' he said, 'with a real plane.'

'Where are we supposed to find a hangar?' I said, suddenly fee
ing this project – as often happened with Dudley – about
become more complex than one might have imagined.

'I don't know. You're the co-producer of this thing. Find us
place. Persuade somebody to lend us a plane,' he said. It was mine
solve.

I was always surprised by how much information could be ga
nered in a few phone calls. For example, the names of all the go
small private airports in New Jersey, and who owned them. It to
one hour. We learned that the owners of Solberg Airport
Readington, New Jersey had a couple of historic old planes. And
small, classic, aircraft hangar.

'Great,' Dudley said. 'I'm sure you are capable of arranging it.'

I dialled the number. 'You don't know me,' I said. 'But I have
slightly unusual request. We are producing a CD. Would you mi
if I bring Dudley Moore over and take his picture sitting on one
your planes?'

'No problem,' the female voice replied.

A few days later, Dudley put on his tuxedo. In exchange for ha
ing their photo taken with Dudley, and a small credit on the C
booklet, the owners of the Solberg Airport were more than cordi
We knew we needed some formal shots of Dudley sitting on one
the wings of the colourful old propeller plane. Once inside t

ngar, Dudley came to life. It was definitely the right environment.
e enjoyed the contrast of being in concert dress and precariously
ositioned on the wing of a plane. After a few shots looking happy,
e decided things were still too serious and wanted to take some
dditional shots lying down on one of the wings, looking startled, as
ough he was falling off the plane. We used that one on the back
ver of the CD.

ch day in the process of CD production was a small triumph, as
udley's timing and notes about the tiniest points in the music or
ords, once clarified, would find their way onto the typed version.
earing it all translated onto the first and second drafts of the
ited CD was exciting.

Most of the major work on the CD was completed. We were up
the third complete editing session, and Dudley was picking at
ny little details that nobody else would have heard. He would lis-
n over and over to the already edited commentary – most of it still
aking him laugh.

Every time he listened to his own story about filming *Bedazzled*
ith Peter Cook, he laughed aloud when describing his bedroom
ene with Raquel Welch. His comments were a prelude to the
unning music he had composed for the film. In his concert perfor-
ances year after year, he would tell the story before playing the
usic.

Describing the bedroom scene in detail, he would explain: 'I was
bed with her . . . That day I wore six pairs of Y-fronts – well, you
n't be too careful, can you, I mean, it was a very intimate
ene . . . She was resting, as it were, between takes – she was lying
1 the bed and I was in the bed and she put her hand down on my

knee and she looked at me very slowly and said, "My God – is that you?" I should have said yes, I did say yes as a matter of fact, but I had to explain that it was my knee – it was slightly less glamorous than what she thought she had landed on. Anyway to cut a long story short . . .' This always drew thunderous laughter from his audiences.

The wording of the story varied slightly, depending on the feed-back from his live audiences. Putting it on CD, he wanted it to be absolutely perfect. He went over the words again and again, cutting it to ramble less and have the right timing and the right punch.

'Stop,' he would say, always as though it was an emergency. I kept the remote control for the CD player in my hand. Previously a job Dudley would have taken on, but he was having trouble pressing the tiny little buttons and getting them right. He still loved his elevator buttons, but had made a big sacrifice in relinquishing these tiny buttons 'for the good of the project as a whole'. It was his job, but 'one step removed' and placed in my hands: 'You may be my deputy button-pusher.'

'Thank you,' I had replied. 'I'll try to do the job justice.'

He still thought of it as his job, and was frustrated having to issue orders. 'I need to hear that part again,' he would say. It was a delicate operation. If the button was pressed too hard, the CD would revert to the beginning of the track and the passage in question would be lost. We would have to go through it all over again to find the spot. Sometimes he would want to hear the same line four or five times because something wasn't quite right.

'There's a space that shouldn't be there,' he said. I hadn't heard it. 'Listen, an extra second or two.' He used the stopwatch, which proved he had been right. There had been two extra seconds, past the time of a normal pause. They had to be cut.

We were nearly finished with the final edits. Dudley was a little sad and didn't want to let go. He had loved working on the CD. We agreed to produce another CD a few months later, but by then he was having a lot more difficulty with everything.

The CD was released in the United States in 2000 and two years later by Cooking Vinyl in the UK.

22

HOW DID WE GET HERE?

THERE WAS ONE LAST trip to Los Angeles to go through Dudley's possessions after the house was sold. It was a difficult trip for Dudley. His balance was declining, and speaking was becoming increasingly difficult. His voice had been slurred for years, but now he would find he could not reply quickly enough. In a conversation, by the time he had formulated his thoughts and was ready to speak, the topic would have changed. For someone previously so quick, this was incredibly frustrating. Sometimes he would begin expressing an idea, but he would lose it halfway through, or his voice would trail away, or a word would be unrecognisable. His frustration would be apparent to anyone listening.

When Lou Pitt announced that he was putting on a party for him in spring 1999, Dudley was excited about once again seeing many of the Hollywood celebrities he had worked with in the past. But he was worried how he would communicate. 'What if it happens,' he began strongly, 'if I start talking and I'm in the middle of a sentence and . . . and–' He stopped abruptly. 'That's what will happen. My thought is gone for ever.' He was still struggling with the stigma, feeling weakened by having the condition. 'But I *want* to see them. Will they be able to understand this?'

He needn't have worried. His old friends and colleagues were there to support him, to remind him how much they loved him. Lou and Berta Pitt were gracious hosts, and wanted to do something special for Dudley. The evening was a reunion on more than one level – the Hollywood community is well accustomed to attending high-profile events, but this was different. They shared the warmth and delight of seeing Dudley, coupled with the unspoken sense of farewell that was in the air. Dudley sat in a big armchair – the 'place of honour', and embraced his old friends, one after another, among them Blake Edwards and Bo Derek, Paul Reiser, Raquel Welch, John Lithgow, Brooke Shields, Sugar Ray Leonard, Cate Blanchett, Nastassja Kinski, former girlfriend Susan Anton, Dudley's ex-wife Brogan Lane. Many others who had worked with him over the years. For some, who were suddenly faced with the reality of Dudley's condition, there were teary moments in another room where he couldn't see them. Bo Derek recalled her own feeling of 'anger, more than sadness' seeing the effect his condition had on him. 'It was so unfair,' she said. But she remembered the sense of support at the party. 'I remember all the women – he had a special thing with the girls. I didn't see him all that often, but when I did, it was really wonderful.'

There were strong words of encouragement at the party. The clinking of wine glasses, and humorous stories from past occasions. Laughter and tears. Each conversation was hard for Dudley – slow halting and, despite the smile on his face, there was his frustration at being a 'diminished version of my former self,' as he had once said when talking about the effects of his condition. It was a reunion that Dudley would speak about for a long time. He held Lou and Berta, a big hug of thanks, before leaving their home afterwards. Their friendship had always been close. The evening had been very special for him.

As we were ready to drive off, Dudley sat in the car and tried to put it all together in his mind. It was 'a wonderful, sad evening', he said, but he did not openly acknowledge that this was a farewell gathering. He was thankful that Lou had given the party in his honour. A few days later, he would leave Los Angeles for the last time.

In the meantime, there was still work to be done – decisions to be made; possessions to examine. And another event to attend – a Music For All Seasons musicale at the home of our board member Jan Turner Colburn, where Dudley once again took his presidential role seriously, encouragingly talking to the young musicians who were the guest artists for the evening.

We stayed at a hotel, and went back and forth to the Marina del Rey house, until Dudley found it all too depressing and asked me to finish the work of clearing it with Stacey Herman. Dudley knew there was no point in moving everything that was left in the Los Angeles house back to New Jersey, but he found it difficult to part with his belongings. Most challenging was the walk-in closet in his bedroom. It contained most of the clothing he had collected since the 1970s. Often, he kept costumes from his films; if they looked like everyday clothing he would adapt them as part of his wardrobe and wear them until they fell apart. He wanted to sort through it all himself, and sat on a chair inside the closet as we went through every piece of clothing, one by one, starting with yellow bellbottoms from the ancient past. At Dudley's insistence (two-hour rule suspended) we sat in the closet for two days, with time out to eat and sleep. Friends would drop by, bringing refreshments and commenting on the enormity of the job to be completed.

Occasionally Dudley would emerge from the closet, saying, 'I am now *coming out of the closet*,' expecting the laughter he would hear from anyone who was in earshot at that moment and had not previously heard the line at least twice.

With his weight having fluctuated over the years, he had trousers with waist sizes from 32 to 38. The clothing in his Marina del Rey closet was a veritable history of four decades of fashion, everything from the white leisure suits of his early Los Angeles period to the more conventional styles and dark colours he preferred. He wore boots that were custom made – a few pairs of smart leather boots, but (because of his club foot) mostly heavy and stable hiking-style boots, ordered in multiples. In the end, he eliminated only twenty-two pieces of clothing – anything torn, stained or obviously a size he would never repeat was placed in a large bag to be given away or thrown out. The rest was left in the closet to be packed and shipped by the movers. My comment – that if he hadn't worn it in five years he probably wouldn't wear it again – was not taken kindly. 'I'm reminded of a comment you once made about a pot and a kettle,' he said, using as evidence the fact that my closet still contained two items I had worn in junior high school.

His history was in that closet. He needed to keep nearly all of his clothing. 'I can always sell them as antiques,' he said. He already had a new wardrobe. He never wore any of the clothes he shipped back to New Jersey, but he liked knowing it was all nearby.

As with food, Dudley went through thematic periods with his clothing. A phase of wearing a particular style of clothing could last for months or years. He would purchase several the same, and would wear one of three identical dark brown tweed jackets with leather elbow patches, for example, over and over, along with one of several silk shirts in a deep maroon, grey or blue shade that he liked. Although his closet was filled with more clothes than he could wear, he would go to the same small area where he had identical shirts or jackets. Then, after a time, and for no apparent reason, the style would shift slightly. He liked to incorporate jackets from his films for two reasons – he would not have to go shopping, and he would be more easily recognised. As his condition declined, he wore ties that would be conversation pieces – one had a map of the London Underground (quite a novelty in America); another had Disney characters.

In clearing out the Marina del Rey house, the other dilemma was what to do with his large video collection. It included his own films, and historic videos that he had been collecting for years, among them many unopened sets ordered from late-night television advertising programmes. He had a large multi-video set on parenting and several sets on world history, with the shrink wrapping still intact. In addition, he had a huge collection of pornographic films that he had ordered, using his own name, from magazines and television shows. They had all been opened. He had previously selected a few to carry back to New Jersey, and this time left Stacey in charge of disposing of the rest. A big problem, as they couldn't be thrown into a dumpster or donated to charity – at least not one that we could think of. Stacey had to arrange for their destruction. Dudley did not really need to keep hundreds of these tapes, as he had painstakingly created a few composite tapes of the most arousing scenes from each video.

Dudley only occasionally watched the composite tapes in New Jersey. In the 'annex' he watched them on mute, but would sometimes press the wrong button. A few times, Elise (whose room was directly opposite his, across the hall) was awakened in the middle of the night by loud moaning sounds coming from the television in his room. The next morning, Dudley would always apologise profusely. 'I'm *so* sorry. I hope you weren't *offended*. I pressed the wrong button.' She would chuckle and assure him she hadn't been offended.

He never paid a formal farewell visit to his house – he just did not go back again. By the following spring, the move was well behind us. Dudley had been able to let go of his attachment to the Los Angeles house. When he spoke about the house, it was with fondness and good memories. He said leaving it behind had not been as traumatic as he had imagined. He had everything he needed in his smaller New Jersey space, and he was comforted being surrounded by the possessions he had always loved.

Having a busy and productive year, followed by another summer in Nova Scotia, helped Dudley to put some distance between his past and his present lives.

Dudley was happy when we had a lot of visitors there, and did his best to participate in whatever trips and activities were taking place. He also spent a lot of time resting in bed. Early one evening Brian, my sister Dot and I were watching a movie in the living room of the cottage in Nova Scotia. Dudley was trying to sleep, and eventually stormed out of his room, saying, 'Some people are trying to *sleep* here. Could you turn that down!'

I turned down the volume and Brian mumbled something about Dudley having slept all day. Normally Dudley would join us for films, so this wasn't a situation that arose often.

The following morning, we were all driving to Lunenburg to show my sister one of the most beautiful spots we knew in Nova Scotia. The tension in the car was thick. Dot was conversational and bubbly, but could not cut through Dudley's seething resentment. Over lunch, while Brian was in the lavatory, I asked Dudley what was wrong. 'It's Brian. He said he couldn't respect anyone who sleeps all day. I'm sick and I can't help it.'

'I didn't hear him say that, and I know he doesn't think that,' I said. 'He said you had slept all day – he wished you would have joined us in the living room; it wasn't an assault on your character – and I never heard him use the word "respect" at all.'

Brian had been irritated by Dudley's rude order to adjust the volume. When he came back to the table I suggested they try to work it through, but both were angry. Dudley repeated his complaint, and Brian said that, yes, he did have resentments, but his resentments had to do with Dudley having more of my time than he did. It would have been hard for anyone to argue with that. It was true, and not likely to change. Brian had every reason to be upset.

I was annoyed with Brian for his comments, although I understood he was being pushed to his limit and that the situation was troublesome. I thought that nobody else would have handled it as well as he did. Our lives were unravelling but we alternated between addressing the problems and trying hard to pretend everything was fine'.

Brian stood firm in supporting Dudley through his illness, in being his family. He loved him as a brother, and he wouldn't

abandon him no matter how difficult the situation became. Whe
Brian made a commitment there was no turning back. But our live
were strained, despite all our efforts to keep things light.

Still, at that moment we had a specific conflict in need of quic
resolution. 'That's not the issue,' I said. 'The issue is what happene
last night. Dudley is telling you how he felt about it – this is wha
you would want him to do, to tell you how he feels. Then you ca
tell him how you feel about that one specific issue – not everythir
else in the entire world that can't be resolved over lunch. You nee
to resolve this one issue before we leave here to go home.'

I was remembering Dudley's comments about women being i
charge, but letting men think they are in charge. I was sure the
knew they weren't in charge, not this time, and I wondered why
had to be ordering two supposedly grown men to fix a tiny littl
feud so that we could go home peacefully. There were bigger issue
that would never be resolved, and I knew we all had emotions tha
weren't fitting back into the neat little boxes from which they ha
escaped. All the lines of these relationships were blurred. I envie
people who could believe their lives were in order, their neatly pack
aged boxes tied up with coloured ribbon, the edges carefully curle
We had lost that ability a long time before this moment. Dudley ha
taught us well that real life is not always pretty.

We were at a table on the deck of a restaurant high up overlook
ing the pier, with all the tables practically on top of each other.
momentarily mused over why these things always had to be dis
cussed within earshot of other people, but I realised that was les
important than resolving the problem. Once they began talkin
about the specific issue, it was quickly settled.

'I would never have said I didn't respect you. I do respect you

Brian said, 'and I always have. I know you are struggling with a dreadful condition. I only got upset because I felt you were rude. You could simply have asked politely for the volume to be turned down.'

'Well I suppose I could have,' Dudley said. 'I was just lying there listening to it, and I didn't realise I had reached the point where I couldn't stand it any more.'

They both apologised. As we walked to the car, Brian turned to Dudley and said, 'So, do we still love each other?'

'Of course we do,' Dudley said. They laughed and hugged each other.

It was the only real argument they had ever had.

Dudley enjoyed having Dot in the cottage, and liked hearing progress reports on her enthusiastic landscaping work. As a fine artist, it had been her goal to spend time on the beach, painting, but that trip she found it more intriguing to explore the woods. Dot and Brian had been walking through the woods near the cottage one day when they heard a deep growl. It was one of the resident bears we knew to be our neighbours but had never seen.

Dudley wanted to see the bears. Whenever he was outside, he was looking for them, but they were stealthy, clever, non-confrontational black bears. We knew they were black bears – not grizzlies or brown bears – because black bears were native to the area and everyone else we knew around us had seen them, at least once. We were finding fresh bear prints in the sand on the beach every morning, but still no bear sightings. We knew, however, that they came out at night, stole our trash, had a picnic and went back into the woods.

Dudley and I spent a long time planning how we could spot the bears at night, finally determining that we would bait the garbage can with fish, set up the video-camera on a tripod near the kitchen window and take turns watching throughout the night. Since Dudley didn't sleep normal hours, he didn't consider it much of a problem to stay up at night. But when I mentioned this to my children in phone conversations, we were reprimanded by more than one of them, in Elise's words, for having 'absolutely no common sense, attempting to tangle with a dangerous wild animal, and not acting like mature adults'. We were *forbidden* to do it. Brian agreed with them. Dudley and I both thought they were being very unfair, but we cancelled the plan. I wondered when the tables had turned.

Just off the path to the beach was a beautiful area that had become overgrown. Dot took it as her mission to clear the area and turn it into a 'grove'. We watched as it was transformed from an overgrown tangle of branches to a beautiful spot suitable for elves and nymphs.

Dudley was impressed to hear about it and wanted to see it. Dot said she would lead the way down the path. We all followed, Dudley with his cane, Maurice, in one hand and Brian holding his other arm. As we came to a large moss-covered boulder that constituted the only danger spot on the path, Dot turned round to warn Dudley. 'Watch this spot. It's a little slippery here,' she said, miscalculating slightly and falling backwards over the rock she was warning him to avoid. Dudley was convulsed with laughter.

The last week of the summer, our cottage was transformed into a film studio. A crew from the BBC spent several days with Dudley and all of us talking about his music and his life. One of the highlights of the experience was a surprise they arranged. Dudley had omposed his first and only string quartet while a student at Magdalen College. He had not heard it played in many years, and with only a few weeks' notice the Halifax-based Blue Engine String Quartet learned the work.

The plan was to surprise Dudley by having the all-female quartet playing on the beach, with the rocks as a backdrop. It was to be the perfect tribute to Dudley – four lovely young women, long hair flowing in the breeze, playing his music.

Director Norman Stone pored over the Nova Scotia tide charts as though he were going to set sail. He had to set up the film session when the musicians could be near the rocks in low tide and not get washed out to sea. As Dudley had to rest every afternoon, the event had to be strategically timed so that he would be awake and it would be low tide at the same time.

Dudley was surprised and delighted when Graham Pass, one of the producers, located the score of the quartet and showed it to him during a lunch that was filmed for the broadcast. 'It's not simple,' Dudley said, looking at his score for the first time in many years, impressed by his own youthful exuberance and complexity as a composer. But he still had no clue that more was coming – that one afternoon during the week, he would be escorted onto the beach, and as he walked towards the rocks, accompanied by Brian, me, and our dog Alexander, Dudley would hear the distant strains of his String Quartet No. 1. Finally in full view of the group, he sat down on a large flat rock to hear the performance, incredibly moved.

Although the musicians were used to playing outdoors in the summer, and had secured their music on the stands, nobody had stopped to consider just how windy it could be on the beach. During one of the quartet movements the wind picked up and one by one

the music stands started to blow over. Norman came up with a sol
tion – a human solution. A couple of the BBC crew, led by Norma
stretched out on their bellies across the wet sand and held the mus
stands in position, while the cameraman filmed, taking care to kee
the camera a foot above ground level. Dudley chuckled over th
image for a long time. On the last day, Dudley and I flew back
New Jersey and the BBC crew came along to continue filming
home for a few days.

After the summer, Dudley's condition took another downturn. Th
crisis of Dudley's illness – his death sentence – had given him a
opportunity to change, to grow, to develop and to understar
himself to a degree he might not otherwise have reached witho
the pressure of a deadline. We were all changing, and too much
the middle of it to see it clearly. Our relationship had been stab
for many years, but unexpectedly came to a crisis point o
afternoon.

Just as things seemed ominously quiet, I had begun gettir
phone calls from friends who had seen a little item in a New Yor
newspaper's gossip column that had casually mentioned 'Dudl
Moore was living in New Jersey with his new girlfriend, pian
Rena Fruchter'. I was surprised that such an item should appear
print, and immediately phoned Brian to tell him about it, and of r
plans to write a note to the columnist setting the record straight.

I sent the columnist a lightly stated e-mail, noting that my hu
band and family were quite surprised to hear this news. I wonder
what his sources might have been. I immediately received a pho
call from the charming but embarrassed columnist, who claimed
would be firing his anonymous source. He wrote a correction a fe

days later, claiming that he had written the column in an 'eggnog-induced stupor'.

When I told Dudley about the incident, I laughed it off. It had not been the most incorrect item that had ever appeared about me in print. But Dudley was annoyed with me. 'I don't know why you are laughing about it. It isn't funny. Why would this be amusing to you?'

I had unintentionally hurt his feelings. 'Dudley, I didn't mean to be insensitive. I just thought putting in print that I'm your new girl-friend was funny. I wasn't implying that anybody could think *being* your girlfriend would be funny.' I wanted to say that it would be funny if he was being amusing, that there were various interpreta-tions of 'funny', but thought I should stop before making things worse.

He was stewing on it. 'Maybe if I weren't so ill it wouldn't be funny to you.'

He was way off track. 'It wasn't funny because of you or your con-dition or anything about you at all.' The word 'funny' was now dangerously close to 'going funny' on me.

'You don't get it, do you?' he said. 'I hate being in second place. Why do I have to be in second place? You and I *connect*. That's what's important – just that we connect.'

'Oh damn.' I hadn't wanted to hear it. I knew it was the wrong reply, but it had jumped right off my tongue. 'Brian and I love each other, and Brian would probably say he feels like he's the one in sec-ond place. And you've always said you felt so close to Brian – that he was like the brother you never had.'

'He is – just like my brother, only a lot bigger. I know he cares about me. He would understand.'

'Why are you telling me this now?' I asked.

'Because you laughed at me. Because you are incredibly naïve. Because life floats by in a little cloud just above your head, and for all your *intellect*, you haven't much of a clue what's really going on.'

'I'm sorry I laughed.' I hated the idea that people could write things about me without knowing my situation at all. 'I used to be a classical pianist . . . and a semi pseudo-intellectual music writer. I worried about whether there was a meaningful amount of tension in a dominant seventh chord before it resolved into the tonic. Now look at me – I'm in gossip columns and tabloids. And you – you're telling me I don't know what's going on.' I was on a tangent that really had nothing to do with the conversation, and he had stopped listening a minute earlier. Or so I thought.

'And what the *hell* is a semi pseudo-intellectual music writer – is that like a semi partially pseudo self-deprecating comment? You wouldn't let me get away with that, would you?' he asked. I opened my mouth to reply but didn't have a chance.

'And I went from one relationship to another because I couldn't *merge* with anyone. I was damaged. I was searching because my emotions were homeless. But with you—' He just stopped speaking. He wasn't going to finish the thought. It was a dominant seventh chord that was *never* going to resolve comfortably into the tonic, but would remain hovering in midair.

I finished his sentence. 'I know that we've merged. There's no barrier between us. This is all about lifelong friendship – closeness and trust.'

'And music, and love,' he said.

'But there's all the rest of my life, and you're an important part of that too, apart from *us* – not that we can really separate one part from the other.'

'I think you should leave Brian. I would take better care of you.'

I was out of words. We both were. There was nowhere to go, and I was watching the walls closing in on me. I wondered how they were doing that. I had been struggling to maintain the illusion that everything was *fine*, and I had liked the illusion.

More importantly, I knew that life was closing in on Dudley, and he didn't want to die alone. He was frightened of everything, particularly the big unknown that death represented for him. He had always had one eye on the hands of his watch, one ear on the ticking of the clock. The hands of all the clocks in Dudley's room were turning faster and faster, at a dizzying pace, and the ticking was so loud it was deafening. He wanted my help to slow it all down. He wanted to be saved from death. As close as Dudley felt to Brian and every member of my family, at that moment he wasn't thinking of my family.

I tried to take his hand and he pulled away. We barely spoke for two days. Every time I saw him, he was angry and turned away. Then, over a tub of gourmet chocolate mousse, he softened and began to talk slowly, determined to get through all the words. 'I didn't mean to upset you,' he said, stopping to think. 'I just wanted you to know how I felt – that's all. What you do with the information, that's up to you. I understand that – and I understand your complicated life, and all your children and grandchildren . . . and *husband*, and so forth and so on. But how I *feel*, that's up to *me*. You taught me to figure it out. You said I need to know how I really feel, and get stuff off my chest – not keep it inside as I always did – festering like an ugly, disgusting, oozing, greenish-tinged, pus-filled wound that will ultimately be compelled to burst and contaminate everything in the vicinity.' He stopped to admire his imagery, and chuckled at the way he had said it. It had taken a very long time to get all the words out, but he had spoken up and was pleased with himself.

This was a powerful and important time in our friendship, a turning point and a major transitional moment for Dudley. I knew that Dudley did not really expect me to pack my bags and move next door. He knew that things could not change. But he needed to identify and to say how he felt, what our friendship was all about, how much we meant to each other, and what it felt like for him, so simply, to *connect*. It was the final piece that had been brewing and left unsaid for a long time. It was reassuring to know he must have felt safe enough to do that. For the first two difficult days, I had worried our friendship would be damaged, but it was only strengthened by the fact that, now, nothing was left unsaid.

I felt inspired by Dudley to be more open, to address the challenges in all our lives as directly as possible; it seemed easier to communicate with him. The situation was no less complex, but the tensions eased. Dudley was able to settle back into the feather pillow my family represented for him. He was part of something big, and comforting.

23

TRIBUTE IN CARNEGIE HALL

DUDLEY WAS SLOWING DOWN. All of his daily activities were more difficult than they had been. He had more care at home, and we had begun the search for a live-in medical aide, which Dudley had resisted because of the expense.

Dudley was trying to keep in touch with friends and family. He phoned his sister Barbara, although not regularly. He had spoken with his son Patrick a few months earlier. Patrick had phoned him on Father's Day in June, and Dudley was happy to hear from him. They spoke for a while, and agreed that they would meet when Patrick, who was in California, was next in New York. Patrick had spent seven months in a treatment programme for young adults, dealing with his emotional and psychological problems, and had previously contacted Dudley in an effort to mend fences. Dudley wanted to be sure Patrick was doing OK, but was having trouble taking the initiative to make contact with him. He was still resentful of the fact that Patrick had moved into Nicole's house for a time after the divorce and he believed Patrick had sided with her. Nevertheless, he wanted to help his son.

Dudley's official story was that he did not want his sons to see him in a declining condition, but the facts were a lot more complicated. His relationship with Patrick had been strained for many years. His relationship with Nicholas had never been properly established, and he did not want to tangle with Nicole in order to see Nicholas. Each year at Christmas he arranged for gifts to be sent to Nicholas, but he did not acknowledge either of his sons' birthdays. He had spoken publicly of his difficulties in being a father, and he would receive letters from complete strangers telling him how they had re-established their own broken parent–child relationships. But it was all too much for Dudley, he said. He was not optimistic that even his best efforts in this area would be fruitful. He regularly asked other people to check up on Patrick. Dudley knew that Tom Leahy, his former housekeeper in California, took Patrick into his home for a short time and was trying to help him find work. Dudley would ask me to phone and find out where Patrick was and what he was doing. Then he would listen carefully to all the details.

'What about seeing him?' I asked every time.

'That's a good idea, but I want to think about it. We'll do it later.' For a while, Patrick had stayed with his maternal grandmother in California. After her death, he began moving again, from one location to another. The tabloid press picked up on one episode, reporting that Patrick was living in his car. It might have been true, and it served to make Dudley feel doubly guilty for a situation he couldn't repair. He gave Patrick money from time to time, but it never solved the problem. A few weeks before his death he had made the decision to help Patrick get into an apartment and get therapy and the help he needed. He planned to set up the long-awaited meeting.

Dudley's daily ritual of talking on the phone was becoming more frustrating for him as people asked him to repeat almost every sentence. In person it was possible to know what he was trying to say, but over the phone it was not.

His friend Else Blangsted knew these phone conversations were upsetting Dudley and suggested that instead of Dudley feeling obliged to talk to her, she would read to him. Else had turned eighty and realised that Dudley would probably not be able to keep his part of their old agreement that he would not die first. Despite Else's intense dislike of flying, she had come to visit him several times in New Jersey, staying at his home. She made a point of visiting on his birthday several years in a row, and she had another trip planned in the spring 2001 to celebrate Dudley's birthday privately at Barbetta in New York, still his first choice of all restaurants. He had not wavered in this loyalty for thirty years.

Else had established a weekly phone call with Dudley at noon on Wednesday. Unlike some of Dudley's friends, Else refused to pretend she knew what he was saying. She would ask him to repeat the words as slowly and clearly as possible. 'I don't want to insult him by agreeing with something I haven't understood,' she said to me. 'I told him it was a combination of my eighty-year-old ears and his trouble speaking.' Dudley was pleased Else had taken part of the responsibility. 'I'm a Jewish mother. I'm used to taking the blame,' said Else.

They had been friends since 1982, when Else was music editor for the film *Six Weeks*, for which Dudley wrote the music and played a leading role. They had maintained an uninterrupted friendship, Dudley visiting Else when she lived in Switzerland for several years, and expressing relief when she finally moved back to California.

Else's powerful story had impressed Dudley. As a sixteen-year-old in pre-Nazi Germany she had given birth to a baby girl. Her family informed her that the baby had died at birth, and Else mourned her baby, later marrying the baby's father and producing a daughter whom they raised together in California. When Else was sixty-four, she got a phone call from a woman in Switzerland who had been searching for her for many years. It was the daughter Else's family had told her she had lost at birth nearly half a century earlier.

After several phone calls cut short by Dudley's frustration and Else's inability to understand his words, she said that starting the following Wednesday, she would read to him.

'That's a wonderful idea,' he said.

'What would you like me to read?' Else asked.

'Dickens,' he replied.

'Which book?' Else asked.

'*A Tale of Two Cities*.'

Else was surprised. 'It's the saddest of all Dickens.'

'Yes, it is,' he replied.

For months, he would look forward to the weekly phone calls. Else confessed that she rehearsed her 45-minute readings before phoning Dudley. 'The last thing he needs in his condition is to hear bad reading,' she said.

Else suggested to Dudley that he might also enjoy books on tape in the intervening days, but he refused to even consider it. He wanted to hear her live dramatic readings. He wanted to hear her voice, even if his own ability to reply was limited.

They never got to the end of *A Tale of Two Cities*. Dudley knew it was impossible, and that had been part of his reason for suggesting the book. He did not like things to end.

Dudley had kept a low profile for a couple of years – a more private life than he had known in a long time. Starting with the Barbara Walters interview, he was catapulted back into the spotlight. Instead of the negative profiles that had taken place for the previous few years, he was once again the respected Dudley Moore. There were several major landmarks on the horizon, all designed to celebrate Dudley's life and his work. While they were all of an extremely positive nature, and Dudley was enthusiastic about each one, he was also well aware that these events were celebrating his life and career in retrospect, the silent undercurrent being that there was nothing more to come. Dudley craved each celebration, but was well aware of the finality.

Dudley took a major role in assembling a Carnegie Hall tribute, openly communicating all of his requests for the programme.

Several of his birthdays had been celebrated in grand style – two had been public events in Carnegie Hall. In 1997, we had managed to rent the hall on his actual birthday. Dudley had performed at every Music For All Seasons event that took place at Carnegie Hall. It was time to turn the tables and for others to do a live performance paying tribute to Dudley. He loved the idea, and the entertainment community offered to help. It was a good way to honour Dudley for the joy he had brought to so many people, and to raise funds for two charities that were important to him. Plans were put into motion for a major New York tribute in April 2001.

Barbara Walters agreed to host the evening, and members of the Hollywood community were ready to participate. The evening was to be presented by Music For All Seasons, with the proceeds shared between MFAS and Dudley's research fund for PSP. Tony Adams, who had produced *10* twenty-two years earlier, agreed to help produce the evening.

A brilliant producer, Tony knew exactly what was needed to pull the event together. With Carnegie Hall finally reserved for 16 April – three days before Dudley's sixty-sixth birthday – all the potential performers who had been on the 'maybe – I'll have to check my schedule' list were suddenly available. Everything was set into motion for a gala production whose preparation would occupy us for the next few months.

This was a lot more than a production to Tony, who had a strong respect and tremendous affection for Dudley. The feeling was mutual. For Tony, it was a labour of love, and he didn't mind volunteering his time and working day and night for several months.

'I had always held a suspicion that Dudley felt unloved and under-appreciated,' said Tony Adams. 'I don't think he had any idea how much his peers and those around him loved, admired and respected him. I find elaborate memorial services and eulogies to be very nice, but somewhat of a waste. How much better for the person to leave this world with all of that information. Here was a chance for those of us to express these sentiments to this gifted man trapped by a cruel disease.'

The tribute was entitled *A Man for All Seasons*. Violinist Robert Mann, with whom Dudley had been close for many years, agreed to participate in the programme, even though Dudley had not been in touch with him for several years. He refused to hold a grudge, and said he now understood why Dudley's medical condition, and, previously, his marriage to Nicole, had stood in the way of their friendship.

We launched the tribute with a New York party several months ahead hosted by Sir Tom Harris, the British Consul General to New York. David Tait, a Music For All Seasons board member and at that time an executive with Virgin Atlantic Airways, made the introduction to Harris. An elegant event with Dudley, Julie Andrews and Bo Derek as the guests of honour served to introduce the upcoming tribute to patrons and supporters.

So many of Dudley's former colleagues wanted to participate that the cast of the tribute was changing up to the day of the performance, with the final draft of the programme printed that morning. Performers flew in from Britain and California. Eric Idle, Tony Randall, John Ritter, Chevy Chase, Bo Derek, Lauren Bacall, Mary Tyler Moore, Cleo Laine and John Dankworth, Jill Eikenberry, Michael Tucker, Anne Runolfsson, and the entire cast of *Blast!*, who opened their tribute with a rendition of *Bolero*. Christopher Cross arrived at the last minute from LA to perform the theme from *Arthur*. Chris Karan and Peter Morgan flew in from London and recreated the Dudley Moore trio, with pianist Benny Green filling in for Dudley. Eric Idle and Jimmy Fallon teamed up to perform Dudley's favourite skit, 'One-legged Tarzan'. Most of the performers were there because they had been inspired by Dudley, or had a strong connection to him. We almost lost Barbara Walters when ABC-TV threatened to whisk her out of the country for a broadcast, but she stood firm and showed her devotion to Dudley, postponing the trip and giving a remarkable introduction to the evening.

Robert Mann put together a quartet to play two movements o
Dudley's String Quartet No. 1. At Dudley's request, my son Joe
took the role of cellist. Robert asked Miranda Cuckson, his studen
at the Juilliard School, to play second violin, and violist Toby Appe
completed the quartet. Dudley was eager to hear his music played
and also participated in selecting the music for a new medley
arranged by Harvey Cohen and scored for piano and string quartet
Dudley said he would attend the rehearsal at Robert's home in New
York. He was pleased to hear the new medley, drawn in part from
his *Six Weeks* score and from *Songs Without Words*, and he wa
impressed by the group's performance, suggesting only a few mino
changes.

Dudley was particularly happy that two movements of his strin
quartet would have their New York premiere, after being played o
the beach in Nova Scotia only a few months earlier. Dudley recalled
writing the work in a very short time – two weeks – saying it was 'a
unbelievably grotesque amount of time' for such a lengthy work. He
remembered the last movement as his favourite. Tony Randal
would introduce the work in Carnegie Hall.

Dudley asked if I would play the piano part in the new medley, a
well as for a Beethoven spoof entitled 'The Green Green Grass o
Delilah' that he had written years earlier and performed many time
himself. At first, I was hesitant, as organising the event was enough
to do.

'I want you to play it,' he said simply.

'I haven't been practising much,' I explained.

'I know that, and I'm wondering why that is the case,' he said. '
think I know why, but I want you to tell me.'

I had never verbalised the reason. Having little time was not th real reason. I was concerned that my playing would remind Dudley of his loss. I didn't really want to say it to him, but I had to.

'I thought it would make you feel sad,' I said.

'That's exactly what I thought. But it's the opposite. I would like to hear you play. It would make me feel *better*.'

Somehow, Dudley got it into his head that he was going to die on the day of his Carnegie Hall tribute. For months, every time he spoke to Suzy Kendall by phone, he informed her that he was going to 'expire' on the day of the tribute. Finally, he confessed to me that he thought it would be a very dramatic way to make his exit from the world. That day, he would have friends and colleagues gathered around him. They would sing his praises and toast his contributions. It would all have been said and done. Then, at the end of the evening, he could simply die. He was not planning to kill himself — he just expected it would mysteriously occur on that day.

After the tenth time of listening to Dudley tell her this disturbing prediction by phone, Suzy told him that she had no intention of coming to New York in April if he was planning to die. 'I'll just come and visit you later,' she said.

'All right. I'll see you later then,' he replied.

Although Dudley was eagerly anticipating the tribute, and was involved in many aspects of the production, including selecting the menu for the post-concert dinner, April 2001 could easily have felt to Dudley like the end. He had already said goodbye to Hollywood and this tribute was another big production, pulling together his whole life's work. It was a reminder that, although everyone could celebrate his past achievements, his future was bleak. A dramatic end would have been fine with him.

On the day of the event, Dudley was in the care of a young nursing student our MFAS intern, Kosha Lerwick, had introduced to us. Matthew Hutchinson had been interviewed by Dudley and Dudley's medical aide, Peter Clarke, and both liked him. Matthew was in charge of helping Dudley with meals and getting him ready for the evening.

An hour before the tribute, we gathered all the stars of the evening backstage as a surprise to meet with Dudley and take photos. There were some who had been to Lou's party in Los Angeles, and many others Dudley hadn't seen for years; he was overwhelmed by the turnout. A large birthday cake had been arranged backstage, and the press snapped away until it was almost time for the tribute to begin. Because of some Carnegie Hall regulations, there would have been a $2,500 fee to eat the cake (security guards were assigned to watch it), so it was saved for the post-concert dinner at the hotel. Dudley asked why he couldn't 'have his cake and eat it too'.

During the tribute, a camera focused on Dudley, who was seated in a box on the left side of the hall, between Karen and Elise. One Hollywood reporter said that Dudley was seated between his two daughters, and they looked proud enough for anyone to have thought that. Not so pleased with the timing of her own production, Ruth had given birth to her second daughter late the previous night and missed the tribute.

Occasionally the audience would get to see Dudley's reaction, as his face was shown on the large screen above the stage. It had been set up to project a short video montage of Dudley's films, and film clips that were introduced by his co-stars. Dudley had agreed that a camera could occasionally focus on him as well and project his face onto the screen. His hilarious Tesco ads, 'searching for chickens', never seen in the United States, were shown in short clips throughout the evening. There were also video tributes from a few of Dudley's old friends who were unable to attend. John Cleese, Julie Andrews and Robin Williams had filmed their messages.

In her filmed message, Julie Andrews looked right up at Dudley in his box, explaining that she couldn't be there because she was 'in sheer terror . . . rehearsing for a live broadcast of the play *On Golden Pond* with Christopher Plummer.' 'Being your on-screen "wife" in *10*,' she said, was 'one of the most cherished experiences of my life.' To a big laugh from both Dudley and the audience, she added, 'And I'm quite proud of the fact that, unlike others I might mention, *our* separation didn't cost you one penny.'

Dudley had always loved the 'Tarzan' skit, and while Eric Idle willingly agreed to play Peter Cook's role, finding someone to play Dudley's part as a one-legged man auditioning for the role of Tarzan, was not an easy task. Dudley had played the part many times, hopping, with his left leg tied up.

Dudley had often quoted both his and Peter's lines from the skit.

'And yet you, a unidexter, are applying for the role.'

'Right,' Dudley would reply.

'A role for which two legs would seem to be the minimum requirement.' [In his recitations, Dudley would always cut to the punchline.] 'Your right leg I like . . . A lovely leg for the role. That's what I said when I saw you come in. I said, "A lovely leg for the role." I've got nothing against your right leg. The trouble is – neither have you.'

Candidates for the role in Carnegie Hall were dropping off like

flies. Chevy Chase, who was scheduled to speak and play the pia
for the tribute, had intended to join Idle for the skit, but had to co
fess to knee troubles that would prevent him from meeting t
physical demands of the role. Chase was very disappointed, b
instead of the skit, he played a jazz piece, *Alice in Wonderland*. 'I w
delighted I got through it. It was a tribute to Dudley's sense of ha
mony, lyricism in jazz. Dudley had a great effect on my playing,'
said.

At the eleventh hour, the young comedian Jimmy Fallon, one
the stars of *Saturday Night Live*, stepped in and saved the 'Tarzan' sk
Eric recalled being inspired by Dudley, and *Beyond the Fringe*, a
wanted to become a comedian. Jimmy Fallon was impressed by t
setting and company. For both, it was a big responsibility perform
ing the skit with Dudley in the audience.

Jill Eikenberry remembered 'one extraordinary moment wh
onstage'. She was reading the script Larry Gelbart had written,
tribute to Dudley. 'I got up there, and was really scared – a mome
of consternation and pause as I realised "I'm in Carneg
fuckinghall!" Then I read something funny and saw Dudley's l
smile projected on the screen behind me. He had sensed my fear
he had been worried . . . then proud of me.'

Dudley was extremely touched by Cleo Laine and Jo
Dankworth. Among Cleo's selections was 'Before Love Went O
of Style', a piece written by Dudley and a work she and Dudley h
performed many times in the past.

At the end of the evening, the audience gave the entire cast, a
then Dudley, a standing ovation. Dudley pulled himself up, holdi
onto the balcony railing. Then he motioned to the audience to ke
the applause coming. There was, of course, nothing wrong with l

nse of humour. He went back to the hotel, where 500 people,
cluding all the stars of the evening, attended the celebration din-
r. Dudley rested for an hour, then Brian wheeled him downstairs
time for his birthday cake to be cut. Dudley said that the entire
ening had been an incredible experience for him.

Although we knew how much Dudley had appreciated the work
at had gone into the tribute, it was hard for him to say so. Hard
cause of the limitations imposed by his condition, and hard
cause these expressions had always been a problem. Tony under-
ood. 'I'm aware that Dudley, as with most of his other feelings, had
ard time expressing thanks. When I saw him after the tribute and
looked at me with tears in his eyes and pointed at me in a scold-
g fashion, it was the greatest thanks that I could ever receive. He
as reprimanding me for making him vulnerable, and grateful for it.
he evening had gotten him . . . and that was the point!

'I felt incredibly grateful that I could play a part in this gift to
m. It was a demonstration of love and tenacity winning out over
ld business and big money. I take great solace in the fact that it
as a bright spot in those last dark days of his life,' Tony said.

24

ICE CREAM AND
ERROLL GARNER

TRAVELLING HAD BECOME DIFFICULT but there were still places Dudley wanted to see. Knowing that something had to be placed on the calendar following the Carnegie Hall tribute, Brian and I began discussing what to do. We thought a cruise would be a good way for Dudley to travel without the usual hassles. As we were thinking of a summer cruise, Brian, who dislikes cruising, preferred to open up the cottage in Nova Scotia after another winter; once again, it seemed a fair trade.

By the time the cruise was arranged, Dudley knew that he was to receive a CBE, and planned to go to England during the fall season. The cruise was no longer the final event on his schedule.

Dudley had greeted the idea of a cruise with enthusiasm; the trip was to take us from New York to Bermuda for one week. His suitcase was on the floor, ready to go, a week ahead; it was stuffed to overflowing, but remained unzipped for the daily addition of extra items. 'I almost played on a cruise once, but we couldn't agree on the terms,' he said. Similarly, a couple of years earlier, Dudley had been invited to discuss his film career with the audience on a cruise, but after he announced his condition the offer was immediately withdrawn.

The cruise line arranged VIP treatment, and whisked Dudley through the normally long check-in procedure. With his condition fairly advanced, he needed a doctor's note to be allowed on board and to obtain medical insurance.

Dudley was glad Matthew agreed to come along. In the short time he had spent with him, he had warmed to Matthew, a lanky 22-year-old with a great sense of humour. Since the Carnegie Hall tribute, Matthew had graduated from nursing school with honours, and had amply demonstrated that he was both bright and practical. He had never cared for anyone in Dudley's condition, but had asked a lot of questions, learned quickly and listened closely to everything that Dudley said.

He waited for Dudley to make the decisions, no matter how long it took for him to get the words out. Knowing that Matthew was religious, Dudley kept his curse words to a bare minimum. Matthew was completely unaffected by Dudley's celebrity status. This was good for Dudley, who found it easy to be under Matthew's care.

Matthew had done a good job of helping Dudley in New York in April and was pleased to be invited to go on the cruise, his first trip outside the United States. He was to take the day shift, with blocks of time off to explore on land when the ship was in Bermuda, or when Dudley was resting during the day. He had his own cabin, and Dudley and I shared a two-room suite, one of two presidential suites on board. My room was connected, and close enough to hear Dudley if he needed help during the night.

On the third morning, I heard childish giggling outside and opened the door of the suite to find two young boys, about eight and ten years old, standing there. They looked like brothers. They had obviously been there for a while, but had been scared to knock. They were a little startled when I opened the door. It was 9:30 and we were having breakfast in the room. The two boys were polite and looked very curious.

'Excuse me. We've just been wondering something,' one of the boys said.

'Wondering what?' I asked. Dudley was on the sofa a few feet behind me, eating scrambled eggs and hash brown potatoes, and drinking freshly squeezed orange juice.

'Wondering who is in the . . . presidential suite. Is the *President* really in there?' the younger boy asked.

'No, not the President,' I said. I almost laughed, but the boys were so serious. 'Just us,' I added.

'Oh,' the other one replied. 'Are you just . . . regular people?'

'Well, I suppose we are,' Dudley said before I had a chance to answer. 'I've never thought of it that way before. I like that . . . just regular people.'

'May we see the presidential suite, please?' one of the boys asked. They were still standing at the door.

'Sure, come on in,' Dudley said. 'I'm Dudley. Who are you?'

They introduced themselves. They had no idea who Dudley was, but were very impressed by the suite. I gave them the grand tour of the two rooms.

'Wow!' they both said.

'You've got two whole rooms,' the younger boy said to Dudley. 'We've only got one room, not as big as this one. You are so lucky. Are you rich?'

'Well, I've got *some* money,' he said. 'I wouldn't say I'm rich.'

'You're not supposed to ask that,' the big brother said. 'It's not polite.'

'Oh . . . I'm sorry,' the boy said.

'That's quite all right,' Dudley said. 'Would you like some chocolate?' There was a perpetually filled bowl on the table. They each took one. Dudley did too.

'Neat. A wheelchair,' the younger boy said, looking at the chair folded in a corner of the room. 'My grandfather uses one too.'

They headed for the door, and I opened it. They had been in the suite about ten minutes. Dudley was smiling. Something about their visit had made him feel good.

'Thanks for stopping by,' he said. They both thanked us, and left running down the hall as I closed the door.

'Nice to be that age,' Dudley said. 'At the beginning of life instead of the end,' he added, slightly wistful but without any hint of sadness. It was just an observation.

That evening, for the first time, Dudley wanted to go to the dining room for dinner. We had been assigned a table for three, but Matthew and I had taken turns eating dinner there, so that Dudley wouldn't be alone in his room. Dudley began getting dressed and slipped on his jacket; he was impatient for Matthew to tie his shoes. He sat patiently through every course of the formally served dinner, not complaining too bitterly about the musicians playing a few feet from our table.

'We've heard worse, haven't we?' he said very softly.

'Yes, we certainly have,' I replied.

Eating had always been among the great pleasures in Dudley's life, and was now one of his biggest struggles. As with most of his symptoms, there was an element of unpredictability. Sometimes the food would go down without a problem. Other times, it wouldn't go down, or he would cough and choke. He could no longer eat foods with a hard or chewy texture. Some PSP patients progress to a diet of thickened liquids, using a specially designed powder so that even coffee is thick. To Dudley, the idea was horrible.

Dudley was afraid of choking to death. He was sure that would be his fate, and every time he began to cough, he was frightened. His panic served to make things worse, and whoever was with him at that moment had to rub his back and remind him to relax and breathe through his nose. Invariably the coughing would stop and he would be OK.

Dudley was very diligent about taking his medication. Somebody was always on hand to help him take the pills. In the face of loud complaints, control of his medication had been taken away from him some months earlier, when he had inadvertently doubled a dose. As his finger dexterity declined, he reluctantly accepted the help. Dudley had always been very precise about medication – taking it on schedule, ordering it from the pharmacy before it ran out, doling it out to himself with obsessive precision. Giving up control was hard for him, particularly since nobody else had it timed to the minute the way Dudley did.

One evening halfway through the cruise, it was time for Dudley's 11 p.m. medication. He had already been asleep for several hours and I heard him from the other room, true to tradition, about to get up without asking for help. I looked through and saw that he was going to grab an unbolted chair for support. I took what I imagine must have been a ludicrous-looking flying leap into the other room. Dudley, still half asleep, was startled, but began laughing.

I caught him just as he was about to lose his balance, and he held onto me, apparently thankful I had turned up at that moment. 'Let me help you with those pills,' I said. I took out one of the smaller pills and put it in his left hand, which he was already holding out, palm up. I helped him to take three steps backwards and we sat on the edge of the bed. The boat was rocking more than usual. He took the pill with his right hand, thumb and forefinger, very carefully, and put it in his mouth. I handed him the juice and he took a sip. He tried to swallow and it wouldn't go down. He struggled and started to become very frightened. I could hear the liquid gurgling in his throat and his eyes were wide. I rubbed his back and told him to breathe through his nose. The gurgling sounds and his panic were continuing. I had never seen anyone choking, but I knew this was it. This was the moment we had feared.

'We've got to get help,' I said. I tried not to let him know how scared I was. I turned and reached over to pick up the phone. He grabbed my arm and was trying hard to stop me. But his eyes were wide and he was hardly getting any air. He was gurgling and gasping for breath. He held onto my arm with all his strength and wouldn't let me pick up the phone. I was terrified that he wasn't getting any air. Finally, the blockage cleared. I heard him swallow and breathe. He was OK.

There were tears in his eyes, and he was frozen in fear, not of the moment that had just passed, but of the future. Since his diagnosis, he had been terrified of the thought that one day he would die just that way – that he would start to choke and that nothing could be done. He was ready to let it happen so he wouldn't have to keep worrying about it. 'It's too hard,' he said. 'My time is up. Just let it be over.' I turned back and held him tightly. He was shaking from the experience, and taking long, deep breaths. Neither of us spoke for a long time. Slowly, I got up. He pulled me back down next to him. 'Don't leave me,' he said. 'Stay with me until I'm asleep.'

For the first time it was entirely clear that the end was coming. Perhaps a few months, a year, but not much longer. We both knew it – it was clearer than it had ever been before. Clearer than any doctor could have explained it. His death sentence was right there in the room with us, staring us both in the face – it might as well have been in flashing lights – and Dudley was more scared than I could have imagined. So was I. There was no way that I could imagine a time without him. Our lives were completely intertwined. Yet we were standing out there, close to the edge of an unbearable precipice. There were only a few steps left, and Dudley was about to jump off the edge.

There were only a few days left on the ship. The time had passed quickly with no further incidents. Dudley bounced back from the choking episode, and I wondered if he felt the need to do more, feel more, live more – to do everything he could to postpone his death. His actions were showing that he was feeling the pressure of time. Dudley was going out more, attending all the shows in the theatre. 'Ever the optimist,' he said one evening when the show was, finally, excellent. 'There's my epitaph.' He was musing on it, not dwelling on it as something morbid. 'Better than "Life's a Bitch, Then You Fucking Die".' He laughed.

After the cruise, I had arranged to be in Nova Scotia with Brian and planned to return to New Jersey after a couple of weeks to collect Dudley and bring him back to the cottage. First, Brian and I needed time together. All the stresses were taking their toll on both of us, and Brian and I had barely seen each other for weeks – not just the week of the cruise; the previous weeks, after the Carnegie Hall event, had been extremely busy. I wanted to get back to the piano and knew the green upright in the cottage was calling my name.

I had only been in Nova Scotia for a few days when Dudley said he hated being at home and wanted to come north. His aide, Peter, was with him during the day, and we had hired a new person for the night shift. Elise was there as well.

'I need to be there with you and Brian *now*,' he said.

'You know that we are worried about your safety in the house and we're looking for someplace close by.' (We had installed grab bars and bars in the shower, and we had a wheelchair ramp to the front door, but it wasn't enough.)

'I know that.'

'Will it be OK with you?'

'Yes,' he said. 'I would rather be in the house, but I understand why.'

During the months we had been away, our friend and owner of a restaurant in Port Mouton had built five vacation cottages for rental, one of them handicapped-accessible. Having two bedrooms, a kitchen and bathroom, all set up for easy wheelchair use, a ramp to the door and a small deck with a good view of the water, it was the perfect setting for Dudley.

Matthew agreed to accompany Dudley for the first week of the trip. We hired a head nurse and her two associates to rotate shifts and stay with him. He could not be alone at all, yet even with 24-hour care from a diligent nursing staff, he would still try to get out of bed without help, and would fall. He required the support of another person in order to walk. All agreed that it was best for his circulation to keep walking indoors, reserving the wheelchair for trips outside. Dudley wanted to be in charge, and would pick the moment one of his nurses turned around, or blinked, to get up from the bed or chair – and fall down.

Now, with his condition declining further, his legs were stiff and his sense of balance almost non-existent. Though he could see, his slowed eye movements meant focusing was a problem. Reading was frustrating and he usually wouldn't attempt it because of the extreme effort it required.

Since the rental cottage was a short drive from our place, it was easy to see Dudley many times each day, to take him out with us and bring him back to our place for meals or visits.

A couple of days after Dudley's arrival, we were having dinner with our friends Gwen and John Hall when the phone rang. It was Matthew, informing us that he was on the way to the emergency room with Dudley. He had been choking on something and Matthew called the rescue squad. By the time they arrived, the blockage had cleared, but they felt Dudley should be checked to make sure his oxygen level was adequate.

We left our dinners on the table, jumped in the car and all went to the tiny Liverpool General Hospital, where Dudley was already admitted to the emergency room under one of his assumed names. He was OK but exhausted from the experience. We confirmed that he was responsive and able to speak, and with all the visitors on hand had not yet begun his now familiar hospital dementia.

The doctor immediately recognised Dudley, and we asked if [] could make sure the press would not get wind of this news. [] knew it would be international news if word got out.

'We keep a very low profile here,' the doctor said. He was exam[] ining Dudley's legs, and smiling. 'But if you are trying to stay out [] the press, you shouldn't be advertising your status,' he said direc[] to Dudley.

'What do you mean?' I asked.

'Well, you only have to look at his socks to see he's a celebrity.'

We all looked down and everyone, including Dudley, laugh[] aloud. Each of his socks had the word 'Celebrity' in large letters [] the cuff. Dudley had been wearing the socks from our cruise – [] the Celebrity Cruise Line.

We were all looking forward to a visit from Suzy and Elodie. We h[] arranged for them to stay in one of the cottages adjacent to Dudle[] and Dudley began preparing for their visit. Instead of staying in [] dressing gown, he practised getting up, getting dressed, putting [] his shoes and going out – anywhere we could persuade him to [] Sometimes he would go to the supermarket with Brian and me – [] would take the wheelchair and go round every aisle of the store, g[] ing Dudley a chance to select whatever he wanted to take back.

Or we would ride round inside the video store and select clas[] movies. They were always available – five films for five days, a to[] of $5 Canadian (£2). Usually we had to take ten films home. Dud[] was in charge of the selection. If he picked the film, he would wat[] it. If somebody else made the selection, he was less likely to watch[]

His weight was declining again. We were able to persuade h[] that he no longer needed to worry about the fat content in his di[]

This had been so completely ingrained from years of controlling his weight that it was a difficult habit for him to break. He had given up ice cream years before, and was happy to add it back, along with the occasional dose of chocolate syrup and whipped cream, all of which usually went down without much of a struggle. Sometimes we would drive ten miles to get a dish of ice cream from the one place he liked best. 'Finally, I've found one good thing about this condition,' he said, holding up his dish of ice cream. In the car, we listened to music played by Dudley, Erroll Garner or Steven Isserlis. Dudley had been completely bowled over the first time he heard a recording by the jazz pianist Erroll Garner. Dudley was in his teens, and he described this as a major turning point in his musical life. He began listening to everything he could find by Garner, and emulating his style. Now, with his condition declining, he seemed to be returning to his fascination with Garner.

Dudley wanted to go to the beach. In the previous summers he had been able to walk with assistance. This time, however, he would have to be wheeled. We had not yet heard of the wheelchairs specially designed with thick wheels for the beach. Brian and Matthew said they would wheel Dudley to the edge of the water, and then help him walk into the ocean. I went along for moral support. They started out on the soft sand and thought it would be easier once arriving at the wet sand. But they were wrong. The wheels were sinking into the sand, creating large ruts. Dudley started laughing, then Matthew, then Brian, then me. No engineers in this group — part of the laughter was the fact that we had all assumed the same thing — that the wet sand would be easier. But the chair wasn't going anywhere. They abandoned the wheelchair; each took one of Dudley's arms, and helped him to walk into the ocean.

Suzy and Elodie arrived towards the end of the summer. Dudley had been looking forward to their visit for weeks and was happy to see them, using the energy he had stored up for their visit. They had not seen him in more than a year, and both were shocked by the decline in his condition, although hid their reaction well when they were with him. Holding herself together for the first short visit, Suzy went back to her own cottage for a break and couldn't control her tears.

We had seen the gradual decline, and knew well that he was in the final stage of the disease. For Suzy, it was a devastating shock to be faced with the reality that she might not see Dudley again after that summer. We all talked about Dudley's forthcoming visit to Buckingham Palace in the autumn, but we weren't sure he would be well enough to make the trip. Dudley and Suzy had long talks during that Nova Scotia visit. Dudley spoke openly to Suzy about his fears about wishing he had faith as strong as hers. Gradually, she was able to accept the change in his condition. When he suggested that we should all go to Charlotte Lane, a restaurant he liked in Shelburne, she was touched. He was very tired, yet struggling against all odds to go out, as he had always done before. Even in his condition, Dudley was thinking of what he could do to make their visit enjoyable.

25

PROUD OF WHAT YOU HAVE GIVEN TO THE WORLD

VE HAD KNOWN FOR several months that Dudley would be
receiving the CBE in the Queen's Birthday Honours. Dudley had
been given a choice of dates, and the additional option of having the
ward presented in the United States. There was no such option in
Dudley's mind. He was going to Buckingham Palace in the autumn
of 2001, and it was not open to negotiation.

For a short while after the terrorist attack on 11 September we
thought about cancelling the trip, but we made the decision to pro-
eed. In mid-November, we arrived in London with a day to spare.
On the morning of 16 November, Matthew (who had taken Peter
Clarke's place for this trip) and Brian helped Dudley to dress in his
morning suit. When he was ready, he stood and stared at himself in
he mirror, admiring the suit and fixing a stray lock of hair. By that
oint he was having trouble showing facial expressions, but he man-
ged a little smile.

Prince Charles was presenting the awards at the Palace. Br
waited in the anteroom with Dudley. The other recipients
honours that day were touched and impressed that Dudley l
made the trip all the way from America. He received a
of attention from others in the distinguished group assembl
When it was Dudley's turn, a palace page wheeled him across
the prince, who stepped down, leaned over and, with his ha
on Dudley's arm, spoke to him for several minutes. It was
important moment for Dudley, and he gave the best smile he co
manage.

After the ceremony, photos were taken in the palace courtya
As Dudley reached the door, he was met by members of the pr
He lifted his top hat and waved it. Being able to attend was a mor
mental achievement for Dudley, and he was proud to have be
honoured with a CBE.

Dudley had made arrangements to use a silver Rolls-Royce
the day, almost the same as the car he had used in *Arthur*. He
pleased that it created a stir at the palace. The only problem
that the wheelchair would not fit in the boot, and a second car
to be ordered just to drive the wheelchair.

Weeks earlier, we had talked about a celebration lunch after
award ceremony, and Dudley said he wanted to go to the Sav
Grill. He was very clear about who should attend the lunch. Beca
of the limited number of tickets allotted, only Brian and I,
Barbara and Bernard, were able to attend the ceremony at
palace. Dudley was disappointed; he had wanted Suzy and Elodie
be there too. There were no such restrictions at lunch. All of us
at the Savoy Grill, joined by Cleo Laine and John Dankwo
David Tait and Matthew – eleven in all.

It was a lively group, and after all the excitement of the morning ceremony, Dudley was exhausted. He refused to leave the long lunch earlier than the rest of the group, despite the fact that he was not able to speak more than a few words. Generally, the more tired he became, the less he was able to speak. He also didn't like the way the sound of his voice was being altered by the condition.

Cleo and John had been close friends of Dudley's for many years and Dudley was glad to have renewed their friendship the previous year, after a lapse of a few years. John and Dudley shared the same reverence for 'appropriateness' in formal settings. Towards the end of the afternoon, Dudley was looking oblivious to his surroundings, barely functional, when John began a joke. 'A guy was discussing his health with a friend at the local pub,' said John. 'He was worried. "I have a terrible itching in my rear quarters. I have no idea what is." "You've got piles," said his pal, "and you don't need a doctor. Just take a few tea leaves from the pot every time you have tea, massage the affected part with them, and after a few days your troubles will be over."

'For the next week the guy did as he'd been told, but it didn't seem to do the trick and he wound up at the doctor's anyway. "Well, I'd better take a look. Whip your pants off and lie on your tummy." Our hero waited for the verdict, the doctor peering at his rear end. "Yes, just as I thought," the doctor said. "You've got a rather nasty little attack of haemorrhoids – and, it may interest you to know, you're going to meet a tall, dark stranger!"'

John was finished. Before anyone had a chance to react, from across the table came a huge, loud laugh – one of Dudley's big guffaws. Contagious as his laugher always was, everyone around the table joined in. This time it was coupled with the relief of knowing

that, despite his appearance, Dudley had been aware of everythi
going on at the table.

There were a few days left before going home, and Dud
wanted to pack in as much as he could. He wanted to spend ti
with Suzy and Elodie, go to the theatre, see his sister Barbara a
her children and grandchildren, and just look out of the window
a car while being driven around London. He had a few visitors
the hotel, including long-time friends Barry Humphries and Stev
Isserlis, who arrived together one afternoon, Barry telling Dud
hilarious stories, and Steven playing a short cello recital. I
conversation was difficult. As much as Dudley tried, he was al
to say only a few words, and they were hard for his guests
understand.

We had learned the lesson well that there had to be something
the calendar. We had been through several of Dudley's se
appointed 'departure dates' – dates when he was sure he would d
They would always come and go and he would simply set a new da

Dudley was very tired after the trip to England – tired of stru
gling, and knowing well that he was close to the end of his time.
the other times we had been to England in the previous few yea
he had been certain he would return there. This time, he said goo
bye. He said goodbye to Suzy and Elodie, who promised to visit h
in New Jersey in the spring. He said goodbye to his sister and oth
members of his family. He said goodbye to England.

Back home in New Jersey, we had a number of small trips sche
uled, including a trip into New York to hear Cleo and John
Feinstein's. There was enough happening to satisfy Dudley. V
talked about celebrating his sixty-seventh birthday on 19 April. V

planned another cruise for the end of April to celebrate both of our birthdays. We were no longer under any illusion that he might recover, and we didn't know if he would really be able to make the trip, but he enjoyed thinking about it and talking about it.

A few weeks after returning home from England, Dudley decided it was time to give away his car. It was a magnificent cream-coloured Bentley with personalised California licence plates reading 'Tndrly'. He had driven it years earlier in Los Angeles and it had been garaged there for several years. He missed having it nearby and had arranged to have it shipped to New Jersey to keep in his own garage. Occasionally he would say, 'Let's take the Bentley out for a *spin*.' Brian, who was familiar with English vintage cars, was the only one brave enough to drive it, and Dudley enjoyed seeing people's reactions when we were out in the car.

Now, he said, it was time for the Bentley to have a new home. He knew he could never drive it again, and taking it out no longer made him feel good. After consulting with his advisers at the Management Group, Dudley made the decision to allow Christie's to offer the Bentley at its classic car auction in Manhattan in May. It would be sold for charity, Dudley said, with the proceeds after auction costs to be divided between Music For All Seasons and the Dudley Moore Research Fund for PSP.

Every day it was becoming more and more difficult for Dudley to eat. He was coughing and choking on both food and liquids and was losing weight quickly, a dangerous sign. Dudley had been told that some PSP patients have surgery to insert a feeding tube directly into the stomach. We read everything there was on the subject, and Dudley said he would think about it and consider having the procedure done. But he kept wavering and refused to make a decision. He said he would try to drink more of the high-calorie shakes, and for a short time it helped.

He was listening more to his own performances on tape and CD, and watching his old movies on video, as though he needed to absorb and remember his work for whatever was to follow. Tony Adams sent him an edited videotape of the Carnegie Hall tribute, and Dudley watched it over and over again.

It was hard for Dudley to talk. He was speaking in a whisper, if at all. One Wednesday, Else phoned me after her weekly Dickens reading call. She was concerned because she had not heard Dudley say anything at all. She wasn't sure he had even been on the phone. I asked Dudley, and he had heard every word. 'My words wouldn't come out,' he whispered. 'Please tell Else that.' His whispers could not be heard over the telephone. Sometimes he would mouth the words without even the sound of a whisper. Dudley resumed speech therapy with Monique, who came to the house once a week. She was able to rescue a little of his diminishing voice and worked with him to produce some vocal tone, but it was a struggle for him. We knew that people with his condition often reached the point where they could not speak at all and would stop even trying to whisper. Yet they continued to be aware of everything going on around them, their alert minds completely trapped in their failing bodies. There were longer and longer periods – sometimes two or three days in a row – when Dudley would not attempt to speak. After the long silences he would invariably try again – he never completely stopped trying to communicate.

Suzy called whenever she knew someone would be in the room to help Dudley with the phone call. He liked to listen, even when he couldn't reply. Hearing her voice always made him feel good. Brogan occasionally phoned and talked to him or left cheery messages. Lou would call to ask how he was doing and offer words of encouragement. Dudley wanted to hold the phone to his ear. He never lost his connection to the telephone.

It was a monumental struggle for Dudley to attend Cleo and John's cabaret evening in New York at the end of January 2002. We arranged for Dudley to stay overnight after the concert, arriving at the hotel early in the afternoon in time to have dinner and rest before the programme at Feinstein's, a small dinner theatre in the Regency Hotel in New York City. Dudley invited a small group of friends to dinner before the concert – but was too tired to actually attend the dinner, and came downstairs only in time for the performance. The concert was an hour long, and Dudley insisted on going backstage to see Cleo and John afterwards. They were touched when they later learned that theirs was the last concert Dudley had been able to attend.

Another few weeks passed, and Dudley was losing weight more rapidly. We had a visit scheduled with Dr Golbe, who had periodically tracked the progress of Dudley's condition. 'The question of the feeding tube may come up during your appointment. Please think about this,' I said. 'You cannot continue to lose weight at this rate and remain alive, but I know it has to be your decision.' I knew the tube might prolong his life for a short while – but he had to decide without pressure from me or anyone else. I held my breath waiting for his answer. He already had a death sentence. The tube might serve as a small reprieve but would not reverse his condition.

'I know it has to be my decision,' he said. His voice was a complete whisper as he said it. 'I don't want surgery. I don't want a feeding tube. It won't help.'

I couldn't fight back the tears. He had tears too, but my reaction made him angry. I had not expected that from him. He grabbed my wrists and held on tight, staring in my eyes.

'Very soon, there will be a time when I won't be here. How can I leave you? I love you, and I need for you to be strong, for you to help me . . . to help us both . . . get through this.' His voice rose slightly above a whisper.

'I love you too,' I said. 'I'll try to be strong.'

'This has been some incredible journey,' he said. 'Do you think there will be music there, wherever I'm going?'

'I'm sure of it,' I said.

'I'm not really afraid. You've made me feel a part of something important,' he said.

He had asked me to be strong, but we held each other and cried together for the last time. I knew I had to accept what was happening, as impossible as it was, and to have the strength for both of us. I promised that whatever time was left would be a time of light, not darkness.

A few days later we went to see the doctor, as planned. Dudley weighed 104 pounds and his face was thin and drawn. 'What can we do?' I asked.

'Try to put a little weight back. Eat fat,' he said to Dudley. 'Butter, cheese, cream, ice cream.'

We both smiled. For Dudley, smiling was very difficult. Facial expressions were almost impossible now. He was told to eat everything I had eliminated from my diet in order to lose weight. Dudley had never stopped enjoying the taste of food, despite his struggle to swallow.

The doctor took me into another room. 'I've never seen a PSP

patient in such an advanced condition,' he said. 'This must be a tribute to his will to live and to the care he has received. But you need to
monitor him very carefully. The next infection he gets could turn to
pneumonia. In his state, that will kill him.' Dudley had recently
gone through two bouts of bronchitis, and was a little weaker after
each recovery. He had not yet developed the dreaded pneumonia,
but we were aware that it was almost inevitable in his condition.

We went home, and Peter helped Dudley climb back into bed; he
was exhausted. He had refused to trade in his king-size bed for a
hospital bed at home, as his medical aides had all suggested. It would
have been easier for them to help him get in and out of bed. Dudley
had said he did not ever want to be in a hospital bed, and he wanted
to stay in his own home until the end of his life. Knowing his fear of
being hospitalised, we said we would do whatever we could to be
certain he would remain at home.

Less than two weeks after the doctor's warning, Dudley began
coughing again. We thought it was a recurrence of bronchitis, but it
was getting rapidly worse. Dr Sharrett came to the house and took
his temperature. He had a high fever. On Saturday morning, he
started liquid antibiotics and appeared to be slightly improved by
early evening. He was still insisting on walking around the house.
During the evening, he was sitting on a chair in the living room and
suddenly became fearful. He was looking at something or someone
in a corner of the room – something that nobody else could see. He
couldn't speak after the experience, but could only nod or shake his
head. Later that evening, he was able to say there had been a presence in the room; someone coming for him. He was frightened. I
knew he had little time left.

On Monday 25 March Dudley stopped eating and was barely

able to drink. We knew he would become dehydrated without intravenous fluids. Two years earlier, when he had prepared his will with Gene, Dudley had signed a living will saying that he did not want extreme measures to be taken. I thought he might not survive the night and I did not leave the house. Dr Sharrett came to the house on Tuesday morning, and, after a few moments with the stethoscope, confirmed that Dudley had pneumonia, although he did not say it in front of him. Through the hospital, he arranged hospice care, oxygen and an intravenous drip with fluids and antibiotics. He told me there was very little chance Dudley could survive pneumonia.

Dr Sharrett had treated Dudley for many years and felt very close to him. They had shared many laughs in his office. Dudley was also a great admirer of Dr Sharrett, who was then seventy-three and had in the preceding few years survived open-heart surgery and two types of cancer. He would bounce back as quickly as he could in order to take care of his patients, many of them elderly. And he was among the minority of American doctors still to make house calls. This time, he stayed with Dudley and encouraged him, talking to him about the medication and encouraging him to take liquids and tiny ice chips to keep his mouth from becoming dry.

The doctor was getting ready to leave and said he would come back in the morning. I walked to the door with him.

'He will probably not survive the night. We can only make him comfortable now,' he said.

Brian came in and sat with Dudley for a long time, holding his hand and fighting back his tears. A few days earlier, Brian and Dudley had hugged as they did every day when Brian left the house. 'It was strange, though,' said Brian. 'He didn't speak. He just held on for the longest time, as though he had to tell me something important.' Now we understood what it was.

The hospice nurse was there for a few hours, and Dudley's aide was preparing cool towels and a bowl of chipped ice. Dudley was able to drink a few sips of ginger ale. I said I would stay with Dudley during the night.

In the middle of the night, Dudley began shivering. I could feel that his fever was high. A small lamp was on, very low, and he seemed frightened again. I remembered how much he wanted me to be strong, not to cry yet. I knew we had only a few hours left and didn't want to waste the time sleeping.

I was sitting next to him on the bed, leaning back against the pillows. After a while he fell asleep, but his breathing was laboured. Sometimes there was a long pause between his breaths, and I waited for the next one, relieved when it came.

I closed my eyes and didn't open them for another four hours. I was still holding his hand, and awoke with a start when he had twitched. He was a little cooler and reaching for his cup of ginger ale. But his breathing was still laboured, with a faint rattling sound in every breath, and it was easy to hear the fluid in his lungs.

Dr Sharrett returned in the morning and was surprised that Dudley had survived the night, but he was not encouraged when he touched his forehead and listened to his lungs. He confirmed that it was time for everyone in the family to gather in the room. We had been listening to Chopin, but it felt all wrong, and we changed it to Dudley's own *Songs Without Words*. He squeezed my hand, as if to say, 'That's right. Thank you.'

We all sat with him, held his hands and comforted him. We listened breath by breath, as they came farther and farther apart, and we waited for the next one. Finally, we knew the next one was never going to come. He was at the end of his long journey, and he was at peace.

I remembered the last conversation we ever had, during the night – just a few hours earlier.

'I hope you are proud of what you've given to the world,' I said.

'Yes, I am,' he whispered.

He was looking out in front of him, at something I couldn't see. He was calm, and I knew it must have been something good, something comforting. 'What are you seeing?' I asked. I was placing tiny chips of ice under his tongue so he could have a small amount of cool liquid. I had just put a cool towel on his forehead.

'I'm sitting at the piano, playing Bach; you are there too.' He was speaking very softly, in the softest whisper I had ever heard, and the words were coming one at a time – very, very slowly. 'I'm happy . . . and peaceful . . . and strong. I can feel the warmth of the music all around me.' He had closed his eyes, and he had just the hint of a smile.

POSTLUDE

IT IS MARCH 2004, nearly two years to the day after Dudley's death. It is difficult not to think about 27 March 2002, and to wonder how two years could pass and it can seem like yesterday; how two years could pass and it can seem like a century. I happen to open a book and there is a note in it written by Dudley a few years ago. He used to write himself notes while reading. This one is cryptic, nothing to do with the book where it had served as a bookmark. The words scrawled on a small piece of lined paper are hard to read. I stare at it for a long time, finally able to decipher them: 'Celebrate the *journey* more than the destination.' I wasn't sure what its context might have been – perhaps just a comment he had read and wanted to remember. His scribbled notes tended to be profound, so I doubted he was referring to a car trip. How appropriate to find it now. Dudley certainly wanted us to celebrate his life more than to mourn his death. At first it was very hard to do that; now it seems essential not to mourn but to remember all the wonderful reasons that Dudley was with us.

Dudley did not just pass through our lives. He was right in the middle of our lives. He changed us and we changed him. He came into the world with a mission and he left having accomplished it. He wasn't finished, but then who is? Through his humour and his music – and through his struggle – he taught us how to communicate, how to be honest, how to strip away the layer upon layer that we pile on to prevent us from knowing who we really are, what we really think, how we really feel. We taught it to Dudley, and he taught it right back to us in full measure. Or was it the other way round?

My family had the privilege of knowing who Dudley really was. Dudley showed us that the only reality is in the truth of who you are, what you feel, how you act. Fame, fortune, acclaim – none of it mattered. Those were a *part* of Dudley's life, but they were not the essence of his character.

We remember Dudley's voice, see his face, hear his music – as clearly as ever. For me and for my family, it is not the face on the big screen. It is the face of Dudley chasing after kangaroos with wide-eyed enthusiasm, or sitting at the piano playing his own music, or laughing his infectious laugh. Dudley was part of my family, but he belonged to the world. We are stronger, better and happier for having shared his life.

March 2004
Scotch Plains, New Jersey

ACKNOWLEDGEMENTS

PECIAL THANKS TO MY husband Brian Dallow, whose
atience, support and encouragement made it possible for me to
rite this book. We have lived through this journey twice – once
ith Dudley and a second time in the telling of it. Brian encouraged
e to continue on a challenging personal journey through all the
oments when I wasn't convinced I could do it.

My warmest gratitude to a group of diligent and perceptive read-
rs, and to my family, friends and colleagues for their support while
was chained to my computer during the past year:

To my family and extended family – to my children and their
ouses, for their care and understanding – Ruth and Stuart
outhland, Joel and Mary Ellen Dallow, Elise and Vincent Latona,
nd Karen and Kevin Burr; to my sister Felice Platt and my
rother-in-law Jay Platt for their encouragement; to my sister
orothea Cahan for perceptive advice and guidance, and asking all

the right questions; to Steven Isserlis for his support and insigh
and for saving me from the disgrace of putting into print th
Mozart died at thirty-six, not thirty-five, as well as finding my sp
infinitives (some of which remain just to possibly prove I
human); to Else Blangsted for providing history and honest insigh
and continuing a caring tradition by calling me every Wednesday
noon; to Suzy Kendall and Elodie Harper for their friendship a
for helping during all the difficult times; to Stephen Rodner a
Nick Goldstone for steadfast personal and legal guidance; to Ja
Mason for her enthusiasm and confidence in me, and for insisti
that you have to take chances in life; to Dudley's son Patrick f
reminding me of all the reasons it was important to set the reco
straight; to Barbra Paskin, who willingly shared her research a
experiences and advised me to get some sleep; to Cleo Laine a
John Dankworth for always being available to help, no matter whe
on the globe they were; to Lou Pitt for being forthcoming with l
thoughts and memories; to Dr Martin Gizzi for guidance and me
ical information.

To my agent Sophie Hicks at Ed Victor Ltd, for her enthusias
encouragement and persistence, and for helping me to keep it all
perspective; to my editor Hannah MacDonald at Ebury for consta
guidance, and reassurance in helping me to overcome my hesitati
and fears; to the wonderful team at Ebury – special thanks to K
Barlow, Claire Kingston and Stina Smemo; to Mari Roberts for h
gracious editing and for gently guiding me in my quest to become
bi-lingual (British/American) author, trading in nearly eve
American Z for a British S and wielding an electronic hatchet
excise vestigial subjunctives.

To those who have helped in so many other important ways,

offering moral support, sharing their memories of Dudley, working with me to piece together the years before I knew him, providing photos, and confirming that both my facts and my hunches were correct, I thank, enthusiastically and alphabetically, the following people: Tony Adams, Deborah Rose Andrews, Dame Julie Andrews, Chevy Chase, Lin Cook, William Cook, Bo Derek, Blake Edwards, Jill Eikenberry, Stacey Herman, Eric Idle, Jim Johnson, Ann Koranda, Brogan Lane, Carol Marder, Bill Miller, Hugh Macdonald, Robert and Lucy Mann, Dr. Michael Palmen, Arthur Paxton, Ann Reinking, Dr Richard Sharrett, Dr Sue Schonberg, and Tuesday Weld.

To the Board of Trustees of Music For All Seasons, for patience during my absence and to Ruth, for doing double duty in the MFAS office for a year.

In memory of Dudley Moore, a portion of the proceeds from the sale of this book will be donated to the two charities that were important to Dudley – Music For All Seasons, taking the healing power of live music into facilities for children and adults including hospitals, nursing homes, hospices, shelters for victims of domestic violence and special schools. And the Dudley Moore Research Fund for PSP, searching for a cure.